KV-576-495

DEATH OF A MYTH

DEATH OF A MYTH:
CRITICAL ESSAYS ON NIGERIA

FEMI OJO-ADE

Africa World Press, Inc.

P.O. Box 1892
Trenton, NJ 08607

P.O. Box 48
Asmara, ERITREA

Africa World Press, Inc.

P.O. Box 1892
Trenton, NJ 08607

P.O. Box 48
Asmara, ERITREA

Copyright: © 2001 Femi Ojo-Ade
First Printing 2001

All rights reserved. No part of this publication may be reproduced, stored in a retrieval system or transmitted in any form or by any means electronic, mechanical, photocopying, recording or otherwise without the prior written permission of the publisher.

Book Design: Wanjiku Ngugi
Cover Design: Ashraful Haque
Cover Artwork: Dapo Ojo-Ade

Library of Congress Cataloging-in-Publication data

Ojo-Ade, Femi.
    Death of a myth : critical essays on Nigeria / Femi Ojo-Ade.
        p.   cm.
    Includes bibliographical references and index.
    ISBN: 0-86543-789-0 (hardbound) -- ISBN: 0-86543-790-4 (pbk.)
    1. Nigeria--Politics and government--1993- 2. Nigeria--Social conditions--1960- I. Title.
DT515.842.O46 1999
966.905"3- -dc21   99-30086
                                                               CIP

In Memory of M.K.O. Abiola
First a menace to the people, then and finally a hero, a
martyr, and the symbol of their struggle; and of
Kudirat, his wife, a rarity of a woman, a revolutionary
towering above the mass of reactionaries

CONTENTS

DEATH OF A MYTH

ACKNOWLEDGMENTS

I express sincere gratitude to my family for both constant support and understanding, without which I would never have been able to write, to survive.

My wife offered much appreciated professional help as a librarian of outstanding quality.

My children and other family and friends lent their moral backing to my seasons of dilemma, and desperate search for answers to impossible questions.

Israel and Valentine, of course, you know I'll never forget your support and brilliant ideas.

Finally, I must admit the inevitable presence of the United States of America, the greener pasture to which many Africans run, only to find that green is often a mask for gray, that the Dream may not be as rosy as we imagined.

PREFACE

These essays cover a period of five years (1993-1998) in the unfolding tragic history of Nigeria, Africa's most populous country. A season of seeming hope, followed by one moment of sudden hopelessness. An instant of unexpected liberation and possibilities. Another moment, just as sudden and shocking, of despair, followed by one more, of supposedly renewed hope.

Much water has passed under many bridges in that short but remarkable period. After eight years of manoevring and mismanagement, General Ibrahim Babangida, the self-appointed executive President, agreed to hold presidential elections on June 12, 1993. Moshood Kashimawo Abiola won hands down in what everyone, including the international community, described as the country's freeest and fairest electoral exercice. By June 23, the crafty dictator[1] and his regime had decided to annul the elections. He "stepped aside" and put in place an Interim National Government headed by Ernest Shonekan.[2] That the new "Head of State" was a puppet, was patent to those that understood the peculiar politics of Nigeria; for, next to him was General Sani Abacha, Babangida's former second-in-command who, strangely enough, had been left behind by the reluctantly departed president. In fact, Shonekan's regime was but a figment of his and his friends' imagination: A high court declared the government illegal, and there was overwhelming civil disobedience in the land. The wily Abacha did nothing to shore up Shonekan's authority. It therefore came as no surprise that on November 23, 1993, Abacha took over, very peacefully and forcefully, after Shonekan had supposedly announced his resignation.

Abiola, who had fled into exile for fear of being assassinated,[3] soon returned home. Word was that he had maintained contact with the regime even while he was criss-crossing the West in search of support for his presidential victory. It was further asserted in many circles, that Abacha had given him his word to spend only a few months to return the country to the path of reason and justice, and then to pass the baton to Abiola, the rightful leader of the country.

In the thick of all those scenarios of rumors, claims, and counter-claims, Abacha gradually entrenched himself in absolute control, to Abiola's surprise and disappointment. Out of frustration, or commitment to justice and fair play, and definitely consequential to the realization of Abacha's determination to self-perpetuate in power, Abiola declared himself President on the 1994 anniversary of his annuled victory. The illegal government promptly arrested and charged him for treason.

From 1994 until 1998, Nigerians witnessed a farcical display of barefaced bestiality by a regime bent upon eliminating any sign of opposition. All institutions were roped into this process of de-humanization. Many once principled human beings lost their sense of dignity and self-respect, in a setting where corruption and oppression reigned supreme. The judiciary, expected to be the firm and fair arbiter in its role as the symbol of justice, sold its soul to a dictatorship prepared to use or waste anyone seen to be in its way as it steamrolled the country towards living hell. Politicians, for-ever symbols of the worst in a country too big and too diverse to establish and encourage any meaningful policy, reverted to their past roles as prostitutes ready to be raped and paid for the abomi-nation by tyrants that proudly and patriotically dug their dirty hands deep into public treasury.

Sports has not been spared from the all-embracing pollution. If anyone ever doubted the linkage between sports and politics, Ni-geria provides definitive proof that our century has gone far be-yond any Olympic notion of competition for its own sake, or for the sake of socialization, or relaxation. Football is the most spec-tacular example. Nigerians have comne to excel in this universal sport, with the best players traveling abroad to sell their God-given talent to the highest bidder; yet, these skillful individuals have not escaped the cesspool of corruption and indiscipline within the larger body politic. Although Nigeria won the soccer gold at the 1994 Atlanta Olympics, it hardly convinced any lucid observer that it could lead the world at the highest level; hence, it was no surprise that, at the 1998 World Cup competition in France, the very tal-ented but disorganized team was humiliated by Denmark.

Journalists are perhaps the only group that has succeeded in maintaining an element of integrity. They never ceased to expose the government's heinous crimes. For their obstinacy in speaking out, many of their number were jailed, including some who were convicted for participating in phantom coups d'etat. A few of the most critical media houses, such as *TELL* and *TheNews* (dubbed the South-West, that is, the Yoruba region's, press), were hounded underground. Thousands of their magazine copies were seized, and their equipment was vandalised.

Meanwhile, the country's economy was being flushed down the drain. Health services, education, industry, all aspects of the country's infrastructure, were being suystematically destroyed. Yet, the dictatorship continued to claim its right to rule, or rather, misrule. Any critic, any dissenting voice, proclaimed Enemies of the Nation, were chased down and thrown into detention. The most unfortunate ones were simply killed off. Others, more fortunate, managed to escape into exile. Among the assassinated were Ken Saro-Wiwa, the Ogoni writer-activist executed in blatant defiance of global public opinion,[4] Kudirat Abiola, wife of the jailed President, and Alfred Rewane, renowned politician and one of the most progressive in Nigeria's history. On the list of exiles are Anthony Enahoro, a prominent politician and activist who first moved the motion for Nigerian independence (1953), and Wole Soyinka, 1986 Nobel laureate in literature and a world renowned critic of military regimes and an advocate of democracy and the people's freedom.[5]

From all indications, General Abacha had, by June 1998, successfully completed his plans to transform into a civilian President. The five political parties organized by his government, had all been forced to draft him as their sole candidate. Stories abound that the land was flooded with posters, badges, and gadgets (television-sets, cookers, refrigerators), all bearing the robust image of the dictator. The government-run television network served as propaganda machine: Before each newscast, there was a rhetorical question on who was most capable of running the country, with several faceless bodies magically coalescing into the one and only face of the master-ruiner. Nigerians abroad continued to protest and to appeal to the West to save the situation. Those at home kept praying and hoping that something would happen.

And so it did, most unexpectedly. In the early hours of June 8, 1998, Abacha died. There was dancing in the streets of many a Nigerian city and community. Free drinks and food were generously offered in bars and restaurants. Hope immediately replaced the hopelessness that had been holding everyone and everything hostage. The religious-minded claimed that the Almighty had answered their prayers by dealing decisively with the devil incarnate. The politically-conscious declared their conviction that they had expected something drastic and definitive to happen to the monster. Even the man's comrades in crime suddenly became his critics as they tried to exonerate their actions as a result of his machinations and mean-spiritedness. The international community gladly joined the bandwagon of those expecting Nigeria to immediately become heaven on earth. Abacha's successor, General Abubakar, made speeches full of promise. He has been treated as the new, ultra-clean messiah, as if he was not a prominent member of Abacha's regime. He released several political prisoners, the most prominent of whom was the former military Head of State, General Obasanjo, who had been sent to life imprisonment for a 1995 coup that has not been proved to be anything more than another Abacha-motivated concoction to rid the regime of its enemies. Abubakar himself oozed confidence and enthusiasm for a better country. He announced the imminent release of Abiola, still the symbol of the fight for freedom and democracy. Everyone was waiting for the jailed President of the people to come out and implement his mandate.

That hope suddenly became a mirage when, in the evening of July 7, 1998, one month after Abacha's passing, the news struck like a bolt of lightning: Abiola had died during a meeting with a United States delegation. The reaction was the direct opposite of what happened after Abacha's death. People wept publicly. Everything stopped, as if life itself had expired in a country desperate to live. Some, out of anger and frustration, went on a rampage, burning the property, and threatening the lives, of those they considered collaborators with their oppressors. Many expressed disbelief at the official announcement that Abiola had died of natural causes. At the same time, stories started making the rounds, that Abacha himself had been murdered by foreign prostitutes who fed him poisoned apple as he tried to prove his vaunted, viagra-enhanced sexual prowess. The result of the much publicized postmortem performed by a team of British, American, and Canadian experts, has been released. Abiola, we are assured, died naturally. Yet, nothing has been said about the conditions of his four-year imprisonment, as if anyone kept in isolation in a cubicle of a cell, irregularly fed with food meant for dogs, prevented from obtaining medical attention for already existing serious ailments, and psychologically and physically tortured, could actually escape dying from "natural causes."

Nigerians have now accepted that Abiola is gone forever. Whether the hope for a better life has not died with him, is a matter for debate. The "new government" has announced a program to return the country to civilian rule by the end of May, 1999. Some Nigerians, and all the Western nations, are satisfied with this arrangement. They believe in Abubakar, "a gentleman without political ambitions." Others, particularly, the long suffering opposition,[6] are skeptical about the regime's sincerity, as well as Abubakar's capability to resist the influence of the Hausa-Fulani oligarchy.

This state of uncertainty, this doubt, this lack of conviction as to the true meanings of actions and realistic expectations from players in the political game, they are all aspects of the confusion and, indeed, the myth named Nigeria. During the five years briefly discussed above, many lives were lost; many destinies, destroyed; many ambitions, fulfilled, frustrated, or fatally shortcircuited. Of course, individuals were the ones that survived, if one is cynical enough to see success in a setting were diseased minds coopt like, materialistic minds into their horror show. The community suffered, in the form of the vast majority of the population.

The author of this book is an individual, a privileged one at that, who, however, believes that, for Nigeria to rise from the ashes, it will take more than cosmetic actions of democratization. It will require a total overhaul of the state machinery, including an honest discussion among the various nationalities with regard to their association in a nation that is yet to be created. The author is a privileged individual, because he has been fortunate -and it is largely a question of material buoyancy- to escape the economic concentration camp established by the set of marauders feeding fat on the people's blood during this season of death. His misfortune has been, that material success has not solved the other, more urgent problem: How to create a viable home in a foreign land where you are considered an alien, no matter your status.

For the author, therefore, home has remained Nigeria, to which he has returned every summer in the past decade of his exile. The essays in this collection are the reflexive results of the past five years. The vast majority address specific issues besetting the Nigerian state. A few others, written abroad, contemplate the essential relationship between Africa (particularly, the writer's Yoruba race) and the African diaspora. The final essay, originally the text of a keynote address made at a gathering of African students in an American university, offers a critical analysis of Africa's present, as well as a vision of its existence in the 21st century.

Overall, the essays express the anger of a frustrated son of the soil reduced to the role of observer in a country where cowards like him dare not stand up and be counted. They also express some notions on how to make his home livable, and attractive, and prosperous, so that exile may no longer be the foremost option for anyone seeking to live the proverbial normal life. Finally, it is the author's hope that the reader will, at least, have an insight into the peculiarities of Nigeria, perhaps the most complex country on the face of the earth; and, that fellow Nigerians will have reason to reflect on the myriad issues addressed here, so that we may all find the way forward.

Notes

1. In Nigeria, Babangida came to be known as Maradona, in reference to the Argentine footballer blessed with unparalleled dribbling skills, and in recognition of the military politician's ability to "dribble" everyone through deceit, manipulation, and machinations.
2. A former chairman of the United Africa Company, one of the most formidable enterprises of the British colonizers that has continued to wax strong in independent Nigeria, Shonekan hails from Abeokuta, the home town of the beleaguered Abiola who, in his own right, was a very rich man and a well known friend of the military, particularly Babangida, whom he, Abiola, reputedly had helped to attain power through a coup d'etat in 1985.

   Shonekan was not new to the task of serving the regime: Earlier in 1993, he had been appointed as "head of government," ostensibly in preparation for a new, civilian dispensation which never materialised.

3. Abiola was then considered a coward in some circles, for failing to claim his mandate from the military. In what was to become one of his legacies, he explained that it would be foolhardy for him, an unarmed, normal human being, to go lie in front of a runaway train. In the five years of his political saga, Abiola showed his extraordinary knowledge of African proverbs, and his spectacular way with words.

   In a similar vein, Nigerian journalists, intellectuals, and politicians, showed their gift for linguistic inventions. At every juncture of what may be called *the era of democrazy,* new words were introduced into the socio-political discourse, and students of the English language, as well as political and social scientists, would have a field day reading the newspaper articles and speeches dealing with *the political logjam, the home-grown democracy, the impasse, the siddon look* [attitude of some Nigerians], *the hidden agenda* [of a government unwilling to quit], and *the five fingers of a leprous hand* [that is, the five political parties created to serve as handmaids and mouthpieces of dictator Abacha's self-perpetuating plans], among others.

4. For a critical study of Saro-Wiwa's life and work, see, Femi Ojo-Ade, *Ken Saro-Wiwa,* New York: Africana Legacy Press, 1998. The Nigerian Provisional Ruling Council (PRC) put paid to any hopes of saving his life and those of his eight comrades by jumping the gun, as it were: According to the law, there was to be a thirty-day grace period, to appeal to the PRC to overturn the death-sentence imposed by the special tribunal. Messages poured in from all over the world. The Commonwealth was convening at Aukland, New Zealand, and Mandela, recognized as Africa's beacon of light, expressed confidence that diplomatic engagement would save the convicts' necks. However, suddenly and shockingly, Saro-Wiwa and others were marched to the gallows and hanged at dawn, on November 10, 1995. The international community threatened to let loose fire and brimstone on the Abacha regime. Britain and fellow members of the European Union, the United States, Brazil, and South Africa, all recalled their ambassadors from Abuja, the Nigerian capital. Abacha remained defiant, and confident that it was just hot air. And he was right; for, soon enough, the threatening storm abated. The ambassadors returned to their posts. Relations were strained, but never severed.

5. See, Wole Soyinka, *The Open Sore of a Continent,* New York: Oxford University Press, 1996.

6. One of the main opposition groups is the National Democratic Coalition (NADECO). Another umbrella grouping, the Joint Action Committee of Nigeria (JACON), has more affiliates than the former, but

with less recognition by officialdom. Within the present dispensation, NADECO has been cooperating with the government. It participated in the ballyhooed "reconciliation" exercise that Abubakar used to elicit support. It also expressed guarded support for the democratization process. On the contrary, JACON, under the leadership of the fiery lawyer, Gani Fawehinmi, roundly condemned the Abubakar agenda. It stated that the regime must leave by October 1, 1998, as earlier promised by Abacha. It rejects any plan that does not include a Sovereign National Conference to discuss Nigeria's future, and a Government of National Unity that would serve as facilitator of that process. One might say that NADECO is flexible, and moderate, while JACON is firm, and radical. Observers contend that such areas of conflict within the ranks of the opposition, make for its inability to stand up to the military and flush it out of power.

NIGERIA, AFRICA, AND AMERICA

> It [Nigeria] is one country that has no
> yardstick for anything whatsoever except evil
> that has managed to triumph.[1]

> Africa is a nightmarish world where chaos reigns.[2]

> The President's [Clinton] visit to Africa certainly is based
> firmly on America's national interests.[3]

Nigeria's political crisis has helped to reaffirm certain facts, while revealing new ones, in regards of the country's importance and potential, as well as other countries' position and posture in the face of those realities and possibilities. For one thing, the self-proclaimed—and sometimes acclaimed, either seriously or satirically—giant of Africa has lived up to expectations, as an unserious and unsettled entity with a special talent for squandering its limitless natural endowments. For another, other countries, both within and outside the African continent, have hardly done anything to nudge the pitiful prankster back to the road of responsibility and dignity.

Before anyone cries foul against the former colonizers and current imperialists, exploiters that they all are, let it be known that, in this author's opinion, Nigeria must bear the brunt of the blame for its own retrogression or, to put it more mildly, stagnation. For, its so-called leaders are guilty of collaborating with the foreign exploiters and, internally, of coercing the support of some unscrupulous elements to dictate and destroy, through deceit. Of course, it matters that the military has clung to power for some thirty of the country's thirty-eight years of independence: With gun in hand, any fool can foist any policy on a cowered people. In the case of Nigeria, another factor is of great significance: The marauding military has had its roots firmly in the North, a region dominated by the Hausa-Fulani nation that, as a result of its cultural particularity, lagged behind the others in the process of Westernization, even as it repelled democracy and wallowed in feudalism. Indeed, the North first refused to board the independence train. For it to agree to join the East and West to form the geographical giant now named Nigeria, the North had to be coaxed (cynics would say, bribed) with political power. That would explain the Northern domination of which many Nigerians are complaining very loudly on the eve of the 21st century.

True as it is that Nigeria cannot pass the buck with regards to its myriad socio-political, economic, and human problems, one cannot but note the shameful contributions of the Western powers to that process. Without Britain's support, and tutelage, the Northern Nigerian oligarchy, mainly through its military wing, would not have been able to maintain and sustain its stranglehold on power. That support has hinged upon the double-edged springboard of British pride in its priced possession, and an economic policy of exploitation. Nigeria, the ex-colony, remains Britain's surrogate child economically and psychologically. One of the worst effects of colonialism is, that the colonized internalizes the master's values and vision. Thus, perhaps the most dangerous demon is the Self. Colonialism, or imperialism. Independence, or neo-colonialism. Development, or despoliation. It is only a question of linguistic manipulation. In reality, the master has never ceased to keep an eye on his servant, faithful as ever, both filled with the fervor of self-preservation, and prosperity. For both to continue to enjoy the booty, change must be repelled by all means necessary, and at all costs.

As for the Nigerian people, they cannot be exculpated in this ce of death. True that they are vastly victims, innocent victims, almost prepared to agree. Nevertheless, their innocence is at wed. It is neither compelling nor convincing. The South struggle immediately comes to mind as an excellent ex-hat the mass of the people can, and ought to, do. Mandela,

Mbeki, Tambo, Tutu, and others who led the anti-apartheid struggle at home and abroad, from the dungeons of Robben Island and the dark alleys of the guerrilla underground, through the torture of exile, and the teasing and tension of life under the watchful eyes and trigger-happy hands of the Monster, all of those leaders' work could not have amounted to much without a committed followership. The school children who, in unison, said a resounding and definitive no to apartheid. The workers who objected to the abomination of the pass. The house-wives who kept intact both family and faith. The thousands that stood strong, and proud, and prepared to make the ultimate sacrifice in the face of apartheid's murderous weapons. These are all symbols of commitment, and courage. They explain why apartheid, that seemingly insurmountable obstacle to African humanity, suddenly was submerged, even as it found subtle and often overt support from the hypocritical Western powers. When Mandela walked free on that fateful day in 1990, he knew without doubt that the victory belonged, first and foremost, to his people.

Sad to say, Nigeria is another story altogether. There, commitment is a foreign word, a strange sensation, the peculiar condition of a handful living in a world of fantasy, far away from the confusion, corruption, and contradictions holding the country hostage. Nobody is ready to die, because it would be dying "for nothing!" Cowardliness, or realism, this lack of commitment captures the dilemma that must be addressed, and resolved, if at all the people would one day be in a position to enjoy true freedom and human rights. On that day, mothers would not teach their children to squirm before criminals trying to mortgage their future. Workers would not run back to their subhuman conditions of service at the mere threat of retrenchment, aware that they would be that, without their blood and sweat, the whole structure would come tumbling down and that, after all, they would be better off jobless than to continue to eke out a living while working for months without pay in a country where individuals have been guilty of stashing away, in secret vaults of private villas, millions and billions of dollars and pounds sterling belonging to the people. Citizens would neither keep quiet, nor close their eyes, before the iniquities of political prostitutes cavorting with the criminal rulers that offer them crumbs of the national cake. People would not run for cover at the sound of a burst tire, because they are scared that it might be the outburst of a bullet shot by the bullies sent to keep them under control and in chains. On that day, at the birth of Revolution and the death of Reaction, the people: mothers, workers, men and women, all citizens, will demand their rights, and refuse to be bullied or deceived by charlatans pretending to be patriots. Cowardliness and collusion with oppressors will give way before the force of a community of freedom-fighters and genuine activists willing and able to dare and defeat the vultures preying upon innocent people. Pity that such a day belongs to a distant, yet unknown future.

Presently, the Nigerian tragedy is probably most graphically highlighted by the projected image of *America*. The very name that originally, and correctly, referred to a whole continent, but now exclusively claimed by one country, makes a loud statement about the power, as well as the presumptuousness, of the United States of America. Nowadays, most people forget that there are two continents, the Americas; that there exists the United States of Mexico, among others; that Canada is part of the North American continent; and that there are many countries in Central and South America. For the *American*, that is, the citizen of the United States of America, his or her country is, simply put, *everything:* The American Dream connotes the possibility of achieving the impossible; to be American means, to be superior to everyone else, to be the supreme human being, to live in heaven on earth. *America* is the world! Its citizens are socialized to look inwards at their land of plenty and their good fortune as its occupants, as if other places do not exist, or, if they do, they are only fit for sub-humans. Non-citizens are called *aliens*, as if they come from another planet. These basic ignorance and xenophobia are hardly recognized as such by a people that believe absolutely in their superiority and supremacy.

If one feels offended by the pretensions of the American big brother and global policeman, one is just as outraged by the attitude of many Nigerians who are ready to die in order to obtain a visa to this promised land. Indeed, Americans' pride in their nation is as strong as Nigerians' shameless alienation from, and deliberate denial of, their hopeless country. Up until the mid-80s, Nigeria as a country enjoyed a certain level of respect in the United States. As a rule, intending travelers from there were warmly welcomed at the American embassy in Lagos. They were treated like human beings. They entered the building in a matter of minutes; they helped themselves to free coffee and coke; they were offered four-year, multiple-entry visas, without asking for one. Once they landed in *God's own country*, the store-owners on Broadway, in New York city, rolled out the red carpet, and accepted the Nigerian currency, the naira, in preference to others.

Now, everything has changed. At Lagos, the embassy shuts out travelers in rain or shine, in heat or cold. Visa-seekers are known to arrive there as early as 2:00 a.m.; some actually camp overnight outside the premises, so as to be among the fortunate candidates allowed inside, come dawn. Consular officers consider it a favor to review applications. The successful applicants jump for joy, praising the Almighty for performing the miracle of having a one-entry document granted, with the ominous warning -a badly veiled threat- that the immigration personnel at the port of entry reserve the right to refuse entry to the elated travelers. In the legendary promised land, the only promise fulfilled is the reality of racism, virulently visited upon any carrier of the green-colored Nigerian passport.

Nigeria's stock has fallen so low, not as much because of the absence of democracy in the country, but mainly because of its economic downturn. The disaster is exemplified by the evolution of the naira: In the good old days of oil boom, when New York stores carried large signs welcoming the coveted currency, one naira was valued at almost two dollars. Today, one naira is worth but ten cents. No wonder why, at this nadir of ridicule, Nigeria's national color, green, turns people off. It has become the color of corruption. Nigerians are now perceived as criminals and pariahs, with a reputation for credit-card scams, drug-trafficking, and business fraud. It is common knowledge that, more often than not, victims of this neo-reactionary policy are innocent, hard-working, and honest individuals. One has never stopped wondering why the State Department does not spend some time to thoroughly investigate the overall activities of Nigerians living in, or visiting, the United States. One is convinced that such a study will reveal one big secret, that Nigerians constitute an asset to the country.[4]

Were the United States to publicly acknowledge this fact, Nigerians would be in a position to demand a change of policy based on a serious, rational estimation of Nigerian realities, which would lead to genuine efforts to resolve the Nigerian dilemma. In this r's considered opinion, such a change, from hypocrisy to st evaluation, would hurt American interests. That might sound ஊ.. ige, but it is the truth; for, the United States would not want to deal with a well organized Nigeria, that is, a Nigeria led by leaders truly committed to establishing and maintaining the country's interests, not those of a clique of robbers whose sole talent is to sell off public resources for fat personal accounts in foreign banks. The United States would appear to prefer a chaotic Nigeria. Evil may reign unfettered; however, any criticism of it would be done more out of concern for the American image as advocate of global human rights and democracy, than for the necessity to place a human face on a fiendish regime. A Nigeria without a yardstick for good, would suit the United States quite well, because that would give Americans a free hand to impose and implement their own rules, particularly with regards to economics.

It is in that light that one understands full well American policy on Nigeria in the past five years. In spite of Abacha's draconian decrees, in spite of his decisively defiant attitude in the face of internal and external criticism, in spite of the regime's bold-faced corruption and the consequent collapse of the economy, the United States refused to impose serious sanctions, under the pretext that such an action would hurt the mass of the people. The bottom line was, and is, oil, the so-called black gold, of which 50% is being exported to the United States. Americans, one daresay, are not only hypocritical, but apparently naive enough to be taken for a ride. On the other hand, maybe both they and their trading partners, have a bond, to play politics with the lives of hapless Nigerians, as long as the oil is flowing in the right direction. There would be no better way to explain the lack of serious action against the Nigerian dictatorship, or the analytic miscue that, somehow, the Abacha coup of 1993, looked like democracy.[5]

Should one have been surprised that, notwithstanding the innumerable facts easily obtained within Nigeria, and the exhortations of credible critics, such as Wole Soyinka and other exiles, the United States hardly modified its position?[6] Should one have wondered why President Clinton, during his 1998 African tour in which he physically avoided Nigeria, averred that Abacha would be an acceptable presidential candidate if he ran as a civilian? Should it come as a surprise that the American president made his statement in South Africa, a country whose struggle against the apartheid monster was championed by Nigeria, and that Mandela, the epitome of authentic democracy and freedom, was a witness to Clinton's gaffe? Mandela's sudden and painful volt-face, from a call for total ostracization of the Nigerian dictatorship by economic sanctions to a call for caution, must be contemplated in the context of African and extra-African politics. He could not act alone, nor did he wish to discuss the expressed desires of Nigeria's West African neighbors. Furthermore, he could not overlook the wishes of the foreign powers with whom South Africa, fresh out of the woods and struggling to live up to its image as the pin-up nation for Democracy, has been working hard to cooperate. In short, it is all a question of politics. Should one blame Mandela?[7] Should one castigate Eyadema (Togo), Rawlings (Ghana), Taylor (Liberia), Kabbah (Sierra Leone), and others ruling their countries as their personal farms, and much relieved to enjoy the financial and military backing of the big brother from filthy rich Nigeria? As already stated here, the United States and other interested parties could not hide their joy at Nigeria's confusion and profligacy: One will never know how many billions of dollars of public funds Abacha, and Babangida (the master dribbler and destroyer) before him, threw away in the name of democracy in Liberia and Sierra Leone. Nary a word was said to underscore the laughable contradiction written all over Nigeria's glorious campaign of terror in those two countries. The great gods of global democracy rushed to congratulate Abacha and his cronies. Abuja became the West African center of the democratic process. The United Nations gave Nigeria a citation of honor for spearheading those spectacular struggles on behalf of humanity. Meanwhile, the citizens of those same countries, Nigerians' brothers and sisters according to the well worn Pan-African ideal, did not mince words in expressing their disgust at Nigeria's intrusive, overbearing attitude and action. Those Nigerians who travel in West Africa are fully aware of this sentiment of abhorrence. And it is not restricted to the West; Kenyans, South Africans, Zimbabweans, they all object to Nigeria's show of shame, in its inability to put its house in order, and in its propensity for poking its crooked nose into their business. Nigeria is in a no-win situation: While other Africans lambast the country's paternalistic and pompous policy, their leaders follow Nigeria's lead like hungry dogs in search of bones. Understandably, after Abacha's death in June 1998, those leaders meeting in Burkina Faso at the annual mutual ego-massaging, honored their fallen peer as a beloved hero.

Understandably, too, the United States and Britain led a chorus of applause from abroad, as if they did not help to prop up the departed dictator while he was alive. Of course, questions remain about the United States' role in his death. Again, since the subject is Nigeria, one may never know the truth. Certainly, if the American leadership eliminated Abacha by poison (allegedly served by imported prostitutes after the sex maniac had finished a long round of fornication), it must be that they had enough of his throwing rotten eggs at their civilized faces. If, on the contrary, they are innocent of any shady deal in the matter, then they must be relieved that they can now work with a reasonable ruler who will help promote Democracy. Whatever happens, and whoever happens along, the essential thing will always be, to watch out for America's economic interests. That much has been stated in all the reports of President Clinton's triumphant trip to Africa. *Time* magazine put out a special number (March 30, 1998) entitled, "Africa Rising." Clinton, at various stops on the continent, praised "African Renaissance."[8] He congratulated his hosts in Senegal, Ghana, Rwanda, Uganda, Botswana, and South Africa, for their open society and, most importantly, for the open market that encourages American participation. The Clinton administration has announced "a new Africa policy [that] will promote greater private business involvement in Africa, trade incentives conditional on democratic political change and military cooperation to produce a collective African peacekeeping force." (*The Washington Post*, March 29, 1998: C1) More revealing comments on the trip, the first extended visit by an American president: "As President Clinton pointed out in his speech in Uganda, the cardinal sin in American relations with Africa has been that of neglect.'

For all the sweet talk about respect -Clinton even made an indirect apology for slavery-and concern for human rights, "the president's visit to Africa certainly is based on America's national [economic] interests." When Clinton talks of "the cardinal sin [of] neglect," this author reads that as the desire to pay more attention to trade, based on Africa's growing private sector and more capitalistic tendencies. That, more than the tired talk of freedom of speech, of free and fair, democratic elections, is the thrust of the African adventure, and the bulwark of the new policy. Respected American political commentators, such as George F. Will ("Sorry, So Sorry," *The Washington Post*, March 29, 1998: C7), have gone as far as to berate Clinton's expression of remorse over slavery. In a piece of parody that carries the lily-white stamp of supremacist posture, Will says that Clinton has given the executive jet, Air Force One, a new name, "Sorry About That!" The fact is, that Americans of Will's ilk consider it absolutely unacceptable that their great, civilized nation would stoop so low as to apologize to savage Africa. Yet, such patriotic Americans must be aware that Clinton has done nothing to deviate from the straight and narrow road leading to American economic supremacy. The African Growth and Opportunity Act, now before Congress, again confirms our assessment. America will help Africa to grow economically, and America will derive maximum benefits from that process.

An interesting, and potentially major, aspect of the new Africa policy is, the central role being reserved for the African American community. On the surface, it would represent the United States' determination to nurture the racial and cultural relationship between continental Africans and their brothers and sisters in the American diaspora. Already, Clinton has been using as his special envoy to Africa, the Rev. Jesse Jackson, former civil rights activist, twice presidential candidate, and now chief executive of the pressure group, the Rainbow Coalition. The reaction from Africa seems to be positive: "Initially considered a potential liability by African policy makers and human-rights groups, the special envoy is now viewed as an asset." (*The Washington Post*, March 29, 1998: C4) An asset, perhaps because African leaders see possibility of exploiting the racial and cultural affinity, which, indeed, would be America's objective in the first place. An asset, also perhaps because the Africans would give credence to Jackson's image as an African American leader. Nonetheless, the aspect of liability has not been erased by the man's performance. In fact, Jackson's pathetic track record in African affairs is representative of the lackluster standpoint of other African American leaders. At least, their performance during the past five years of Nigeria's season in hell, has left much to be desired. It is on record that Jackson was a good friend of the Babangida regime. When Abacha seized power and began his despotic rule, Jackson was one of the signatories to an open letter to him, written by **TransAfrica**'s Executive Director, Randall Robinson, condemning the dictatorship's move away from "democratic reform and reconciliation, to the detriment of its people."[9] That 1995 document turned out to be the high point of African American solidarity with the Nigerian people, and the zenith of their protest against Abacha. Soon after, everything went south, as it were. Quite a number of the protesting elite found their way to Abuja, supposedly in an attempt to assess the country's conditions first-hand. But, in reality, those travelers were either deliberately or subconsciously playing into the tyrant's hands. He welcomed them with his special brand of African hospitality, with wads of greenbacks, and sumptuous, state dinners, and state-managed visits to sites and citizens enjoying excellent health and full of praise for the self-declared father of the nation.

Senator Carol Moseley-Braun was one of the prominent travelers. She went to Nigeria in August 1996. Abacha feted, and fawned upon her, so much so that rumors surfaced about a personal relationship. Rev. Henry Lyons, head of a major American Baptist convention, went, too. While he was relaxing in his five-star hotel suite in Abuja, and offering Abacha spiritual support,[10] news broke back in his homeland that the good reverend and a female associate were engaged in affairs of the heart and hands, that they were practicing adultery and picking the heavy purse of the vast Baptist congregation.[11] Another major player in the Nigerian game was Marion Barry, mayor of the American capital, Washington, D.C. He was reported to have kindly bailed out a group of local government appointees sent out to clean up Abacha's image. When Washington journalists failed to cover their press conference, slated for a big, downtown hall, the coordinator, Roy Innis, he of civil rights fame, sought out Barry who was generous enough to host the delegation in his office. Abacha must have been pleased, and sincerely grateful for such black solidarity. Hence, Barry later attended the "World Conference of Mayors" conference held in Abuja, in November 1997. Although Barry claimed to be unaware that the Nigerian government subsidized the event, the conference organizer, Johnny Ford, former mayor of Tuskegee, Alabama, confirmed the fact. Barry was confronted in Abuja; but he did not for one second think of leaving. Not until he had fulfilled his objective. "They [the local government chairpersons] are thirsty for information, thirsty for ideas that many of us could give,"[12] he declared with a flourish. He went further, to boast of his impeccable record, and clean character: "My civil rights background is so strong that I never could be duped into something." To add insult to injury, Barry bragged about his influence on the Nigerian politicians, as well as their imagined integrity: "They're not going to be dictated to by the military or anybody else." Many were perhaps not surprised that the Black Muslim leader, Louis Farrakhan, also went to Nigeria. He was given a welcome befitting a head of state, and the government named a Lagos street, the location of the American embassy, after him. Naturally, the United States resented the blatantly spiteful gesture of honoring the man who has stated that his country is the devil incarnate. Barry, Lyons, Moseley-Braun, and Farrakhan cannot hide their materialistic goals. If they had been honest, they would have stayed away from Nigeria.

Jackson's case remains the most unfortunate of all. A man of his experience ought to have known better than to go dining and dealing with those engaged in ungodly acts. Some African Americans are of the opinion that Jackson has actually lost credibility in his own community. Would that be why the American president appointed him as special envoy, that is, with full knowledge that Jackson would do nothing meaningful for Africans and African Americans?[13]

Jesse Jackson could have, should have, been more vocal against the Nigerian regime, just as he and others had been during the civil rights struggle. What is particularly galling about this African American silence and complicity is, that Abiola, winner of the 1993 elections, was not only a bosom friend to many of them, but also a comrade-in-arms. He was at the vanguard of the movement for reparations by Euro-America, to Africans on the continent and in the diaspora, for the pogrom known as slavery. He spent his time and money to promote programs of African solidarity. He was an active supporter of the Congressional Black Caucus. He was a generous contributor to Black colleges. When he fled to the United States in 1993, Abiola was very confident that his many friends— his African American family—would rally round to help restore his popular mandate, and rescue Nigeria from socio-political abyss. Given that letdown by family, one may not have any cogent reason to complain about the behavior of the American government.

Abacha's death, a metaphor for the birth of hope, and Abiola's, signifying the very opposite, the death of hope, have left Nigeria high and dry, in some people's opinion. Now, going by American and European expressions of relief and their show of solidarity with the Abubakar regime,[15] one is expected to have faith in future peace and prosperity. Past events, however, point to another possibility, that our dear imperialists will be glad just to return to a situation that they can control. It is becoming clearer by the day, that these democratic missionaries and exploiters will not, cannot, should not, be Nigeria's messiahs.

And that is one of the many myths that have to be exploded before we Nigerians can begin to address the hydra-headed problems facing them. Soyinka and other exiles shuttling between Euro-American cities, often in varying disguises and aliases meant to preserve their lives, have to come to terms with the reality, which they do know already.[16] They probably will continue to be welcome to live, work, and talk, in those countries, which certainly will project the image of Democracy. Unfortunately, that does not mean that the exiles would be able to impact policies in Nigeria, or that their hosts would help them overthrow any reprehensible regime at home.

One may then ask: How should those opposed to dictatorship seek change? What exactly should they do to search for meaningful solutions? And, perhaps the most bothersome dilemma of all: Is exile a viable option for the committed Nigerian? This author is himself involved in these dilemmas. The essays in this collection proffer some answers, but no definitive solutions. Exile, one might say, would be a provisional option, a sort of half-way house in which batteries for the ultimate battle are recharged; a conditional distancing from the war-zone, so that the combatant may reflect on what weapons to choose, and how to use them. But, then, those caught in the war-zone have a right to complain about what they consider as the cosy conditions being enjoyed by the exile. A question of broken bridges. Both the exile and the prisoner of war would do well to communicate, to combine their efforts.

As for Nigeria's destiny, the belief here is, that the ci\
[Biafra] days are long gone, when "to keep Nigeria one ['
task that must be done." That was the ploy of the military m
who commandeered everybody and everything to maintain a unity
that did not go beyond shared geographical space. Whether now,
or later, Nigerians must sit down, peacefully (a hope that some
might call hopeless!), to discuss their future. And Britain, or the
United States of America, or any other nation, no matter how powerful, will have no influence over decisions honestly taken by Nigerians, hopefully. And the rest of Africa will appreciate that event
as a harbinger of peace and prosperity for all, because it would be
the first major step towards the creation of a new Africa with a
voice all its own, no longer the ventriloquist standing in for Euro-
America.

Notes

1. John Oyegun, former civilian governor of Edo State, forced into exile, in *TELL*, July 8, 1996:14.
2. Editorial opinion in *TIME*, special issue, "Africa Rising," March 30,
1998: 34.
3. Salih Booker, "Is This the End of Africa's Invisibility?", *The Washington Post*, March 29, 1998: C1.
4. Far from being parasites and leeches, Nigerians are present in every
major profession in the United States, including the vaunted space
program, NASA. The refusal to publicly acknowledge this fact is an
aspect of the racist system.
5. See, Cindy Shiner, "In Nigeria's Confusion, Military Coup Looks
Like Democracy," *The Washington Post*, Dec. 4, 1993: A24.
6. Soyinka, in particular, has not missed a beat in vilifying the Nigerian
dictatorship. He was charged with treason in 1997, accused of being
the brain behind the spate of bombings that rocked certain parts of
the country. Soyinka's growing frustration at the international
community's lackadaisical attitude, is easily visualized in his many
writings and speeches.
7. Besides the political constraints, Mandela also expressed his anger at
the lack of courage of Nigeria's opposition, a point already made by
this author. See, for example, Emeka Nwandiko, "Mandela Blast for
Abacha Foes," *Voice*, Dec. 5, 1995:15.

8. In addition to *Time*, major newspapers followed the president's trail. See, John H. Harris, "Clinton Hails 'African Renaissance,'" *The Washington Post*, March 24, 1998: A1/A13.

9. For the full text and the list of signatories, see *TELL*, March 27, 1995: 14-15. Also, Karen de Witt, "Black Group Begins Protest Against Nigeria," *The New York Times*, March 17, 1995: 17.

10. Abacha established a reputation of pretending to be very religious. Rumors have it that, in the presidential mansion, *Aso Rock*, he had special marabouts praying for him round the clock. At the very tense, final months of his life, when all the political parties had, as expected, drafted him as their sole candidate, Abacha invited to Abuja leaders of all religious denominations, to pray so that he could decide on the patriotic invitation. The amount of money that exchanged hands at that prayer meeting, has been a source of much speculation.

11. Rev. Lyons has been indicted for fraud, and embezzlement of church funds. The prosecutor claims that he and his lover bought landed property together. During Lyons' visit to Nigeria, his wife set fire on one of the buildings owned by the man. The reverend's notoriety spread largely as a result of his unholy alliance with the Nigerian regime. (Lyons has since been jailed for his crimes.)

12. See, Vernon Loeb, "Barry's Nigeria Trip Angers Human Rights Activists," *The Washington Post*, Nov. 18, 1997: B1.

13. It would be useful to study the lack of real leadership in the African American community. The travails of such personalities as Marcus Garvey, Martin Luther King, and Malcolm X, make one wonder why black solidarity has been problematic. American officialdom always seems to succeed in sowing the seeds of friction, so that it is impossible to work on a common agenda. One perceives a similarity in America's dealings with a country like Nigeria. The fact is, if genuine leaders emerge, any policy of exploitation on the part of the American government, would fail.

14. One story often heard in discussions on Abiola's saga, is the claim that he had contributed a large sum of money to the Clinton campaign. This author has not been able to verify the statement. Another story, confirmed this time, was that the Abacha junta was a generous supporter of Clinton's reelection campaign in 1996. The funds were routed through the Arab business tycoon, Chagoury, who holds multi-million-dollar enterprises in Nigeria, and is well known as Abacha's friend and partner in grand theft.

15. General Abdulsalam Abubakar, Abacha's Chief of Defense Staff, took over the reigns of power immediately after his boss's demise. Reports have it, that the new Head of State was propelled to the hot seat

after some political maneuvering, since he was not the most senior officer. Thus, it is implied that there remains within the hierarchy serious in-fighting. By releasing political prisoners, promising to hand over to a democratically elected civilian president in May 1999, Abubakar won many people to his side, and convinced the foreign powers of his honesty and capacity to do the job.

However, the aforementioned military politics, and his close relationship with Abacha's predecessor, the self-declared evil genius, Babangida, have left some doubt about what the Head of State would be allowed to do by forces that may be beyond his control.

16. See, Steve Visser, "Message to U.S.: Help Me Fight Back," *Toronto Star*, July 12, 1997:m6.

CHAPTER I

DEATH OF A MYTH

INTRODUCTION: BIRTH THROES OF A NON-NATION[1]
I would like to begin this essay by relating three events that occurred to me in the United States and Africa; for, contemplated together, they underscore the problematic condition of both the Nigerian and his society. I was a Visiting Professor at Spelman College, Atlanta, when the great news broke about Wole Soyinka winning the 1986 Nobel Prize for Literature. I was naturally very excited to learn of the success of Nigeria, Africa, and the African world. I phoned everyone I knew. Very few were interested. Nobody called me first. Many did not respond to the messages I left on their answering machines. Now, in 1998, I am a Professor in the United States at a time when the American press is obsessed with scams and cocaine-deals of unscrupulous Nigerians. When my phone rings, I am almost sure it is a friend ready to pass information on the sad story of another poor, innocent American fallen victim to a devilish Nigerian. On the other hand, the press is almost silent on Nigeria's political situation. My mind flashes back to another recent moment: In 1994, I am back home in Lagos watching on television the World Soccer Cup quarter-final encounter between Nigeria and Italy. It is thirty-two seconds to the end of the match, and Nigeria is leading by a lone goal against almighty Italy. Many Nigerians are praying for a sudden change of fortunes, that our dear Nigeria may lose the game! And, lo and behold, the Almighty hears their prayer: Italy forces an overtime and wins the match. Nigeria is out of the competition!

You might wonder why some would exhibit such blatant lack of patriotism; why people would be so cold towards the achievement of an African son; why all the zeal about the iniquities of a handful of Nigerians, while the good deeds of the others are never heralded in the American press. The answers are, of course, complex, but they must go back to the context and condition of creating the entity called Nigeria; they must refer to the history of Africa within a world society that has long placed Africa last on the hierarchy of humankind; they must take cognizance of the implacable racism that we continue to face even when our human qualities place us at the top of the ladder. In order to fully understand Nigeria's present dilemma, one needs to look at how the *COUNTRY* (mark that word) was put together. Students of African politics and history must recall the glorious days of the Discovery and the subsequent Scramble culminating in the Brazzaville Conference of 1884 where the European masters carved out colonies and protectorates to facilitate exploitation and the play of power and self-aggrandizement. As for Nigeria, its history as a country dates back to the earliest days of this century when the two protectorates of North and South were created, and Mrs. Lugard, wife of the famous governor, stamped the name (the area around the River Niger) on the vast land populated by nations with no aspirations or intentions of coming together. From 1901 until now, the country evolved into:

a. Three regions (North-East-West), based upon the three main national groupings in the respective regions, Fulani-Hausa, Ibo and Yoruba; and

b. thirty States, in post-independence. In the interim, the English-speaking Protectorate of the Cameroon was passed over to France, to form the new Republic of (Francophone and Anglophone) Cameroon. In recent times, the Nigerian capital has been moved out of Lagos (on the Atlantic coast to the South) to the more "central" (actually in the North), newly constructed city of Abuja. These new creations (States and capital), do they represent a sign of breaking down elements of fragmentation and division, the so-called tribalism? an attempt to form a nation? just one more show of fragmentation and tribalism or, worse still, a display of political manipulation by new masters trying to use every trick in their bulging bag, to please themselves and their lackeys?

Political independence was attained in 1960. Until that very instant of hoisting the new flag and singing the new anthem which, by the way, has been changed by one of the military messiahs into a supposedly more nationalistic one, the North had insisted on not wanting independence. The first national anthem composed by a white woman, included the words, "though tribe and tongue may differ, in brotherhood we stand." In the opinion of the military masters of the mid-70s, those words highlighted and encouraged division. Hence, the anthem was thrown out the tribalistic window and replaced by another, compoed by a Nigerian, and more nationalistic composed; "Arise, o compatriots, Nigeria's call obey..." A call to unity, a call to sacrifice, a call to commitment. Unfortunately, there is a patently shallow ring to those words, because the leaders who chose them did nothing to prepare the population; nothing to nurture the very notions vocalized by the words that every school child and civil servant were compelled to learn by rote and repeat either at school, or- in the case of the civil servants- as part of the preparation for any promotion they might expect. At the same time, the educational system, and the civil service, were set on the path to decay. Regarding the country at large, the anthem, its lyrics, and the manner of its sanction by the regime, became one symbol of the people's condition: They were servants or, indeed, slaves of the system run by dictators without any thought for their welfare, or will. When the master commands, the servant must obey without complaint. Compatriots became the synonym for foot-soldiers; and Nigeria, a metaphor for the military. It did not matter that the patriotism which everyone was called upon to express was non-existent, a fabrication, a lie.

That absence of unity has always been a looming presence. When the motion for independence was moved (by the exiled mid-Westerner, Enahoro) in parliament in 1953, the Northern representatives vehemently rejected any notion of detachment from Great Britain. It took the perseverance and compromise of the Southerners, as well as a lot of negotiations, to bring the unwilling *dependents* of the Commonwealth Queen to cut off the umbilical cord and climb on the freedom train. Britain, master of divide and rule, had always played the North against the South. So as to agree to accept Independence, the North insisted upon having their choice as first Prime Minister. So was it. And so it has always been since 1960. Counting both civilian and military Heads of State, the North has supplied all but two, from 1960 to 1994: the first non-Northerner, General Ironsi, spent less than six months before he was assassinated by disgruntled Northern soldiers. The seond, General Obasanjo, came to power when the substantive Head of State, a Northerner, was assassinated in a failed *coup d'etat* in 1976. He, the replacement, was second in command and was virtually forced to take the post. No wonder that he was largely considered to be a figure-head. The second (1994) non-Northerner, a civilian, was hand-picked as Head of a redundant Interim Government by Babangida, the out-going Northern military *Executive President* (the first ever to so name himself) who had run out of tricks. It is said that the executive master-dribbler actually meant to sell the unwary country a dummy (to use the soccer parlance), to use the interim arrangement to buy time, and prepare the way for a glorious return as a civilian President. Unfortunately, however, he played into the hands of a fellow gangster, his deputy and surrogate for eight years, Abacha, who, tired of playing second fiddle, drove out the hapless civilian and became Head of State.

The events of 1993-94 would serve as sample of what I call the continuing sickness of the child of circumstances called Nigeria. The military regime of the one called Maradona, the one that spent all of his years in office preparing the ground for what he and his comrades-in-arms proudly and regularly called "true and lasting democracy," finally (after several canceled primaries) organized a presidential election in June 1993. International observers were invited in order to give the exercise a semblance of authenticity and approval. The observers expressed their satisfaction as the votes were being counted. The results were being announced. Infact, overseas radio and television had projected a winner when, suddenly (and I would say, not that suddenly to those of us that had expected the usual, strange abortion of reason), the Savior of the Nation called off the whole thing because, according to him, the process was tainted by corruption and graft, by rigging and all the iniquities of which he and his regime were definitely guilty. The unofficcial winner, Abiola, fled abroad when he realized that his life was at risk. The United States, Britain, its European Community allies, and others, expressed outrage and called for release of the final results. Hemmed in by those criticisms and, more importantly, by his cohorts hungry for their own taste of the national pie, the Maradonic messiah "stepped aside for the sake of peace and progress." His hand-picked civilian surrogate was enthroned without any legal or law-enforcement backing. Many remain convinced that it was all well contrived so that the second messiah could accede to power (which he did in mid-November 1993).

The new savior, spitting a similar language of deceit and deviousness, employing the very tactics of divide-and-rule and arrant inhumanism, making false promises to a resigned populace, and encouraging thievery and thuggery among an ambitious minority of rogues, remained in office until his sudden death in June 1998. To placate the foreign governments asking questions about *democracy*, which is supposedly the watchword for Progress and Modernity, the regime set up an "election" of delegates to a "National Constitutional Conference,"[2] to coincide with the period when, the year before, any thoughts of true democracy died a death of disgrace. All of an officially announced number of 300,000 total votes were recorded (note that Nigeria's population is an estimated 100 million). Of the 275 seats at the Conference, the regime reserved 96 for its own chosen representatives. To form a quorum, 1/3 of the total membership was needed. Among those elected, that is, voted for, we had a slew of ex-military men and members of past reactionary regimes that ran the country aground. In *The New York Times* (Oct. 25) and *The Washington Post* (Oct. 27, 1994), in *Time* Magazine, on *CNN*, we read and watched paid propaganda filled with blatant lies about how the great government of Africa's giant was doing its level best to establish "long-lasting democracy" through the Constitutional Conference. Meanwhile, the undeclared winner of the 1993 Presidential election was languishing in jail. The regime's opponents were hounded and harassed; anyone that dared say a word of criticism was jailed or cajoled into joining the army of patriotic tyrants and thieves, democracy-seekers democratically lynching the very people they were pretending to serve and protect.

POLITICS AND ECONOMICS: TWINS IN THE GAME OF CONTROL AND COLONIALISM

Politics, of course, goes hand in hand with economics. Nigeria's oil boom has been a bane from the very start. A mid-70's military Head of State declared: "Money is not Nigeria's problem; it is how to spend it."[3] Since those heady days, we have seen a series of big spenders taking the country to the cleaners. White elephant projects show-casing senselessness and obsessive sham grandeur, have become the order of the day. We have five-star hotels galore to host local robbers and foreign collaborators holding the people hostage. Budgets are not meant to be balanced but to be mind-boggling, open-ended in their possibilities for providing the empowered with endless wealth, like fleets of luxury and sports cars, mansions at home and abroad, and dollars in the millions and billions in Swiss bank accounts...

Let us take a couple of concrete examples of profligacy:

i. Nigeria, as usual, was a willing supplier of cheap oil during the Gulf War. Of the approximated $12.5 billion revenue lodged in what was called a *dedicated account*, some 12.2 billion was clandestinely disbursed, that is, unaccounted for.

ii. Nigerian National Petroleum Company (NNPC), the major unit for organizing and controlling the oil industry, was shown to have engaged, right from its inception, in games of gangsterism in which each and every head, or high official, made away with millions. No data reliability and completeness. No rigorous strategic capital plan. No visible mission. Indeed, only NNPC officials know (do they, really?) the amount of oil exported by both individuals and foreign companies, such as Shell, and Mobil Oil.[4] And one is not even talking of the flagrant violation of laid-down laws by these companies willing and able to bribe the country's leadership for favors unheard of in any nation worthy of the name. To deceive critics, the authorities set up all sorts of committees and panels to investigate corruption. But the results of such inquiries invariably found their way to the garbage-can.

iii. Some years ago, the government (it *was* a civilian regime headed, naturally, by a Northerner) decided to construct a cross-country pipeline from south to north to a brand-new oil-refinery at Kaduna, that is, from an oil-producing area to a faraway location, to make sure that the national industrialization process was equitably distributed.

One could continue to list such examples *ad infinitum*. Let us move on to the matter of *EDUCATION*. Nigeria has always prided itself in having a high quality system. Ibadan, the first university established in 1948, used to be recognized as one of the best in Africa. Others in Ile-Ife, Zaria, Nsukka, and Lagos used to produce graduates that compared favorably with their counterparts anywhere in the world. But, then, as in the socio-economic sphere, things began to deteriorate when institutions of higher learning were created according to political expediency. Each new State, carved out of regional and other larger entities to please or impress particular groupings and cause friction among perceived government opponents, wanted its own hardly viable university. Existing institutions started to suffer from neglect and loss of substance. There are now more than thirty universities, and numerous Colleges of Education and Technology. Not that these establishments are enough to meet the numerical needs of those sections of the country firmly rooted in the belief that education *a la Euro-America* is the passport to earthly paradise. The tragedy of the system is, that one sees no meaningful policy. Regimes, both civilian and, in particular, military, have (one can only say, deliberately) downgraded the quality of education. Universities are regularly shut down either by striking professors and administrators, or by a government unwilling to deal with the volatile psyche of students on campuses. College posts have become pots of gold to be scrambled for by paperweight professionals dancing to the beat of the bullies at the helm of power. One probably should not have expected otherwise in a country where the ruling class is made up of men in uniform whose knowledge of education was acquired in the classroom of combat and consisting of orders given and carried out, with hardly an inkling of initiative or reasoning. The Nigerian public calls them *Kill and Go:* All they can do is snuff life out of anyone trying to breathe or make them see reason. They just kill and continue in their relentless march towards nowhere. The minority that can read among them are known for reading books upside down.

In addition to the bungling armed masters, let us note that intellectuals lend their support to the process of prostitution and pauperization. That should be understandable in a society where money talks above everything else. You make money and you become a god. No one ever asks you how you came about it. Before Nike company ever knew about its advertising catch-phrase, Nigerians were already aware that you must "just do it!!!": Steal! Kill! Do anything! Just get rich, now! So, people seek positions for power (money-making machinery) without giving any thought to productivity or progress. And, since intellectuals are traditionally empty in the pocket through a combination of circumstances and a deliberate punishment meted out by an empty-brained public leadership, they are often tempted to join the band of robbers rolling in green-backs all the way to Swiss banks.

Now, in spite of the system, Nigerians still rate very high on the ladder of knowledge and competence. Here in the United States, for instance, individuals are found at high levels in almost every field imaginable. Nigerians live in, and contribute positively to, many countries world-wide. Furthermore, in these days of economic exile, Nigerian young men and women are finding their way to America in increasing numbers. Those who enroll in colleges perform very well. Which proves that they are as brilliant as anyone else; all they demand and deserve is the opportunity. Another point: Those of us privileged to have taught in both Nigeria and the United States, are convinced that, on the average, Nigerian students, due to the discipline instilled in them, to the seriousness of purpose with which they are made to approach the educational experience, and to their professors' competence and single-mindedness, are able to compete with their peers abroad, and American students have nothing to teach their Nigerian counterparts.

SOLUTIONS, OR MORE QUESTIONS
Let us finally address the following questions: Why and how did it all go so wrong with Nigeria? what to do? how to do it? As mentioned above, Britain created and encouraged disharmony. Besides, some "freedom-fighters" were opportunists militating for an independence allowing for their accession to power, even when it should have been clear that it was a prologue to doom to build a nation on

compromise. That first sell-out has left an indelible mark upon the country. To my mind, the North ought to have been left alone to choose its own path. One thing is now undebatable: whether one likes it or not, the Northern culture stands at loggerheads with the ethos and beliefs of the rest of the country engaged in openmindedness and a desire for progress and complementarity with the outside. The North, so we are told, must hold onto political power because the South has cornered socio-economic supremacy. That very notion reeks of parochialism, a spirit of stagnation and resignation, all of which does not bode well for a so-called nation interested in forging a common path to progress and development. Nigeria will remain nothing but a country, a geographical entity for as long as the leadership remains selfish and short-sighted. Religion is a factor because the idea of secularism embedded in the Constitution (how many constitutions are there?)[5] is just that, not practised or practicalized. There appears to be an ongoing competition (crusade or jihad) between Christians and Moslems, with the latter seemingly winning out, and the former ever so deeper into the bible in search of miracles.

We must, however, state that religion does not have to be a determining factor. For one thing, there are now infiltrations of the two imported religions in both North and South, although Islam is still rooted in the powerful North where the belief seems to be, that non-Hausa-Fulani cannot be true, totally accepted Moslems. For another, those foreign religions should not make us forget African religions and cultural practises that are more open, less combative, more accommodating and adaptable, in essence, more human and therefore better suited for inculcating the idea and ideal of Nation in people's minds. It is noteworthy that, while we are bickering about the qualities of two imported religions, our cousins forcibly carried away to the Diaspora have been resilient in retaining our original religion which has been a major factor in their survival in places such as Brazil, Cuba, Peru, and indeed, the United States.

The people, the legendary *mass of the people*, always being trampled upon by stampeding dictators, the Nigerian people are rather unusual. They are so resilient, so long-suffering, so easy to manipulate, because they have been pauperized and mesmerized by religious and political pranksters. They have apparently resigned themselves, as they sit, or sleepwalk to their grave. In 1994, oil-workers went on strike to push the military regime to release Abiola, the undeclared winner of the 1993 presidential election. The industrial action lasted over two months. The price of petrol at gas-stations skyrocketed from 3 naira 50 kobo per liter to 30 naira. People suffered. The regime survived it all. People were begging for mercy from the current messiah. He obliged. The striking workers' leaders were arrested.[6] The official price of gasoline went up to 11 naira (great news really: only half of the exorbitant price paid during the strike!). Prices of basic consumer goods, including food, keeps heading to the skies. People continue to suffer and smile. The fact is, in a ruined economy, in a State constructed upon corruption and the supremacy of material, all sense of reason and quality is lost. From top to bottom, the power of money and material has become almost absolute. Almost everyone wants to join the bandwagon to the paradise of plenty. The people, poor spectators, want to become players. They do not question the presence, or the action, of those using their, the people's, heads as soccer-ball. They are simply hoping and praying that, some day, they, too, will have the good fortune to don a green jersey and begin to roll in money, and kick some head!

THE FOREIGN CONNECTION: HOPE FOR A SOLUTION?
You have probably been thinking: "What can the United States do?" First of all, Britain, the ex-mother-country, is hesitant to strike against the Nigerian government that it more or less placed, and has been propping up, on the throne. Britain has to be aware of all those criminal activities; it has to know that those brigands should be thrown out. It is doubtful, nonetheless, that Britain would act accordingly. Nigerians have billions of pounds sterling in British banks (it's their right, says Democracy!).[7] Nigerian rulers are Britain's foster-children, and allies.

And the United States? We all know that American policy is dictated by economic interests. In the past, perhaps due to a certain political correctness and diplomacy, we used to read about America's love for Africa, and the desire to work with African countries for peace, progress and prosperity, all in Africa's interest. Today, as the climate becomes clearer, we are witnessing more forthrightness and, naturally, a more glaring (but not surprising) selfishness on the part of America and the entire West. For example, in its editorial of Januray 13, 1995, *The Washington Post,* chastising the in-coming Republican chairman of the Senate foreign operations subcommittee, expresses outrage at his opinion, that Africa is unimportant to the security interests of the United States and that foreign aid to Africa would be slashed while funds for the Middle East and Europe would be heavily boosted. *The Post*'s attempt is, to affirm that Africa is strategically important, that, as President Clinton has said, "Africa matters to the United States." But only a bad reader would mistake the newspaper's statement as genuine interest in Africa's destiny. What is being stated is, that whatever is done to and in Africa is necessary for America's "long-term economic and political interests." In short, as always, any notion of love or empathy for Africa comes dead last.

Nigerian oil has always been very useful and Nigerian dictators, smart dogs that they are, always make extraordinary efforts to please the master who will rant and rave about the absolute necessity to establish democracy while doing nothing to concretize his outcry. Nigeria, one is fully aware, is not the first example of such dodginess. Zaire has been ruled by a dictator whose savvy for survival was truly astounding. But it should not be, because he enjoyed America's support for over thirty years. South Africa suffered through almost a century of apartheid while America threatened and taunted the apartheid monster, and Nelson Mandela spent 27 years locked away.

The United States once insisted that the aborted 1993 election in Nigeria, must be completed and the results declared. Granted that the winner, a non-Northerner and a Moslem, was not perfect; but he did enjoy widespread support all over the country, and he won the election. Pity that the United States suddenly became silent. The kind of silence one observes in a cemetery. A silence loud enough to shock one into submission in the face of human-looking monsters armed to the teeth. The Congressional Black Caucus sent a team to Nigeria to discuss with Abiola and the military ruler. They were welcome with open arms and given promises of *a genuine, home-grown democracy*, through the actions and decisions of the same Constitutional Conference that was actually being used to push for the dictator's continuation in power until, some said, the year 2000.[8] Jesse Jackson, too, went there. He came out under a cloud of controversy because he could not impress perspicacious observers who remembered that he was a friend of the Nigerian military rulership, just as has been Andrew Young, who has led teams of businessmen and women to Nigeria. So, it is a question of economics, not democracy. The American public is not involved in what is being done over there. Here, the press is supreme and, if it is not Somalia, or Rwanda, or Liberia, anywhere offering really sensational stories, the press would hardly bother.

If the United States had wanted to help, it should have insisted on the immediate release of the imprisoned Abiola. It should have placed total embargo on trade, especially oil. It should have imposed sanctions. It should have pressurized other nations to cooperate in this process. But, it was the same old song: Poor Nigerians would suffer! They would die! There would be chaos!! There would be a civil war!!!

CONCLUSION: HOPE FOR WHAT?

Yes, indeed, we had a civil war before (1967-70) in which millions died. That war was the consequence of the egos of pig-headed individuals and the self-serving desires of confused groups. Result: the fire raged for nothing. Nobody learned any lesson besides the fact that Nigeria was/is not worth dying for. And that brings me back to that anecdote on the World Cup match. A nation is a notion, a state of mind, a dream concretized in acts giving reality to common concepts of life, growth, and survival. You live together, and die together, willingly. One single word, such as, *America*, makes many a heart beat umpteen times. One envies Americans for that oneness of attitude and action, although one often complains of its excessiveness. For Nigerians, the attachment is to other nations, simply because the necessary notion of the larger state was a sham from the start. For that reason, many see the need to create a Confederation where power would rest mostly with the states, not at the center. Others would like an outright break-up. Yet others think it possible to stay together, with changes, such as a rotational presidency.[9]

The tragedy of our present estate stems from the fact that nothing positive or meaningful is being done to address the myriad problems facing the country. Some individuals are entertaining hope in the activities of the self-proclaimed democrats, some of whom fled abroad to seek the support of foreign governments. If past experience is anything to go by, one must be skeptical of the outcome of such efforts. Moreover, there is ambiguity in the camp of these *militants/activists/democrats*. Some of those gone overseas are known to have contributed, by their acts of collaboration and corruption, to the decadence now dogging the country. It is also hard to explain how some of them got away while their comrades are rotting in jail and detention. Maybe there is coordination between the two groups. But maybe it is more a question of opportunism and confusion, which has been the norm in the history of the misguided giant of Africa.

Nigeria is feared for its potential. And it has played significant roles. For example, without its militant position backed with billions of dollars, anti-apartheid South Africa's final victory might not have happened as early as it did. Nonetheless, it is foolhardy to now compare Nigeria to South Africa, as certain ignorant impostors are shamelessly doing. I, as an intellectual, privileged, exiled, believe that pressure has to be exerted upon the military to leave, not with the intention of establishing democracy (a too often misused, meaningless word), but with a view to finally giving the country a chance to determine its destiny. And we must not ever forget that, in the final analysis, only Nigerians --and nobody else-- can save themselves (and I should say, ourselves!). For, contrary to the false dream of democracy choreographed by some humanitarian Afrophiles from abroad, the reality is, that those foreign friends are masters solely interested in keeping alive their economic supremacy. As it was in the days of colonialism so it is in today's imperialistic ventures and adventures: the master wishes to exploit while imploring his servants to espouse his way of life which we have learnt to call Civilization. The master knows that his servants are not at all interested in the development of their so-called nation. Even a blind man can see that Nigeria's educational, socio-economic and human systems have been savaged by a gang of armed robbers and their hare-brained collaborators. Yet civilized observers and advisers have kept calm, playing the waiting game, while the victims of the holocaust have themselves been busy praying and waiting for miracles from hell!

Soyinka, the Nobel laureate, calls his generation, just before mine, "the wasted generation." I call mine, "the wasteful one."

The hope is, that those coming behind will not be "the wiped-out generations," that Nigeria will not cease to exist.

Notes

1. Essay originally written in 1994. Updated for this book.
2. The arrest and subsequent death in prison of Shehu Yar'Adua, former deputy head of state to Obasanjo (1976-1979), has been linked to that controversial conference. Yar-Adua was an elected member. With his strong political pull, he had pushed for a January 1996 handover date by Abacha, to a civilian government. Before the motion could gain any force among the politicians and the people, the conference was sent on a strange recess. It reconvened about two months later, only to sing a different tune, giving the regime a free hand to decide its exit date. Meanwhile, the constitution supposedly crafted by the wise men and women, was tinkered with and torn apart by several government-appointed panels and, finally, taken into custody by the head of state who refused to release it until his death.
3. Yakubu Gowon, the acclaimed hero of the civil-war era, whose name became the source of a popular slogan, *Go on with one Nigeria.* He was ousted in a 1975 coup, after reneging on an announced promise to quit power. He fled to Britain, obtained a doctoral degree in political science, escaped prosecution for complicity in the aborted coup that eliminated his successor, Murtala Mohammed, and later returned home in triumph.
4. The world was alerted to Nigeria's oil tragedy, and the sad role of foreign companies, by the late Ken Saro-Wiwa.
5. Nigeria has fashioned several constitutions, a fact which underscores the confusion entrenched in the polity. Constitutions exist for the years 1956, 1959, 1979, 1985, and 1996. The last two remain the most baseless and redundant of all: The former, made public, was never implemented. The latter has remained a secret, although the new head of state has promised to have it published, and debated, so that his government may promulgate it into law. Many Nigerians find this to be unacceptable because, in their opinion, the conference that put together the document was unrepresentative of the people.
6. The most prominent architect of that strike, Frank Kokori, was released from almost four years's detention without trial, by the post-Abacha regime. Kokori has lamented the lack of solidarity among workers, and the necessity for true revolution in the land as the only

means to change. See, Adeniyi Ojebisi, "Kokori Mobilises Nigerians for Armed Struggle," *Post Express*, August 26, 1998.

7. At Abacha's death, it was revealed that he had over 3 billion pounds in a single British bank account. During her tenure as British prime minister, Margaret Thatcher once answered a question on Nigeria's wish to have its foreign debts cancelled, by stating that five Nigerians were rich enought to pay off all the country's debts. Meaning: Five persons had over $30 billion in their personal accounts. Mrs. Thatcher, however, never opted to have such people's accounts frozen, so that the cash could be returned to Nigeria's public coffers where it belonged.

8. One of Abacha's pet programs was called *Vision 2010*. It was a panel of almost 200 members mandated to draw up a vision of what Nigeria should be in the year 2010. No one knew why that particular year was chosen. The logical conclusion was, that Abacha intended to stay put until then.

9. The idea of a rotational presidency among the newly declared (by the 1995 constitutional conference) six regional zones, was reportedly one of the main aspects of the 1996 constitution. How that would play out is anybody's guess.

CHAPTER 2

NIGERIA[1]

One must admit that Nigeria is a unique country (no, not a nation), created by the brilliant Britons. Think of the very name, *Nigeria: land of Negroes*. Think of the principle and policy behind the country's creation: As a matter of ambition, power, and greed, the great Empire (may the King-Queen Kong rule forever!) successfully scrambled for an unwieldy, expanse of land made up of irreconcilable parts. Arab—Black; Islam—Christianity, imposed upon African Religion; Feudalism—Communalism; Koranic Education, with a tendency towards Fundamentalism and Southophobia—Traditional and Western Education marked by Adaptability to the Outsider; Exclusivism—Inclusion; Superiority Complex stemming from a certain Insecurity—Equality based upon Individual Quality; North—South.

That merger of totally incongruous, incompatible, vast components, must be the only one in the whole world, particularly now that the fabricators and beneficiaries of the farce are adamant in keeping it one. Remember the civil-war slogan which hid the fact that, were it not for the always brilliant Britons, the task to be done would have been one of separation?

Nigeria is the only country in the world where a civil war was fought, won, and lost without winners or losers. Where, until today, nobody is sure of the reasons for the tragicomedy. Where there are no statistics for the event that devoured millions of lives. Where villains replaced heroes who became villains only to transform again into heroes. Where the war, though supposedly finished, is yet to begin.

Nigeria is the only country where disunity is defined as unity. Where slavery is called freedom. Where dictatorship claims to be democracy. Where hate is paraded as love. Where the worst is presented to the world as the very best. And, most significantly, the claim in each case is, has to be, absolute, irreversible, because, as the civilized masters would have us believe, what God has put together no human being can put asunder.

Nigeria is the only country ruled by a Maradona, the one with mesmerizing moves and tricky tactics, feigning and flaunting his skills with flourish, smiling and scheming his enemy to death. And he is proud to call himself an evil genius. Yes, the people are his *enemy* to be dealt a merciless death, physical or psychological, while they -fools mistaking their destiny for a game of football- are applauding his every move. And they forget that Maradona, even with his billions, is just an entertainer playing to the gallery, a cocaine addict who, in his nightmarish dreams, would hardly distinguish between a man, a woman, or, indeed, a monster.

Nigeria is the only country held in bondage by a military fronting for an oligarchy, with both representing a backward, reactionary nation (note: not Nigeria) bent upon ruling the country forever. The military, lest we forget, was fashioned by the brilliant Britons who saw the need to provide a useful career for strong-bodied young men. But, we must remember, too, that the military quickly became brilliant: Rather than stay in the barracks, or go die in the Congo, those fully grown men realized that it was worthier to plunder than to protect; more profitable to give than to obey orders; to live in comfort than to die in trenches; to play the enjoyable game of politics, than the excruciating game of war. And so, the military pounced on the opportunity to snatch power from the hapless politicians by pretending before the people that discipline and probity and integrity, all qualities required in the armed forces, would be cultivated in that country created by the brilliant Britons. And the people applauded and acclaimed these newly born and well armed patriotic heroes of fortune.

Nigeria is the only country where the people are so stupid as to worship villains; so indolent as to want millions without working for it; so resilient as to find a way to survive under conditions that would destroy normal human beings; so cowardly as to adapt themselves to, and even with, enslavement. The people would welcome with glee a change, any change, in government because they are restive, impatient, and too crooked for their own good. Somebody once said that we might be an accursed lot destined to be governed by the worst elements in a country providing experts in almost every field of modern endeavors. Maybe that would not be completely true; maybe it is a result of the unwieldiness of the unique country. And, lest we forget, Nigeria is the only country the population figures of which nobody really knows.

Nigeria is the only country where elections are organized during a period of eight years with estimated billions of dollars, or pounds sterling (of course, it is the only country where everyone prefers, and calculates, everything in foreign currencies), only to have the whole process abruptly annulled at the very end. It is the only country where criminals working on behalf of a criminal regime succeed in causing chaos, and are commended for their patriotism. Where the judiciary is a willing and obedient servant of the autocratic executive. Where life and death are decreed by the whims and caprices of God-forsaken goons. Where the number one criminal steps aside for the next in command who immediately claims ignorance of each and every crime committed by him and his departing boss. And the politicians, those ever so malleable and mindless chameleons, promptly line up to obey and share in the booty.

Nigeria is the only country where politicians are prostitutes and pranksters. Where to be progressive means to participate in any program affording you the opportunity to make your pocket fatter, to obtain and maintain a position of power, to move up the ladder of official looters and robbers. And every politician is a progressive and a democrat, even when he or she is not intelligent enough to spell either of the two words. And the politician may wear khaki or caftan, provided he or she is able to prove that he or she belongs to the right tribe, either by birth or by affiliation. Note: If you were not born right, it is your right to right that wrong by learning the correct language, by changing your culture, or your religion.

Nigeria is the only country where religion is the yardstick for defining and asserting secularity. Where a military government insists on making the country a member of an international religious organization while shamelessly denying same to the surprised populace. Where a mosque is an essential component of the presidential palace. Where pilgrimage is part of official responsibilities. Where a Christian turned Moslem overnight can snatch a position of power for which he or she is not qualified. And there is a proliferation of Alhajis as well as Alhajas on the landscape of officialdom. A federal managing director may have been seconded from a meaningless state position where he spent all of two years. An executive chairman may have been a trainee under several of his new subordinates who are the very experienced professionals that trained him and were convinced of his mediocrity. A minister of education may be a political professor with no publications other than the documents in the bulging file that he carries from one administrative meeting to another. For the women, added to the quality of mediocrity is the willingness to provide succor in bed to the starving masters.

Of course, Nigeria is the only country where the rulers do not give a damn about women's issues. Yet billions of dollars are wasted on something called "Better Life for Rural (Ruling!) Women." You may say that yes, indeed, some progress has been made, from women to family, with the latest gimmick called "Family Support Programme." Those in the know would tell you, however, that both programs are only a means to one end: To provide an avenue for the female arm of the ruling class to corner their own piece of the national cake. Lest we forget, women in Nigeria are generally among the most victimized lot, but, similar to men, they are either silent or submissive to their victimizers. Like the men, the most vocal among them are the greatest prostitutes, painting and toning their skins until the veins shoot out, changing color like chameleons, conniving with criminals in the name of progress.

Nigeria is the only country where the ex-colonizers have succeeded in not only maintaining the *status quo ante*, but in convincing their allies in the West to support their imperialism. The brilliant Britons imposed divide and rule, and Northern dominance, as essentials of the so-called nationhood. They left and left behind these sacrosanct ideals which their brilliant successors have continued to propagate as the only passport to earthly paradise. You dare not query the word brought down from the tower of London. You dare not question the imposed paper-unity. You traitor, you felon, you unpatriotic element! Meanwhile, everyone who has not become an animal (understand that animals cannot think, they only react, out of instinct), can notice the progressive decay and destruction and, for fear of being silenced forever, is making plans to run away, very far away, if only he can find a way.

Nigeria is the only country where exile, even if it means enslavement, is now preferred to life at home. A common joke in Lagos is, that a slave-ship from America anchored off the shores of the ex-capital city, will be so overfilled with elated candidates, that it will sink right there, before setting sail for the New World. And the government is not at all bothered. And the authorities claim that life at home is more abundant than ever before. And they accuse any critic of collaborating with those Western enemies seeking Nigeria's downfall. And they tell everyone that hungry workers are excellently remunerated; that ill-equipped hospitals are providing first-class services; that everything is functioning superbly where there is nothing at all; that everyone is happy to be in Nigeria, including professors, and other professionals, who are dying to leave for greener pastures.

Nigeria is the only country where universities are shut down for the better part of every academic year. Where academic staff are expected to work almost for free under conditions least conducive to the pursuit and dissemination of knowledge and, whenever they dare complain, are threatened with mass retrenchment, so that they may be replaced by foreigners that will come from the moon. Where education is deliberately being destroyed as an aspect of national development.

Nigeria, the best named country in the whole world. Where the long, crooked, winding, pot-holed road is preferred to the short, straight, and smooth one. Where wrong and might make right. Where nobody knows *our destination.*

Notes

1.   Essay written in 1993. From then until now, nothing has really changed.

CHAPTER 3

AWOLOWO AND AZIKIWE[1]

When icons die in any country, they are serenaded as extraordinary, mythical beings. Nigeria is no exception, with the passing of Nnamdi Azikiwe during the 1996 summer of general despair and desperation. His death at the age of ninety-two has given everyone reason to celebrate and to reminisce, to feel good at a time when most are feeling very bad, battered as they are by a retrogressive regime insensitive to the free-falling economy and socio-political entity, and the potential death of a tenuous unit gingerly controlled by the British colonialist and ruthlessly bullied along by the local military politicians. So it is that Azikiwe, "Zik of Africa," is being praised to high heavens with all sorts of superlatives. A great pan-Africanist. Owner of the foremost seat at the fountainhead of Nigeria's modernization. One of the founding fathers of the nation. A Nigerian detribalized to the core. Universal reconciliator. Eclectic, pragmatic, and accommodating. Statesman, philosopher, sportsman, and poet. And so on and so forth. Zik's name is mentioned in the same breath as those of other acclaimed departed architects of our independence: Ahmadu Bello, Aminu Kano, Tafawa Balewa, and Obafemi Awolowo. By coincidence, Awolowo, who died almost a decade ago, has had his body kept intact until now. His family had his corpse embalmed, preserved for posterity (so we were told in 1987). Then, quite unexpectedly, it was announced that his remains had finally been interred, soon after Zik's death. Maybe it is providential; maybe it is contrived by Awo's family out of a sense of history, or selfishness, or financial expediency, or something else. Anyway, the death of the two men, titans of Nigeria, makes one think of a comparison, as a commentary on the country's past and present, and a comprehension of the characters that helped craft the content and context of our complex dilemma.

After Awolowo's death, similar songs of praise as are being sung for Azikiwe, were unloaded upon the people. There is a noticeable difference, however. No one, absolutely nobody, called Awo generous, accommodating, detribalized, nationalist, sportsman, pan-Africanist. In fact, many people perceived Awolowo's importance only in terms of his *tribe,* the Yorubas. Many believed that he was too rigid, unforgiving, and vengeful. Nonetheless, the then military president, Babangida, did take out a full-page advertorial on Awo's last birthday, in which Mr. President proclaimed the "tribalist" as "the best president Nigeria never had." Regarding tribes, I somehow have the impression that all those singing about Zik's detribalization are inferring that Awo was the epitome of tribalism. My intention here is, to comment on the two revered personalities, and to determine whether one was more detribalized than the other; whether, consequently, one was greater than the other; and whether, ultimately, one did more than the other, for Nigeria.

In terms of the struggle for independence, both activists were in the vanguard. Zik's travels as a journalist in Ghana and as a student at Lincoln University in the United States, to where he lured the likes of Ghana's first president, Kwame Nkrumah, gave him the grounding for a pan-Africanist perspective lacking in Awo, trained locally and in Britain, and more traditionally oriented than Zik. Zik's pan-Africanism was, however, less striking and less successful than Nkrumah's. Zikism turned out to be a Nigerian phenomenon, whereas the Ghanaian's name came to be the one single symbol for the African ideal culminating in the Organization of African Unity (OAU).[2]

Zik's commitment to the Nigerian struggle, just as Awo's, led to the passing of the political touch from London to Lagos, in 1960. However, instead of either one achieving the glory of national political leadership, it was a Northerner, Tafawa Balewa, who became prime minister, with Zik being handed the figurehead position of, first, governor-general and, then, president. For his part, Awo was condemned to the second-fiddle post of leader of the opposition. One cannot but wonder why the two men acted as accessories to the bastardization of the decolonization struggle. If their commitment was genuine, if their desire for a true nation was sincere, why did they insist on dragging along an unwilling partner? Why did they cede political power to that group whose culture of feudalism and non-adaptability to modernity centered upon Westernization, constituted a contradiction of the unity and freedom entrenched in the long struggle? How come Zik and Awo never thought of working together for the good of Nigeria? Awo's tenure as opposition leader may, indeed, be a sign of his continuation of the struggle but, then, his comrade, Anthony Enahoro, had moved the motion for independence in 1953, to which the North said no. So, why had Awolowo and his people not left the North behind?

Zik's capitalism and what has been called his Fabianism, would probably explain his flexibility in dealing with socio-political issues. Awo's socialism would blend with the rigidity that irked many people. While Awo harked upon the preeminence of the group, the policy and program of the party, Zik encouraged and epitomized a liberal individualism allowing for easy maneuvering of positions and programs, and giving room for free alliances with limitless possibilities. But Awo's socialism did not prevent him from accumulating personal wealth; one remembers his famous line, that "socialism does not mean poverty." And Zik's individualism did not stop him from using his charisma to bring together people from different cultural, linguistic, and social backgrounds; his National Council for Nigeria and the Cameroons (NCNC) was definitely more national than any other party of their times. Even though he had personal wealth, Awo did not flaunt his money. His legacy of free education for the masses must stand out as the most socialistic, popular, and progressive development program in Nigerian history. Indeed, the Western Region of the immediate post-independence period was the most developed area of the country, boasting a first-class university, the first television system in Africa, an excellent agricultural program generating money used for the kind of industrialization envied by others in and outside the country, a modern banking system, and an outward-looking civil service with offices abroad.

Zik, it must be said, suffered from a lack of base due to his "detribalization." By the time he was forced back to the East after his associates had crossed the parliamentary carpet in the West, the man had lost steam, as it were; his liberalism succumbed to the forces of ethnocentrism that he and Awo had failed to finger and eradicate at independence. Furthermore, Awo's success in the West can most logically be assessed and appreciated as an aspect of his character. What critics call rigidity would thus be perceived as principle, a sustained quality of excellence in both self and others, a single-mindedness without which success would be but a never realized dream, and a refusal to stoop to the beckoning sewage of corruption. The Western Region was built with money from agriculture. Its university at Ife, taken over by the federal government when Nigeria became cursed with the unfathomable wealth of its oil, has since gone from grace to grass, from boom to bust, in line with the tragic fortunes of the country.

Awo's much debated quarrel with his very eloquent and smart political deputy, Akintola,[3] is often cited as an example of his vengeful nature. According to the story, Akintola, who had been left to man the affairs of the West as premier while Awolowo went to the center as opposition leader, wished to be a substantive government leader, not a surrogate doing the bidding of an absent master. Awo objected to such individualism and insubordination. He was convinced that Akintola should represent the party's program. It was also speculated that Awo wanted to return to the West as premier, a plan that was adduced to his obsession with power. Akintola ultimately apologized to his angry leader who reportedly refused to accept the apology. The break-up of that friendship and fellowship, which subsequently led Akintola and his faction into the fateful pre-civil-war alliance with the Northerners, will forever arouse questions in the minds of many Nigerians. If Awo had been compromising and forgiving, would Akintola have joined in entrenching a Northern-based political power that has been trying, rather successfully, to perpetuate itself since the 60s? Would Nigeria have avoided the tragedy of the civil war? Would the Yorubas have been in today's position as exiles in their own country? Awo, the leader,[4] was no doubt ambitious, very ambitious; some would actually say, too ambitious. His hope to be president of Nigeria was all-consuming. He could not countenance any competition, or contradiction. As with many a highly talented person, he was caught up in his superiority complex, sometimes mistaking that for the omnipotence found only in God. That obsession would also explain why, come the 1983 elections,[5] he chose to run again, after his failure in the 1979 elections deemed to have been his best chance to attain power. Many people believed that the younger Lateef Jakande, his close disciple and, reputedly, a man of honor and great promise, ought to have been given a chance, especially due to Jakande's popularity, earlier performance as governor of Lagos State, and his understanding with Northern progressives. Awo insisted on running, and he lost, again. Before one gets carried away by Awophobia, hindsight shows that, maybe, just maybe, the man saw through his supposedly exemplary disciple, Jakande; for, today, the latter, the highly touted "Action Governor," the respected progressive, has joined the train of retrogrades backtracking towards the tunnel of darkness, disease, and destruction in the name of patriotism. Jakande shocked many compatriots when he accepted a ministerial post in the Abacha regime which had replaced the spineless interim government put in place by Babangida to prevent Abiola from becoming president.

Zik's vaunted virtue of being flexible and generous, could be seen as a lack of principle. At times, the man came across more as a journalist than a politician. The journalist is the conscience of the society, an observer, an analyst trying to make sense of nonsense, an adviser blessed with a soft spot for opposing entities from which he would like his society to forge a complementarity. A secondary, indirect activist at best, the journalist enjoys a certain aloofness unknown to the politician caught in the web of contrasts and contradictions called the Nigerian nation. The politician is compelled to take a firm stand. He cannot tergiversate, or else he will fall from the tight rope made to twist and turn by the whirlwind of intrigues and supplications of foes and friends bent upon influencing the society's destiny to suit their selfish ends. Zik was a man of honor, and one has the feeling that he recognized his inability to play the political game seriously: For all of the tales of principle and honesty, the Nigerian politician was often a prostitute, and a multi-faced prankster. Hence, Zik, rather than be a prostitute, declared himself a prospective bride, to be properly wooed and wedded and bedded by the best suitor. The problem is, that the bride remains attached to the bridegroom, and lacking in freedom and originality, and power. In 1983, Zik's party was, to all intents and purposes, an appendage of the Northern-based rulership. Some cynics might say that, in Nigeria's unprincipled political quicksand, the prospective bride could easily transform into a prostitute.

Awo's principled politics did not help him win elections at the national level. Of course, he did not aid his cause by failing to court voters in the North, where he pointed out the educational backwardness and nakedness, and in the East where he vowed to abolish some of the lucrative trade carried out by the people. Most likely that his failure to dent the latter's core resulted from his actions during the civil war of 1967-1970. Awo had been prosecuted and sentenced to life imprisonment for attempting to topple the government through a coup. With the country on the threshold of disintegration, Gowon, the Middle-Belt military officer chosen head of state as a matter of compromise, saw the wisdom in releasing Awo, who soon became minister of finance, and practically the head of government.

This is not meant to be a critical history of the Nigerian civil war. That notwithstanding, we must emphasize certain inevitable facts: conditions and circumstances preparatory to the mass murder and suicide included the absolute disorder and misrule in the West under Akintola; Awo's incessant conflict with the Sardauna of Sokoto, head of the Northern oligarchy. When the young Igbo officer, Nzeogwu, and his mates -both Igbo and non-Igbo- decided to cleanse the military and civilian mansions, Akintola and the Sardauna were swept into the cemetery. Nzeogwu and company's coup did not last long. His superior officer and the most senior in the army, Aguiyi-Ironsi, himself an Igbo, became head of state, but only briefly: Northerners, angered by the murder of their leader, decided to take the law into their own hands. They began by blowing away thousands of Igbos living in the North, as well as soldiers not of their ethnic stock. Aguiyi-Ironsi was cornered in Ibadan during an official visit to the military governor, Fajuyi, a Yoruba. They were both led away and assassinated. After the head of state's demise, Gowon, a Christian and Northern minority, was planted on the hot seat, all to the disgust of Ojukwu, his military superior, but Igbo. In brief, a combination of murder, mayhem, political and ethnic manipulations, as well as distrust, desperation, and determination not to give in to common sense, everything pointed to the disintegration of a country held together by compromise, connivance, and cowardice.

As he and Ojukwu were meeting to match wits, as Nigeria's political tradition was being born and honed by men in uniform supported by civilian collaborators, Gowon wisely chose Awolowo to lead the one-Nigeria crusade. Awo's superior leadership qualities, his insight and foresight, his control and creativity, his discipline, and his financial astuteness, helped the federal government bring Ojukwu's Biafra to its knees. There are many who believe until today that without Awo, Biafra would have triumphed in its bid at secession.

When Ojukwu threatened to secede, Awo was supposed to have made a statement that was to haunt him till his death, and that has continued to hound all Yorubas, and to hamper any potential alliance between Igbos and Yorubas. "If the East is allowed to secede, the West will follow," supposedly said the man, or words to that, or other, effect; for, when Ojukwu declared Biafra as a new nation, Awo was expected to declare the West's freedom, too. The Igbos saw in his refusal to secede a betrayal for which they have not forgiven him and the Yorubas. Awo's critics overlooked Ojukwu's personal ambition for power. They did not wonder how such a major move could have been taken for granted, without proper consultation and cooperation that would have culminated in a common standpoint. They were not concerned with the real conditions of the defenseless West swarming with Northern troops and therefore at the mercy of those marauding forces ready to destroy any opposition. Awo, the reputed repudiator of compromise, the legendary master of rigidity, revealed another side of his personality: He was thoughtful and realistic, he saw sense in dialogue, that is, in give and take, and, most significantly, he was a patriot with faith in a united Nigeria which he had sacrificed to nurture and, yes, which he was hoping to lead in future. He maintained that he had made no promises to secede. The Biafrans called him a liar, and a collaborator with their enemy.

Meanwhile, Zik's role in the events of that tragic era, although less controversial than Awo's, was made significant by its very secondary nature. It must have been a dilemma of vast proportions for the man acclaimed as undisputed leader of his people, to be relegated to the sideline as an interested spectator in the unfolding drama of Nigeria's destiny. Was it a sign of weakness, or conflicted loyalties, that Zik sat on the fence during the civil war? While the war was raging, he was in voluntary exile in London. If he had stood firmly behind Biafra, would the war have been won? If he and Awo had been on better terms and had cooperated in giving direction to the floundering country, could the war have been avoided? Of course, such notions must be understood in the shadow of the gun-toting commanders whose patriotism ended at the tip of the trigger. The civil war apparently ended any possibility for an Awo-Zik alliance, and Nigeria naturally has been the worse off for it. Biafra's defeat also heralded Zik's passing into a dusk of mysteries, with rumors of his death, and of various political affiliations, sporadically bringing him back into the limelight of the Nigerian tragicomedy.[6]

Awo, on the contrary, basked for a while in the sunshine of the civil-war success which served as leverage for his continued presence at center-stage. He lived unhappily after, however, because the military masters made him realize that, once the war had been won and the secessionist menace snuffed out, he was no longer relevant to the establishment and that, as it used to be so it must be again. Awo, the uncompromising genius, became opposition leader, again, this time against a regime armed with the gun and prepared to blow away any critic. Stories abound on how Awo was pushed to resign in disgrace from the Gowon government, and how, during an executive meeting, a Hausa-Fulani officer slapped him and a Yoruba colleague returned the favor in defense of the assaulted Awo. The long and short of it all is, that Awo had striven to keep Nigeria one, only to be reminded that Nigeria was never one.

Awo and Zik's politicking in the short-lived post-military era (1979-1983), was marked by a certain fatalism, or frustration, even though the former appeared to be particularly feared by the powers that be. Obasanjo, a Yoruba head of state, it was who, in 1979, proudly, patriotically, and prophetically affirmed that the best candidate did not necessarily win elections; hence, naturally, the Northern candidate, Shagari, was declared winner over Awo, in circumstances as controversial as those establishing the supremacy of night over day. Zik's party worked out a flawed alliance with the Northerners, in which Zik himself stood to gain nothing more than a reputation for propping up those continuing the domination of the majority by means of manipulation and ethnomania.

The 1980s, it need be said, witnessed the living death of the two extraordinary personalities and patriots, as well as the birth of the hybrid of the soldier-civilian in regimes mired in corruption and confusion, with one constant, the retention of power by the North. Did Awo and Zik know that? Did they care? Zik proffered diarchy as a solution to Nigeria's problem. One remains surprised that a man who fought for freedom from the chains of colonialism would see a possible, free cooperation between unarmed civilians and soldiers armed to the teeth; between individuals encouraged to express their opinions and those, discouraged from such a notion of originality and engaged in obeying orders; in short, between citizens desirous for democracy, and the minority trained to submit to dictatorship.

Although he fought for democracy until the very end, Awo himself showed signs of weariness, or, could it be resignation to fate? Awo, the nemesis of dictators, suddenly became the darling of one of the most notorious and cunning of the Nigerian model, the self-declared evil genius, Babangida. Awo visited the dictator's official mansion to thank him for his congratulatory message on Awo's birthday. What was supposed to be a private visit was transformed by the host into a most public affair. Press men and women surfaced from nowhere, to Awo's consternation. The aged man who took immense pride in his wisdom, had been outwitted by a master tactician. Awo, we were told, later warned those accompanying him to beware of Babangida, that he portended evil for the country. Surprisingly, Awo never warned the general population, nor did he propose, with his followers, a strategy for fighting and finishing off the menace. The image left in the minds of many Nigerians is that of an old, tired warrior reduced to hobnobbing with the people's oppressor who, perhaps to confirm the old man's fall into mediocrity, and to reaffirm Northern supremacy, honored the dead man half-heartedly: Awo's supposedly national burial was markedly at best a Southern affair; the televised event was blacked out in the North; his name has not been given to any national building or establishment, which seems to be the preserve of Northern patriots (just think of Nigerian airports). "The best president that

Nigeria never had" was therefore buried as the only leader that the Yorubas have ever had. Maybe, if he had not been too patriotic, indeed, too Nigerian—an irony very painful to bear—"the best president that the Yoruba nation should have had."

At death, Awo remained more controversial than Zik; perhaps, more bitter, too. He cursed Nigeria when he reviewed our sad society that makes virtue out of vice, that enthrones mediocrity, that manipulates facts to suit the designs of autocrats and ethnomaniacs, that prevents those with the ability from resolving our problems. Awo said that we would for long not have progress, not enjoy peace, because we refused him a deserved presidency. His critics, of course, sneered at him for sowing sour grapes; yet, everyone would agree that the man had immense qualities and that, when given the opportunity, he performed admirably. One recalls that smile fixed upon the face of Awo's corpse as it was carried across Yorubaland; it appeared to be expressing pity for his people, or could it have been a sign of better days ahead?

Zik's death in 1996 has also revealed one fact, that, in spite of all those songs of praise about the man's patriotism and pan-Africanism, he remains primarily the Owelle of Onitsha, leader of the Igbo nation and, indeed, as tribalized as Awo was because, simply put, there has never been a Nigerian nation. Besides, if being detribalized means, reaching out beyond one's ethnic group to actively seek the actualization of the dream of national unity, then one can confidently claim that both Awo and Zik were detribalized. Their struggle to liberate Nigeria from colonialism, is more than enough proof. In fact, the most tribalistic of their generation, Ahmadu Bello, the Sardauna of Sokoto, somehow escaped the epithet that he surely deserved. Bello refused to deal directly with the Southern politicians. And no one complained; nobody dared call him a tribalist. Among the most pertinent issues to be discussed about Awo and Zik is that of succession. Who will succeed Zik? Who will fill his shoes? Who will rise beyond his larger-than-life shadow? Who will lead the Igbos out of the no-man's-land into which the civil war drove them? That there is no genuine candidate in sight, underscores Zik's extraordinary character, but also the problematic of heroism and messianism in the colonial context where leaders, become mythical figures, are irreplaceable gods. Just as it has been with Awo, Zik has not groomed anyone to pick up the baton of leadership. To some extent, neither he nor Awo can be faulted, considering the changed circumstances of the neo-colonial struggle in which the foe may be your friend, and in which the Northern oligarchy has largely succeeded in cowering and conquering, or coopting through corruption, those standing for true federalism. On the other hand, Awo and Zik can be blamed for not fighting against the forces of that oligarchy with as much passion and devotion as they had done against colonialism.

Talking of succession, it is also noteworthy that the two men's offspring have, to date, done nothing to write home about, regarding Nigeria's destiny. It is generally agreed that Awo's first son, a lawyer who died young, represented the best potential for service and relevance on the public scene. Among the surviving children, one does not see that discipline, that disinterested desire to contribute, that generous attitude, and that charisma admired in the man who, according to the myth, was diagnosed by medical experts as having the intelligence of a man and a half. Awolowo's children often appear to be less than men. Their performance is disappointing when not disgraceful; their attitude, astonishing when not atrocious; their overall disposition, too selfish to count in the context of the embattled society.

It is still too early to assess Zik's children, although events that occurred immediately after his death are not very encouraging. Two sons with two different mothers engaged in a war of words over burial arrangements. Which reminds one that, unlike Awo who had one wife and who boasted of his abstinence from sexual intercourse for almost fifty years, Zik, a women's man, married again after the death of his first wife. His second wife was some fifty years his junior; in contrast to Awo, he enjoyed making love, wining and dining, and dancing. Zik was a sportsman; Awo, a serious man. If psychologists would find these distinctions useful in analyzing both men, they would find it difficult to use such data to explain their children's behavior.

In the final analysis, Obafemi Awolowo and Nnamdi Azikiwe remain the two most outstanding public figures in Nigerian history. Perhaps, due to the particular circumstances of the artificially created country, one should think less in terms of comparison, but more in terms of mutual criticism and appreciation. Within their respective nations, the Yoruba Awo and the Igbo Zik were unquestionably the leaders. During the difficult days of 1966, when the country was on the verge of crumbling, Awo was unanimously elected "Leader of the Yorubas" at a gathering for peace and unity by distinguished Yorubas in the Western Region capital, Ibadan. An interesting observation: The convener of the ceremony, Adeyinka Adebayo, military governor of the region, spoke of the Yorubas' "determination to come together as *one people with a common identity, common destiny and common objective;* namely, peace, tranquility and progress of Western Nigeria in particular, and the republic of Nigeria in general." (*The Daily Times*, August 13, 1966: 1; emphasis mine). The military officer was subconsciously reminding one and all of the absence of unity in Nigeria.

Within Nigeria, Awo and Zik were both patriots, with different perspectives and potential. And they contributed beyond the fact of independence. Awo opened the doors to Israeli expertise at a time when the Northern masters, imprisoned in their Arabophilia, were slamming the door against that means of material development. Zik showed the excellence of American educational system and technology, during a period of pro-British tradition. Unfortunately for Nigeria, however, the two men failed to see through the sham of Independence. Their error has meant not only the continuation of colonialism in the form of imperialism, but also the entrenchment of the North in power, that is, the succession of the same colonialism by neo-colonialism. So, when one reads all those encomiums being poured all over Zik's body, still lying and waiting for burial weeks after his death,[7] one can only smile ironically, wondering about what might have been. In these NADECO-crazy days,[8] it comes as no surprise that, in order to spite the Yorubas and to inadvertently slur Awo's memory, Zik is being praised for the qualities of *understanding, dialogue, patriotism, and Nigerianness,* all mere catchwords for condemning anyone perceived as the enemy of the military dictatorship.

Notes

1. Written in 1996, upon the death of Nnamdi Azikiwe, one of the founding fathers of the nation, and first President of the country.
2. All independent African countries are members of this political organization, modeled after the United Nations. There have been many

reasons to question its effectiveness, particularly given the fact that many African countries are under one form of dictatorship or the other.

3.   Ladoke Akintola, premier of the Western Region after Awolowo had moved to the federal house, became an ally of the hegemonic Northern rulership, and was murdered during the 1966 coup. The breakdown of the relationship between him and Awolowo was believed to have had a personal edge to it, as an extension of the disagreement between the two men's wives.

4.   Upon his release from prison in 1966 (he had been convicted of treason, for allegedly trying to overthrow the government), Awolowo was publicly acclaimed as "Leader of the Yorubas." See, *The Daily Times*, August 4, 1966:1; August 13, 1966: 1.

5.   That has remained the last electoral exercise, to date. The military seized power in December of 1983.

6.   The Nigerian press carried stories, on at least three occasions, claiming that Zik had died, only to recant and apologize. When he finally died, most were very cautious not to be embarrassed again.

7.   The corpse was, indeed, kept for several months, while the family, as well as the government, kept wrangling over burial arrangements, including where, and how, to lay the body to rest, not to forget what roads and other physical structures needed to be repaired and rebuilt to give him a fitting ceremony.

8.   NADECO, National Democratic Coalition: the grouping of those elements opposing the Abacha government that refused to cede power to Abiola, winner of the 1993 presidential elections. In Nigeria, NADECO became the symbol of the government's Enemy, considered too dangerous to accommodate, and therefore fit to be eliminated by all means necessary.

CHAPTER 4

OF GOOD GOVERNANCE
AND THE RULE OF LAW[1]

One of the major problems that have dogged Nigeria during the Abacha years, is lack of good governance exemplified by a constant and deliberate disregard for the rule of law. This probably should be expected, since the country remains chained to the boots of military regimes with little or no understanding of human rights. Everyone and everything here are ruled by decrees, not by laws. Decrees—and I bet, nobody, not even the supreme commanders themselves, can tell us how many there are—are orders imposed upon the people according to the whims of rulers not required to account to the people for their actions; hence, the orders address the masters' wishes, naturally, to oppress and repress, not to uplift and redress. Decrees, usually draconian and devilish, have one ultimate objective, to legalize illegalities, to put a stamp of righteousness on an act marked by and made for wrongness. The military, having abandoned the barracks for the ballroom of the political dance, would like to hoodwink the people into believing that the mechanical march of their big boots is a match for the free, rhythmic flow of the civilian feet. Imagine the music: The martial sounds resembling a funeral dirge, the one we usually hear on radio and television on the day of another, inevitable (?) *coup d'etat*[2] contrasted with the joyful, popular songs and their unregimented, spontaneous, thumping beat that awakens the core of the soul, and lifts the spirit. Decrees kill the people's freedom. They instill fear in them. They express the masters' desire for, and claim to, absolute power. They create a series of dichotomies, between the superior rulers and the inferior masses; between oppressors and the oppressed; the privileged and the unprivileged; armed robbers, and their helpless victims.

Decrees are the direct contrast of laws. A law is enacted constitutionally, that is, after proper debate among men and women elected by the people to represent and express their interests in a body accorded the responsibility to coordinate the country's affairs. One can, indeed, correctly affirm that laws are made by the people for the people. Laws serve two basic purposes, to preserve an individual's freedom, and to prevent him from impinging on the freedom of others. Laws strive to eliminate dichotomies. They endeavor to emphasize positivities, to promote happiness, and to remove or reduce hardships; for, they constitute the foundation for life and survival, they are the source of strength of a society consisting of human beings, not beasts. In order to guarantee the rights of the people and to discourage any tendency to manipulate, everyone has the right to question the legality of a law in court. Any citizen has the right, not only to sue, but to appeal, from the lowest to the highest courts in the land. To be certain that the citizen is adequately treated within the law, and that he understands and fully benefits from his rights, he enjoys the services of professional lawyers. He is client to a lawyer trained to represent his interests before another professional, the judge.

Before the law, everyone is deemed to be innocent until proven guilty. On the contrary, one is deemed guilty by decrees which, by their very source and nature, seek to shackle, and to condemn, without possibility of appeal. Having understood the facts of the matter, one remains rather cynically amused at the endless charades choreographed by Nigeria's military messiahs, whereby courts are allowed to listen to political detainees' lawsuits against illegal incarceration by the government, with the latter invariably refusing to obey the courts. Hardly a day passes without such a scenario, underscoring the inhumanity of a clique claiming to have come to save our society from its sins. When a court ordered the government to allow doctors to administer special, and necessary, drugs to Gani Fawehinmi, one of the military's most prominent critics,[3] they shrugged, smiled, and went away unmoved by the law that does not apply to them. As an after-thought almost a month later, a letter was sent by a lawyer in the Attorney-General's office, directing prison officials to comply with the order. They refused. The foolish Fawehinmi may die for all they care! From the contemptible attempt to scuttle the 1993 presidential elections by the collaborating parasites misnamed Association for Better Nigeria (ABN),[4] to the series of farcical processes in 1996 to chain people's souls while proclaiming to the world the patriotic desire at democratization, one has been witnessing the unraveling of Nigeria's judiciary in the hands of an executive of executioners. So as to abort the presidential vote, the ABN obtained a court injunction on the eve of the vote. The electoral commissioner was ordered to stop an exercise that had already cost the Nigerian public billions of naira. The judge, some faceless woman owing her position on the bench to her mentor and master, the country's Attorney-General, conveniently forgot the decree giving the commission immunity against prosecution in exercising its duties. She passed judgment in the dark of night, just to be certain that her dastardly deed would precede the action of the coming day. The electoral commissioner did try: He ignored the groundless court-order, and sanctioned the elections. He went ahead to have the results released. But he did not take cognizance of the might of the gap-toothed supreme commander aptly named Maradona. The latter, sly decree-maker that he is, simply ordered a stop to the whole process. His first public explanation was, that he wished to stop the judiciary from being ridiculed. When people, both at home and abroad, expressed their disdain and disgust, he offered other, more ridiculous reasons: The candidates had bribed their way through everything; the government was heavily indebted to the presumed winner, Abiola, and it would therefore be wrong to allow him to become president; and the military, a powerful class in the country, would raise hell were the man to become their commander-in-chief.

It is noteworthy that Babangida mentioned the insult and injury being visited upon the judiciary. Nonetheless, one must remember that, in Nigeria, there is no one-way traffic when it comes to corruption and destruction of the system. The giant of Africa has always paraded the excellent rewards of cooperation and collaboration in the corridors of power. Some judges are good candidtes for corruption. Not for them the ethical code of integrity, honor, selflessness, and devotion to justice and fair-play demanded by their profession. Not for them that element of autonomy and objectivity that has made judges symbols of a people's hope in moments of hopelessness. Not for them the refusal to support the raping of a people by reactionaries hiding behind a mask of nationalism. These judges in their large numbers are fence-sitters, at best; at worst, they are lame-duck arbiters always deferring to decrees aimed at sealing the fate of innocent people as slaves in a police state.

Some judges refuse to question the right of dictators to detain, and destroy, lives by decree. They are often appointed to chair military tribunals set up to try, and condemn, civilians. Remember Ken Saro-Wiwa, the Ogoni writer-activist, who, along with his comrades, was summarily sent to the hangman in November 1995, without the right to proper counsel, or recourse to any appeal. Once the death-penalty had been passed, the head of the national con-centration camp immediately ordered execution, while the world was still hoping for some humanitarian review.

But, not all judges are easily bought over as servants of the country's destructive saviors. A few, called rebels, have stood up to the tyrants. The only problem is, that their judgment is either ignored, or annulled by another, higher, and hypocritical, judge. Of course, the masters of the land know that the higher they go, the easier they will find collaborators. Thus unfolds the tragic story of the annulment of Nigeria as a country dying to be ruled by a law-abiding government. Abiola has won several cases asserting that he was imprisoned illegally. Judges have instructed the government's agents to release him on bail, or to allow him to read newspapers, to be visited by his family and doctors, in short, to live as a human being. The government has turned a deaf ear to all the court-orders. When the fancy catches them, its legal officers go to court to file an appeal. The judges, ever so considerate, ac-cede to their requests, and adjourn hearing until, maybe, never. And Abiola is rotting away in jail. And patriots are pleading for his release as a sign of the government's magnanimity. And those that dare mention the authorities' injustice are thrown into deten-tion, or warned to shut up, or else their bodies may be found in some dark alley pelted with bullets.

A decree has given the government the right to detain anyone for any, or no, reason, for any length of time.[5] The list of detainees is endless; one is not really sure whether the detainers themselves know all those, and how many are, in their hell-holes. In a few cases, the mistake has been made, by simply arresting people without using any decree. For example, the nonagenarian, Michael Ajasin, leader of the military regime's nemesis, NADECO, and thirty-six of his political associates, were arrested while they were gathered in his house at Owo (Ondo State), for a meeting. Apparently, the government's intention was, to harass them as a warning to stop opposing the train of progress heading for a destination called Destruction. Upon their release, they sued the state military regime for unlawful arrest and detention. The regime's plan of action has been, to disregard the whole case; its attorneys hardly go to court. The presiding judge, after running out of patience, finally felt insulted. He lashed out at "the most backward and moribund ministry in the country." (*Concord,* July 3, 1996: 10) He continued: "Law officers pursue political interests, rather than commitment to their legal duties."

Indeed, the very name, NADECO, makes Nigeria's military authorities cringe so much, that they would love to eliminate anyone whose name bears any of those abhorrent letters, or whoever dare mouth any word beginning with the letter, *N.* Perhaps that is why, after the assassination of Kudirat, Abiola's wife, the crack investigating team pounced upon four NADECO "saboteurs," as their prime suspects. The investigators' professionalism was never in doubt: It is usual for Nigeria's excellent police to chase shadows instead of substance; to solve crimes by absolving the criminal, and convicting the innocent; to arrest and condemn suspects before finding proof of their guilt. That, in their patriotic opinion, is the intelligent interpretation of the law. Meanwhile, the four NADECO old men went to court to seek their release, as well as redress for the inconvenience and inhumanity suffered in the hands of those agents of lawlessness. The judge agreed with the plaintiffs. He ordered their immediate release, with two-million-naira damages. He also admonished the law-enforcement agents to learn to respect the aged. He reminded them that power is never permanent, that they themselves could be on the other side tomorrow. He stated what everyone should know, that each of us is innocent until proven guilty of whatever crime.

As must be the case in a police state, the judge's verdict was ignored for weeks after its delivery. Weeks might turn into months, into years. Lest we forget, the police, magnanimous, did release one of the detainees, an eighty-four-year-old who had fallen dangerously ill in the cell. Such generosity must merit promotion; and a parcel of land in millionaires' row, for everyone involved in the matter. As long as the other three old men are not on the point of death, the police might hold onto them while investigations continue, forever. What may annoy their unpatriotic critics is, that the police, rather than shut up, are now busy trying to rationalize an irrationality. Firstly, they stated: "The law must be obeyed but, then, the court cannot order and we will carry it out without following the proper channel." (*The Punch*, July 19, 1996: 2) That means, that the order would go from the Inspector-General (IG) down the line, until it finally reaches the officer responsible for the case. When that statement was made, Mr. IG was away in his hometown, receiving visitors there to condole him on the passing of his wife. Before the public was privileged to know the IG's next line of action, his deputy gave a glorious interview to the Cable News Network (CNN).[6] Responding to the question on why the police was still detaining the NADECO officials, the honorable protector of the people said: "That does not arise. That is why we are not leaving any stone unturned. In the course of investigating a serious and very callous murder like the one that took place, we don't exclude anybody as far as evidence..." (*TNT*, July 24, 1996: 7) In other words, the old men are deemed guilty until proven innocent, or until the police can, if ever, find the real assassins who have long disappeared into thin air. The people's oppressive protector, in a sudden show of humility and honesty regarding the force's incompetence and inability to perform their duties, then seized the opportunity "to appeal to the general listening (not watching!) public that whoever has any information, they should just give us." (sic) The man's style, circuitous and incongruous, befits the police force that he represents.

Nigeria must deserve to enter the Guinness Book of Records, as one of the few countries with the propensity for flaunting its disgraceful image before the whole world, and for flouting judicial orders, regularly, proudly, and patriotically. Imagine the police refusing to produce Abiola in court, on the excuse that the court's warrant looked like a forged document.[7] Since the NADECO members' case began, nobody has questioned the conduct of the police. After the first few days of sensationalism in reaction to the verdict, newspapers found peace in silence over the whole issue. The police has appealed to the Court of Appeal, a higher court with a more patriotic judge who, they no doubt expect, would set down the earlier judgment and sanction the detention, -and subsequently the conviction?—of the old men. Such is the logic of Nigeria's superior system. In the meantime, Kudirat Abiola's killers will be found when Nigeria becomes a nation; hence, some would retort, never![8]

Nigerian judges themselves have come to accept the military's privileges as normal. Listen to one of their number in an interview on the rule of law: "When he [the head of state] is occupying that office he is higher than most courts." (*TELL*, July 22, 1996: 18) No wonder many cases instituted against the government by illegally detained citizens, are thrown out because they are "beyond [the judges'] jurisdiction." As I mentioned earlier, people's lives would have been much easier if the authorities had categorically declared that nobody has any rights under the military dictatorship; that they are living under the yoke of a police state; that they are puppets on a string compelled to react to the manipulations of the puppet-masters empowered absolutely. Once those facts have been established, everyone would live happily ever after. The courts could be canceled from the system. Indeed, that is already almost the case with the Supreme Court: Due to the fact that Abiola has won an unconditional bail at the Kaduna Court of Appeal which, naturally, the government has refused to implement, a no-case submission has been filed at the Supreme Court which, however, cannot meet, because the country's commander-in-chief has refused to fill the vacancies on the court.

Our submission at this point is, that he should not make any appointments: he merely has to eliminate, nay, annul all the courts. The executive should, instead of manipulating the courts, as has been the general practice, take over their duties. Military men and women, those heroic patriots blessed with exemplary character, should take charge in every area, including education, health, technology, and, of course, law. Solutions to problems would be all too easy to come by, through more decrees. For instance, so as to solve a murder, such as Mrs. Abiola's, a new decree would be promulgated, arresting every innocent soul in the country, and put them in jail until they all die. At that time of total patriotic imprisonment, there would be total peace. And it would not be necessary for a military chief to get angry and blurt out, as one did in the heat of the Abiola treason case: "We shall know whether it's the court that controls Abacha, or Abacha that controls the court!" Long live Nigeria!

Notes

1. Written in 1996.
2. Nigerians have become used to this military music which, strangely enough, they used to welcome with enthusiasm, in the false notion that the successful coup-makers were messiahs sent by the Almighty to deliver them from the fangs of the corrupt civilian leadership. (Now, in 1998, that perception has changed, radically: Every right-thinking person knows that the military themselves are super-corrupt, and must be driven back to the barracks where they belong.)
3. Fawehinmi must be one of the most arrested and harassed Nigerians ever. The joke is, that something must be awfully amiss if one month passes without the man being in some confrontation with the authorities. Perhaps the most interesting comment on his virtues and values, came from Maradona himself, Babangida. In a post-presidential interview, a rarity for him, Babangida confessed his respect for Fawehinmi.
4. An amorphous association that never hid its objective, to scuttle the democratic process, so that Babangida might continue in office. Its leader is, Nzeribe, notorious for his involvement in shady political deals. His biodata includes activities in Ghana in the days of Kwame Nkrumah.
5. The two most notorious decrees are nos. 2 and 4. Sometimes, a decree is specially made for a person, or a group, or an issue. To catch and convict Saro-Wiwa, a special decree was enacted in 1994. (The post-Abacha regime has not yet done away with these decrees. Their very presence makes the regime less humanitarian, less democratically-inclined, than one would like to think.)
6. Nigerians are hot on CNN, where one is likely to learn of matters concerning one's life, or death, long before the local networks carry the already stale story, if at all. Important to note that cable television is the preserve of the privileged minority who are in a position to

maneuver within a polity where the majority are just resigned to prayers and hopeless hope.

7. Hopefully, some day soon, someone would write a book on the political tragedy of Abiola. It no doubt will reveal a great deal on the fascist-like military, legal, and political system in Nigeria, and the sickness of the human mind.

8. The NADECO leaders were finally released after months of illegal detention. In all likelihood, Kudirat Abiola's killers will never be identified to the public, although the general belief is, that the government does know who they are.

CHAPTER 5

THE GOVERNMENT AND UNIVERSITY LECTURERS[1]

Having once belonged to the academic community of the Obafemi Awolowo University, Ile-Ife,[2] I feel ashamed and depressed to witness the current condition of my colleagues. Ashamed because, as I visit the university, I see glaringly -right from the gate- the decay. Depressed because, observing the personae working in the place, I easily read on their faces the feeling of helplessness and frustration, and there does not seem to be any hope in sight, besides the hope for a position (permanent or temporary) in America, or Europe, or Southern Africa, anywhere but Nigeria. Let me inform the reader that I am one of the number considered fortunate to have escaped from what has proven to be a concentration camp, indeed, sometimes worse than a slave plantation. At least, in those other places, the inhumanity was expected; there was no pretext at being civilized; and, it was possible to have some hope, because there was a concerted struggle against the devilish systems. On the contrary, in Nigeria, nobody, apart from the academics themselves, appears to realize how rotten the universities have become; how determined the dictators are to stifle education; how academe has been reduced to a state worse than that of the homeless.

I am visiting home from my American institution where, before my departure, I obtained every single information on my responsibilities for the next academic year, and even beyond. I arrived at home to find lecturers on an already three-month-old strike, just as they have been doing almost every year in the past decade.

Talking to them and others, reading newspapers and statements by the Academic Staff Union of Universities (ASUU), I have come to some conclusions: The government of Nigeria does not give a damn about education; the press and public do not understand the plight or importance of academics; short of a miracle, Nigeria may remain an undeveloped country for many years to come.

Now, I would like to refer to *The Guardian*'s editorial, "Ending the University Crisis" (June 19, 1996).[3] I disagree with the views expressed therein, that the meetings of vice-chancellors, deliberately scheduled for the deadline of the education minister's ultimatum to the striking lecturers to return to work, or else, "offers a good opportunity for a quick and satisfactory resolution of the current stalemate; [that] the tough measures may be expedient in the circumstances;" that the government's directive for local negotiations with each governing council as an aftermath of the proscription of the national academic union, contains a "logic [which is] unassailable [because] an employee can only negotiate with his employer." To my mind, the newspaper's only valid point is, that negotiations should be resumed with the national ASUU.

Without debating the rightness or wrongness of the system, let it be categorically stated that, in Nigeria, the government, and not its surrogate political stooges called university governing councils, is the lecturers' employer. From the mid-seventies when, in their dictatorial wisdom, the reactionary rulers seized the governance of all universities, there has been no doubt about who wields the hammer.[4] The destruction of the universities began at that very moment. At least, it is true for Obafemi Awolowo University (formerly the University of Ife), a true citadel of "learning and culture" (the institution's motto) built with agriculturally sourced money through the hard work and progressiveness of the people of the Western Region. Ife created, cultivated, and deserved the epithet of *Great Ife*, for which it became known throughout Africa. Its first vice-chancellor, Hezekiah Oluwasanmi, symbolized its excellence. Oluwasanmi, a totally devoted professor and professional, has remained unique among the university's executive leaders. Not a single one of his successors has approached his level of performance and integrity.[5]

Since the government has always insisted on flaunting its absolute power over the universities, how come, all of a sudden, it is now directing local chapters of the academic union to negotiate with their respective councils? Using as yardstick the fate of other unions (labor, medical, legal, press, nursing, lower-level teaching, etc.), one realizes that it is a matter of the well known *divide and rule* policy introduced by the great colonial masters, and continued by the even greater, neo-colonialist successors: Set the dissenters against one another! Break their already bent backs! Destroy their tenuous unity! And the pranksters cooperating with the repressive regime, are working hard to ostensibly save the nation from anarchy whereas, in truth, they are helping to eliminate those elements who have an idea of how to make the country grow.

Among the pranksters are the university councils and vice-chancellors. How could you expect these government servants to go against their masters? How could you imagine an interested party, already biased in favor of those providing him with loaded perquisites meant to lighten his financial burden for years after his meritorious disservice to academe, how could you imagine him telling the truth, or mediating with a mind to stating and supporting justice and logic? I bet that the meeting referred to in *The Guardian*'s editorial was called at the government's directive, to give the unwary the notion that the vice-chancellors are concerned about their colleagues, and the students, and their parents, and Nigeria's future. The behavior of vice-chancellors could be considered outrageous when one recalls that they are *supposed* to be professors (competent, and proud of their profession) before being vice-chancellors (circumstantial administrators).

Nonetheless, one is hardly surprised these days; for, vice-chancellors are politicians, having begged to be appointed, forgetting that seven years will come to an end, sooner than expected.[6] One Ife professor in charge of an Eastern university, and chairman of the Committee of Vice-Chancellors (CVC), claimed that they had worked out a great welfare package for the striking lecturers. His chest-thumping braggadocio reminds one of the self-congratulatory nonsense reeled off by each and every dictator choreographing Nigeria's rush to doom. As if these vice-chancellors do not know the salaries of their colleagues. (Think of a full professor of some twenty years taking home all of 8,000.00 naira per month, allowances inclusive).[7] As if they know nothing of laboratories occupied by rats and cobwebs and corroding concrete, or hostels housing hordes of half-educated students who spend more time demonstrating, or finding food to eat at home, than studying in the classroom. As if they are ignorant of the overall lack of quality in the tower of ignominy that they are helping to lay to waste. If these vice-chancellors were really interested in resolving the university crisis, they would send the government one message: Negotiate with ASUU now, in good faith, or else we ourselves would go on strike, or resign our appointments.[8]

With regards to the government, its actions are normal because, from regime to regime, they have shown their disinterest in education, and their desire to destroy the fabric of an institution which, in any society desirous of development, is accorded priority. In Nigeria, the rulers, democratic dictators that they are, decree everything since it is within their right; and the public is free to carry out the order, or else to face the freedom to be fired from jobs, or to face a firing squad made up of other free men... If not, how do you explain the practice of always threatening striking lecturers with thunder and lightning? Actually, one regime threatened to transform the university at Ile-Ife into an army barracks. Let us take for granted that the almighty rulers did sack all lecturers, who would stand to gain? Definitely not the students, and not the country.

A government that refuses to adequately fund education, is the same government that proudly informs the public of its decision to pay almost 400 million dollars to two foreign companies to monitor the amount of oil lifted from Nigerian wells. The same government, through its agents, siphoned some 100 million naira into the pockets of *matriots* running the Family (Self-) Support Program. The same government spends billions on a spurious transition program. The same government regularly creates superfluous committees and commissions that gulp millions and divert attention away from the problems preventing the country from becoming a nation.

Maybe ASUU will not win this war against the regime: Imagine unarmed, starving intellectuals pitted against an organized army with all sorts of weapons. Maybe all lecturers will be driven out of the campuses. Maybe foreign lecturers will come and teach here for free. Maybe.[9] One fact remains indubitable: Nigerian universities are in ruins, a legacy of regimes ready to hold on to power at all costs, and we know that Western education is anathema to these power-mongers. For one thing, their culture calls for other ways of life. For another, in order to keep a stranglehold on power, they can always send their own children abroad, with public funds. Upon their return home, the lucky kids will simply take their places at the top.

Now, lest we forget, not all intellectuals are opposed to the marauding forces of the military. Many eminent professors are definitely survivors. While some are prostituting themselves by seeking contracts from the government, others are busy preaching the gospel. Self-avowed born-again Christians or Moslems, they can recite the Bible or the Quoran upside down. Naturally, the time spent in studying God's Word limits the attention being paid to their various fields of expertise. Thus, scientists (both physical and social), linguistics, lawyers, engineers, doctors, computer analysts, and others trained to lead the country's children into the age of technology and progress, are congregating in churches and mosques, in search of miracles. If you dare criticize their intellectual fundamentalism and stupidity, these godly academics would quickly condemn your paganism. Their disease has rubbed off on many students who are competing in their commitment to the heavenly cause, to the detriment of the brain work necessary to prepare them for future survival and, indeed, leadership on earth. Stories abound of professors threatening to flunk any student that refuses to ascend to the religious faith of the professor's choosing, even if that would mean a descent into academic void. And, when professors claim that lack of achievement in their professional fields is a result of lack of incentive, particularly, funds, on the part of an illiterate government, they forget that they themselves are guilty of collaborating with the murderers of the educational system. One may, nonetheless, wish to rejoice with these flunkees who are forsaking the useless things of life for their reward in heaven!

I feel truly sad for the ASUU members who cannot leave. Their ghostly figures trudging along deserted roads, their gaunt faces wondering why intellect has been so disgraced, their cars running on empty, or jerked up on stone and wood, all these things make me want to cry. And, finally, I am wondering what parents, fathers and mothers of students, *people* just like ASUU members, precisely, the Nigerian public, are doing, are going to do, besides begging the government to "dialogue," and to exercise fatherly leniency, and ASUU, to go back and continue to suffer as enslaved servants in an inhuman state.

Notes

1. Essay written in summer, 1996, during a visit to Nigeria while college professors were on strike.
2. The author spent all his career in Nigerian academe at Ile-Ife (on and off, from 1969 until 1990).
3. *The Guardian,* published in Lagos, is considered to be one of Nigeria's most progressive and objective newspapers.
4. University of Ibadan, founded in 1948 as a college of the University of London, used to be the only federal university. Subsequently, new universities (at Nsukka, Ile-Ife, Zaria, etc.) were established by regions. In 1976, the military regime, under Obasanjo, took them all over. A third phase in the process was, the establishment of state universities, after the government had decided to fragment the geographical giant, partially to please sectional sentiments, and to facilitate its own political agenda.
5. Oluwasanmi, a product of Lincoln University in Pennsylvania, epitomizes the honest professional who, however, suffers from his honor and honesty. He was forced out of office as a result of a construction project scandal in the mid-70s. He later died of depression, forgotten in the new Nigeria where the corrupt and the incompetent hustlers too easily become heroes.
6. Nigerian vice-chancellors used to have two-term appointments, for four and, then, three years, if re-appointed. The system has been changed somewhat, although one remains uncertain of the real policy. Apparently, vice-chancellors were to be appointed for one term only, of five years. But, as at now, some of them have been able to obtain two, four-year terms, for a total of eight years. A more ludicrous turn of events is the appointment of sole administrators (a purely political posting) in place of vice-chancellors. See chapter 7.
7. At the exchange rate of 85 naira to one dollar, that would translate to less than $100.00. The differences in living standards and salary scales dictate that one exercise caution in such comparisons. Which does not lessen one's alarm at the ridiculous salary of the Nigerian academic. The post-Abacha regime recently announced a salary increase of up to 500% for all public service employees.
8. Vice-chancellors, no different from other Nigerian power-mongers,

claim that they are representing those courageous enough to jump into the fray, to contribute their talent to educational development, no matter how shallow the quality of those in power. The refrain: "If we don't do it, who will? By refusing to work with the oppressors, we would be giving them a free hand to continue to oppress our people, and to destroy the system that we all worked so hard to build."

9. Such were the threats of the minister of education, who made it appear very easy to replace Nigerian academics with foreigners. His attitude was symptomatic of the government's open cynicism towards those lamenting the brain drain to foreign countries. It would be useful to find statistics on those qualified Nigerians who have left home in the past five years, or decade.

CHAPTER 6

UNIVERSITY REGISTRARS AND THE REST OF US[1]

Lest we forget, Nigerian universities are not exempted from the sickness threatening to destroy the whole society. This sickness may be called *irresponsibility*, consisting of lack of commitment, and a whole load of mismanagement at the top. While it is true that the people share in the fast spreading sickness, those saddled with (or, rather, those who have seized) the power to govern them, have to take the lion's share of the blame. I disagree with anyone who would include incompetence as one of our basic problems, because Nigerians are present, and performing admirably, in nearly every field of human endeavor. It would be interesting to provide statistics on those Nigerians helping to develop other countries and cultures across the globe, while their homeland continues to wallow in undevelopment.

With regard to the universities, there is no gainsaying that they have almost lost touch with modern reality, and its demands. Universities in other countries are preparing for the twenty-first century; on the contrary, ours are trying not to be dragged back to the nineteenth. That is to be expected in a system badly funded, badly nurtured, and much maligned by the State which believes that universities are a breeding ground for unpatriotic elements. When the federal government took over universities in the 70s, the decision was controversial; the controversy has not abated since: Partisans of central governance saw it as an aspect of common national development, with all institutions of higher learning enjoying equal rights and standards, and moving together in the march towards educational paradise. Opponents feared that the task would likely prove too massive and messy, considering Nigerian socio-political complexities and particularities. No doubt that the nay sayers are right, because successive regimes have mismanaged education, and universities, both federal and state, have descended to the level of glorified secondary schools. As with everything else, policies have changed with each regime, each minister, and each vice-chancellor. What has remained unchanged is the fact that the university is made up of students and faculty, and administrative staff. Let us be very clear on this: Without, firstly, students and, secondly, faculty, there cannot be a university. Administrative staff are *supporting* employees, useful but dispensable to the system. Pity that this distinction has not been made in Nigeria; hence, the confusion and conflicts aggravating the other matters of infrastructure and development.

The current university crisis would be more easily resolved were all of us honest and honorable enough to understand the above fact, known and accepted anywhere boasting of real universities. The Academic Staff Union of Universities (ASUU), the body consisting of *faculty* -the word, I believe, is preferable for distinguishing between those who teach and the supporting staff- has been on strike since April 9, 1996. Before that industrial action, the junior administrative staff union, Non-Academic Staff Union (NASU) had caused unrest on campuses, hounding authorities into paying them salary adjustments, approved on paper but never implemented by the government. Meanwhile, the Senior Staff Association of Nigerian Universities (SSANU) has also used strong-handed means to achieve changes in its conditions of service. In each of the cases concerning administrative staff, the government has generally acceded to their requests. The university administration, represented in the person of the vice-chancellor, has too often allowed them, most especially the junior staff union, to run roughshod over the whole system. The events of 1996 at Obafemi Awolowo University, serve as a perfect example of this system gone crazy: The NASU executive deliberately lied, informing their members that the government had made available funds to cover some approved arrears. Of course, the university pointed out that it was only paper-work and nothing concrete. The stampeding army of aggrieved workers bombarded the VC and other principal officers with threats as horrifying as murder. They almost brought the place to a stand-still. Academics were even threatened with summary elimination for making efforts to carry out essential duties, such as organizing examinations. The Council and the VC were forced to pay the san-guivorous horde. Nobody knew where exactly the cash came from. Which, in a way, would raise the issue of the administration's own honesty, or rather, lack of it.

In all these events, the pattern has been that, somehow or the other, the administrative staff have had their way. Both the govern-ment and the university authorities are at once sympathetic to their cause, and prepared to condone their excesses with the attitude of a doting father. The enemy would appear to be the faculty.

By their profession, vice-chancellors are professors, suppos-edly; in reality, the contrary is the case: Once they move to the mansion on the mountain (images of the colonial administrator looking down upon the indigenes), they immediately metamorphose into mysterious masters, and messengers of the regime that em-ployed them. They become *management*, and the faculty, now con-sidered their employees, become *labor*. Note that we are talking of the faculty alone, not the administrative staff. Vice-chancellors find it easy to make this distinction because, in spite of their complicity with those destroying the system, they, as academics, realize that faculty, along with students, constitute the essential, necessary components of a university, and are therefore the group "to be dealt with," that is, to be disciplined, cut down to size, cowed, indeed, conquered, in order to truly control the institution.

This is how we arrive at contemplating the annoying role of registrars in the Nigerian university system. The top guns in the administrative hierarchy, the registrars seem to have forgotten that they are neither equal nor equivalent to vice-chancellors. The title, *secretary to the council*, appended to the registrar's name, categori-cally describes his or her duty: to serve as secretary; to carry out directives; not to make, but to implement policies; to advise; in essence, to facilitate activities and oversee the running of the ad-ministrative affairs of the *academic* institution. It is understand-able that, in the current problematic of Nigerian university system, registrars would see fit to take sides with the administrative staff. Nonetheless, they must be reminded that, willy-nilly, they and their underlings are secondary to the survival and success of the system. When registrars are instructed to make official announcements -on strikes, opening and closure, conditions of service, appointment, termination, etc.-, they should not forget that they have not taken those decisions. Others have so decided; their own duty is to pass information to the necessary parties. In other words, they, registrars, are in the service of the institution, as medium of action, not policy-makers. In such service, they should refrain from being over-zealous, or overbearing. When registrars meet and make recommendations on universities, they are certainly stepping out of bounds, that is, if their opinions are posited as registrars, not as ordinary citizens concerned with the resolution of problems.

The Committee of Registrars of Nigerian Universities (CORNU)[2] met recently to discuss the current ASUU strike. With tongue in cheek or, should one say, with their tails between their legs, the very patriotic body repeated the tiresome tirade against the academics, whose action "has imposed additional hardship on parents, guardians as well as on students and, indeed, the entire university system, including the striking staff themselves." (*Concord*, June 25, 1996: 13) They made the usual, cowardly, and hypo-critical appeal "to both ASUU and government (...) not to take a hard line but to embrace dialogue and compromise as a credible alternative to ensure the survival of the system." Most importantly and, no doubt, most patriotically, they urge the government to har-monize all the university unions into one body, to facilitate nego-tiations, and to help eradicate the ever-increasing dilemma dog-ging the system.

Before any other patriot begins to praise this most honorable men and women for their most intelligent, most forthright, and most logical suggestions, let us note that the same body has re-mained very loudly silent on the state of stagnation into which the universities have fallen headlong; on the barbaric behavior of the administrative unions in several universities; on the country's de-cline in nearly every facet of life. Registrars have continually seen themselves as an arm, or the handmaids, of the administration and, when it is convenient for them, as civil servants. Some registrars are actually failed, or fake, intellectuals: They could not go higher than a first degree or, where they have done so, it has been as an after-thought or, an aftermath facilitated by their presence on the university campus, that is, through the good grace of understanding lecturers. Registrars regard the latter as being undeservedly privileged on campus, as cry-babies accorded unnecessary rights and respect and, yet, always seeking more exclusivism. Registrars want a unified salary structure, and the same conditions of service as faculty. And, somewhere in each one's psyche, there must also be the desire to enjoy equality with vice-chancellors.

CORNU's recommendation on unions, cannot but be perceived as a representation of the above attitudes and beliefs. It might naturally, be most welcome by the country's rulers, who would prefer the easy road that leads to lies, to the winding road leading to truth. In addition, registrars are encouraging academics to dialogue with the deaf. CORNU has suggested a great way to cut ASUU down to size. It is all in line with the regime's program: Remember that each ASUU branch has been ordered to enter negotiations with the local governing council, not alone, but in the company of the administrative unions. The latter complied immediately, and announced their agreement with the government, and their contempt for the recalcitrant ASUU.[3]

But we all know that such short cuts will not lead Nigeria out of the woods. As each university senate is announcing that students should return to campus, as registrars are signing all sorts of outrageous communiques on behalf of the council, let us bear in mind that, without the faculty, the university is nothing more than another playground, or another parastatal with only files, but no programs to implement. I wonder, how does the senate form a quorum in the absence of the faculty who are its heart and soul? I note that, in some universities, senate consists of a small group of privileged, reactionary professors working with the vice-chancellor.

Maybe registrars and other administrative staff should begin to teach the students, and to direct their research projects; do individual and group research in various fields; establish and encourage post-graduate studies; nurture the dissemination of knowledge and the kind of atmosphere that would make for progress and development due to the engagement of intellectuals in human activities and exchanges. Maybe, as the first step towards sanitization of the university system, vice-chancellors should be asked to move back to their commoners' quarters among their peers, and registrars should move up to the mansions on the mountain. I recommend this most patriotic action to the patriotic government.

Notes

1. Essay written in 1996, during the industrial action of university lecturers. Read in conjunction with chapters 5 and 7.
2. One interesting development in recent years, is the proliferation of associations and unions, simultaneously with the government's myriad committees. A sign of confusion and weakness, or of solidarity among protesting parties, these creations have not done much to promote the cause of their members. Invariably, the leaders' hands are easily soiled by a regime engaged in the business of buying over, or beating down, all opposition.
3. That, happily, did not come to pass. Abacha held ASUU at bay until his death. He proscribed the union, along with other "troublesome" associations. They have been de-proscribed by his successor, Abubakar.

Chapter 7

OF SHAM AND SHAMELESS INTELLECTUALS[1]

For our particular purpose, and especially since we are dealing with a sick society, let us define *intellectual* with three simple but complex words: *prostitute-pimp, pauper, politician.* And one can immediately hear some readers murmuring, or shouting, objections and mentioning supposedly more adequate words, such as, *intellect, intelligence, academic expertise, clear and progressive thinking, knowledge,* and other terms applicable to learned men and women perched on the heights of the ivory-tower from where they disseminate knowledge to the select group of youths and adults being groomed to lead the nation into a haven of prosperity, peace, and progress.

But, alas, remember that this is a sick society! That is why our honorable intellectuals are perched on top of paper-towers being blown all over by the wind of mediocrity and mendacity manipulated by mindless individuals who have nothing to prove their claim to humanity besides their billions of public money hidden away in coded accounts. As they say, a beggar has no choice; on the contrary, our intellectual beggars do, from among the choicest charlatans and cheats of God's creations. Our dear intellectuals are downright poor professionals unfortunate to have chosen to go reading books, big books, when their fortunate friends went off to learn to wear big boots and win big booties, either with weapons or words. So, the latter, smart as foxes, have made easy money and, realizing their intellectual inadequacy, have used the money to win titles for which the former worked day and night. Chief the Honorable Sir Senator Moneybag has just been awarded the degree of Doctor of Letters, for emptying the coffers of his state and giving the dictators a helping hand in their duty of killing the very notion of a nation. Chief General Sir Doggone Death has become a Doctor *Honoris Causa* of Laws, for turning the law of the land on its head, and for breaking every law of nature, and for patriotically helping to murder the constitution in the company of unjust justices and lying legal luminaries. And, sure enough, the honorees have been begged to take the awards by zealous intellectuals who worked night and day to attain their own three degrees, namely: B.A. (Born Again), M.A. (Mad Again), and Ph.D. (Power Hungry Derelict).

The Nigerian intellectual would like to have us believe that the university, his hallowed ground, his heaven on earth, has been the innocent victim of government mismanagement, meanness and madness; that the education system has been deliberately and systematically destroyed by certain nitwits fearful of the intelligentsia and hellbent on dragging the populace back to the stone age of feudalism. Pity that he is a lying paperweight professor, or a lily-livered, boot-licking lecturer or, indeed, a cowardly, conniving vice-chancellor. And there is ample proof of this sad state.

First and foremost, Mr. Vice-Chancellor, the Chief Executive of the Citadel of Learning and Intellectual Leadership. In his status as a *progressive* professor, he participated in, and provided the push for, the system's evolution from an autonomous entity into an automaton manipulated by society's politically empowered solely interested in shackling minds, enslaving souls, and preventing real progress. He calls his reactionary radicalism, Revolution. No wonder when, after spending sleepless nights shuttling between the presidential mansion and other gilded fortresses occupied by self-appointed fathers of the still-born nation, he finally obtained his letter of appointment, his first step was to ban every attempt by anyone to use his brain in his, Mr. Vice-Chancellor's, plantation naturally modeled after the larger one outside. Aided by his cabal of colleagues with barren brains and money-sniffing minds, he is now playing savior and messiah to his confused community of faculty, students, and staff. Now, Mr. VC is an astute businessman, always on the lookout for capital projects, which means big contracts and, of course, his ten percent cut every time he puts pen to paper to sanction a glorious, developmental project.[2] He is also busy calculating his generous estacode as he flies from Lagos to London to Los Angeles to Lusaka, and to Rio de Janeiro and Johannesburg and Paris and Pretoria and Madrid and Moscow, and wherever, in search of nothing but money. Meanwhile, his dear university is rotting away. It is shut down by the government, or by himself, every year. He, Mr. VC, and his counterparts in other citadels of ignorance, are in full support of this policy, because they apparently believe that the best education of the children is given at home. And you must remember African tradition and culture...

For their part, the professors and lecturers have been trying to protest against that policy. According to them, on this the eve of the twenty-first century, Nigeria can ill afford to rely on simple home cooking when other countries are doing theirs on Mars, and the moon. For those concerned intellectuals, however, their past actions—they forget too fast—led to today's dilemma. Quite a number of them were well on their way to attaining the professional paradise when, some twenty years ago, a gun-toting, local colonial master, poised to save Nigeria from civilization and to carve a niche for it in savagery, ordered academics to call off a legitimate strike, or vacate their campus residences to go lecturing to hobos and hoodlums. Rather than maintain their stand, the cowards scurried back to the classroom.[3] Thus began the era of intellectual perversion and prostitution. The military masters gradually took charge and successfully reduced the universities to camps for conquered prisoners of war kept in check by their obedient empty-headed servants ready to rule over an academic desert, or wilderness, as long as the place is called a university, or college of education.

Nigerian professors would love to forget that many of them are guilty of encouraging the humiliation of intellectuals. Many professors did everything essential to attain a professorship as a means to a political end; to use the title to gain entry into the world of graft and greed presided over by men doling out perquisites. Our sham, shameless professors go peddling their curriculum vitae at the capital; they panhandle and pick up crumbs from the masters' tables, their toilet-paper vitae ever ready in file-folders; they beg to apply for anything available, from special assistants to uneducated ministers, to company directors; from cement and rice suppliers, to road contractors, and special advisers to nit-wits in power.

Professors rush to Abuja to report their peers, "insane saboteurs threatening state security and national peace and progress," all in the hope of a handsome reward for their patriotic snitching.

Some people would say that there have been truly progressive elements in the universities. Yes, indeed, progressive in the manner of loud-mouthed, publicity-seeking, marxism-spitting individuals quick to snatch a chance to turn coat (go to newspaper boardrooms, or the ministry of education), or to flee to greener pastures abroad (socialism must be a great preparation for adapting to capitalism). The great leadership of the Academic Staff Union of Universities (ASUU) has bred such self-serving demagogues who, in their grand-standing, refused to heed the warning, that Nigeria's ignorant, self-proclaimed saviors were not the least interested in Western education, or in any kind of education for that matter. By making industrial action (strike) the centerpiece of academics' struggle, ASUU has simply played into the destroyer's hands.

Students constitute the most important and least considered component of the intellectual community, and of society at large. Granted that they are hardly in a position to determine their own destiny. Nonetheless, they have, either by commission or omission, contributed to the bastardization of their citadel of mis-education. On one hand, Nigerian student leaders are as corrupt and as criminal-minded as the armed robbers running the country aground. Irresponsible and irrepressible, they rely on the law of the jungle, unwilling as they are to adhere to rules meant to educate and prepare them to assume roles as responsible citizens. A number of them now carry guns, eliminate opponents, dare the university administration to expel them, and generally reduce the place to a microcosm of the lawless and leaderless country. On the other hand, the student body plays patsies to the leadership, in a vein similar to the mass of Nigerians resigned to their fate as victims, full of prayers to a God that might soon be tired of listening to the exhortations of these apathetic millions.

The article, "ASUU's Ordeal" (*The Guardian*, June 11, 1996: 35), brilliantly crafted by an Ife professor, A.E. Akingbohungbe, details the issues of bad conditions of service, inadequate funding of universities, the spate of abandoned projects, and overall stagnation of the universities. Of much interest is the fact that it is the minister of education, a member of ASUU,[4] who abruptly announced the proscription of the union, and the termination of negotiations and, thus, caused the *impasse* (one of those Nigerian terms invented seasonally). No one should be surprised at this development, because professors, may they be ministers, vice-chancellors, company directors, or cement suppliers, are too often given credit for intelligence and integrity, which they may indeed, lack. In today's situation of economic miasma, professors are willing and able to compromise their principles, to ridicule reason, and to prostitute their very soul. ASUU itself has aided the universities' descent towards destruction, by wavering on many important issues, such as, appointment of vice-chancellors who, by the way, are not ashamed to brag about their position as government servants; bad prioritization of needs; loss of autonomy; relegation of students to the back of the academic bus; and the militarization of academe, with professors forgetting their ideals in their desperate rush after money and material. That would explain why some professors lose all sense of dignity and ethical consideration, to accept the ridiculous post of sole administrators in universities. Note that vice-chancellors are normally appointed through a laid-down process: Nominees (full professors) are voted for within the institution's organized units, specifically the senate and council. A final list of three names is then sent to the Visitor (the head of state), who is free to appoint any one of them. Even though this leaves room for political manipulation, it is still much more equitable than the latest innovation: Any pretext of democracy is eschewed, and the head of state simply appoints anyone, professor, or military officer, to be *sole administrator*, just as has happened in local councils, companies, and states. In essence, the universities have become glorified political playgrounds.

Ultimately, the problem is, that academics have lost their sense of self-respect and direction as they continue to be battered psychologically and economically. Contrary to the widespread belief that all the damage has come from external forces, there are proofs galore that intellectuals, too, are culprits. There are matters specifically arising from within that have been mishandled, as if the intellectuals have not passed through the doors of any university. On many occasions, academics act as do administrators; they are rigid, and retrograde; they act as if the institution were a military unit, not a center where intelligent, open-minded people strive for excellence, and cultivate the excellence without which the products would be only fit to live in the nineteenth century. In some professors' opinion, regulations are apparently made to stop students and teachers alike from making a headway, not to encourage their success in a well-organized, lawful manner. For example, at Obafemi Awolowo University, the course unit system, established in the spirit of facilitating a broad-based, liberal education *for the students*, has been run with the rigidity of robots, without any room for flexibility. In an ideal system, every course ought to be available every semester. Since logistic constraints do not allow such a luxury (dearth of teachers is the major hindrance), the least would be, to mount certain courses essential for those students on the verge of graduation. The sad truth is, that some lecturers object to this flexibility. They reject what they perceive as "unnecessary favors," or "contravention of regulations." They would rather make students wait for a whole year, just to take one outstanding course.

In that setting, where students are treated as if they have no rights, the academic staff union has often tried to play the role of advocate. ASUU's image is a dichotomy of the sublime and the ridiculous. One would expect progressive intellectuals to set excellent examples for students, by acting responsibly; by constructive criticism, and by positive contributions that would enhance the quality of both the academic programs and the general life within the community. Pity that ASUU, with its suspect leadership, sometimes is irresponsible, shallow-minded, and, indeed, a sham. Its actions and attitudes are often destructive, not constructive. It encourages anti-establishment thuggery and terrorism. It tends to always oppose everyone and everything, for the sake of it, without rhyme or reason. As with the student leadership, ASUU is led by a handful of vocal and volatile characters with the knack for stanching the muffled complaints of the silent, indifferent majority.

So, what could be done to save Nigeria's moribund university system? As a microcosm of the country, the institution would probably require many miracles (the Born-Again may have some function, after all!). But, seriously, all intellectuals would do well to search their conscience in order to return to the state of integrity, dignity, and quality that used to be essential to their profession. For example, the vice-chancellors might begin by tendering their letters of resignation, unless the political masters show necessary commitment to education. Come now, do you really expect those leaders of ignorance to write such letters? They would rather ask for life-vice-chancellorships, to give them a chance to complete their programs of transforming their campuses to Sahara Deserts, or plantations. By the way, a friend told me a joke, that the Nigerian government was mulling over the revolutionary idea of appointing military administrators for all universities. That may not be far-fetched: One university, Ahmadu Bello at Zaria, already has an ex-military sole administrator.

Notes

1. Written in 1996, during the ASUU strike to which the government responded with threats, and its own strike, against some vocal lecturers who were given the boot although, according to their status as confirmed employees, they were legally secure in their posts until retirement age.
2. In Nigeria, it is taken for granted that the person in charge of any project, has a right to a 10% reward (bribery, or deserved profit?) from the contractor, as an integral part of the process.
3. It happened in 1975. The military ruler, General Gowon, still basking in the fame of his civil-war victory and unwilling to accept any challenge to what he considered his absolute power, ordered striking professors back to the classroom, or else they must move out of their living quarters which were subsidized with public funds. Since nearly all of them had nowhere to go, the paupers were blackmailed into compromising their principles. Such coercion has become the regular trait of the Nigerian authorities. It is noteworthy that, in that 1975 disaster, senior professors led the government's anti-intellectual strategy.
4. Dr. Iyorchia Ayu, was once an ASUU executive with a reputation for honesty and progressive ideas. He used to fight for university autonomy. As minister, he came to stand against everything he used to represent

CHAPTER 8

ACQUIRING BOOKS FOR NIGERIAN UNIVERSITIES

Anyone reading this title would probably wonder why. It appears simple enough: The library is responsible for acquisition of books and journals for the university. That is expected in a normal system, in a normal society. However, in an abnormal society, the expected might be the exception. And so it came to pass in Nigeria, as the result of a brilliant proposal by the National Universities Commission (NUC), endorsed by the Committee of Vice-Chancellors (CVC), and being implemented by some universities.[1]

To clarify the situation, we ought to introduce the reader to those two eminent bodies. First came the NUC, established by the military government after it had federalized the universities in the seventies. The NUC, we are told, is patterned after a similar commission in the United Kingdom. Nothing wrong with such an imitation, the only thing being that, as usual, the Nigerian copy is a confused image of the original. The NUC may be compared to the central government itself, dictatorial and destructive, mired in discrimination and favoritism, with certain sectors savoring the meat while others, left with bones, are expected to suffer and smile. It is one of those unwritten laws, that the executive secretary of the commission must be a Northerner, because he must be in tune with the rulers' music as conducted by the education minister. The NUC proposes policies on university education, such as admissions, funding, infrastructure, and general development. From the very beginning, it has been accused of bias and backwardness and, naturally, the government has never bothered to address such unpatriotic complaints.

The CVC's mandate is not as clear as that of the NUC. It was a later-day creation, a kind of club where vice-chancellors could socialize, massage their egos, discuss matters affecting their various institutions, and, when necessary, develop common strategies. The exchange of views would help in resolving particular problems, and offer each executive an opportunity to benefit from his colleagues' wisdom. Once again, the ideal has proven to be far removed from reality. The CVC is an aberration because, without a firm footing in the decision-making process, it hardly does more than making unheeded suggestions. It is another forum for *dialogue,* that misused word in a land where monologue has become an absolute. In addition, the CVC actually increases the confusion already crippling the university system: It seems that the only recommendations coming out of those brilliant minds, are those liable to make the institutions pawns in the games being played in the polluted political arena.

In short, when the NUC and CVC put heads together, the result is a recommendation rooted in retrogression. That should be an eyeopener to those Nigerians who are too easily hoodwinked by meetings of the ever-increasing committees, to discuss Nigeria's ever-protracted problems. As the government's deadline to the striking academic staff approached in June 1996, the CVC was meeting frantically, to address the matter, and to recommend something glorious to the government. That was everyone's misplaced expectation. When the CVC chairman proudly announced that an excellent welfare package had been put together for the restive lecturers, a fellow executive quickly retorted, that Mr. Chairman was only expressing his personal opinion.

It turned out that the lecturers' problem was not the only item on the agenda: The acquisition of books was also on the table, and the wise men took a prompt decision. The NUC executive secretary quickly produced a Special Report. "Arising from the benefit of the experience gained during the implementation of the World Bank Adjustment Credit Facility, [the two bodies met] with a view to planning and working out the implementation strategy for central procurement of books, journals, laboratory equipment and essential staff development for the Federal Universities and Centres." The stated objective is, to improve upon cost effectiveness of book-acquisition. Centralization, it is claimed, will reduce overhead and fund diversion, improve input quality, and produce faster "the desired impact" of the government's increased funding of the universities. According to the document, the exercise will ensure "immediate and full use" of all funds, and eliminate the "perennial claims" of inadequate supply of the items needed by the institutions. All requests from each university shall be submitted on a prioritized list. The governing councils and boards will constitute a tenders committee to approve contract awards, and contracts will be signed by the chairman of Committee of Pro-Chancellors, that is, university council chairmen. More on the question of money: The federal military government is requested to approve foreign exchange at the official rate (22 naira to one dollar), instead of the other, commoner's rate of more than 80 naira, and to allow duty-free importation of materials.

The World Bank facility referred to above, is a program of central material procurement whereby some 40 million dollars was spent on behalf of 20 universities.[2] From all indications, the NUC has no reason to think or talk of success. In reality, there was no proper accountability on its part. University libraries have complained that there is as much as 200% discrepancy between what they believed they had spent, and what the NUC claimed to have ordered for them. Since the NUC is the arbiter, the master, the libraries can only complain, to no avail. The whole notion of centralization is doomed to fail because, one, only professionals are competent enough to handle procurement of materials in their given areas of expertise; two, experience has amply shown that, in Nigeria, the larger the entity being serviced, the less the quality of service; three, each university's needs and interests are definitely particular to it but, with centralization, there exists the strong possibility of making universities coordinate their procurement, purportedly to avoid "duplication," and to "cut costs;" four, Nigeria must be the only country in the world where some administrative body would want to centrally procure books for universities.

In all the reported deliberations of the NUC and CVC, in all the committees, in all projected actions, not a single reference is made to *librarians*. It were as if university librarians are simple technicians whose responsibility is, to receive materials, catalogue them, and distribute them to the users. While it is true that, in the new centralization, each institution is to make a list (supposedly with the help of librarians), it is also striking that the eminent administrative bodies at the center have the final say on what to actually procure. Librarians would thus become useless in the university setting. To cut costs, it might be advisable to retrench and replace all of them with school-certificate holders!

One stands convinced that, with the dollar windfall of the World Bank exercise, the beneficiaries would love to continue their blissful performance, even if the almighty dollar would be replaced by the lowly naira. To make up for that depreciation, they recommended that the government approve foreign exchange at the official rate. The latter happily obliged. This move, in my humble estimation, reveals the quality of the NUC and CVC, made of individuals ostensibly interested in academic progress and development, including autonomy which is essential for promoting knowledge. But these bodies are reactionary, consisting of collaborators in the oppression of the people. One would have expected them to advise the government to eliminate the discrepancy between the official and regular exchange rates or, at worst, to recommend that, if universities must enjoy official privilege, the government reinstate each university's right to the official rate.

University librarians must protest, if they are real professionals. Lecturers, already engaged in a struggle for survival, must also register their revulsion at the reactionary centralization. The NUC and CVC must be informed that there are more sensible ways to reduce overhead and fund diversion, to improve cost effectiveness, and to maximize the benefits from funds given by internal and external bodies. Each university already has in place human resources for handling procurement of materials. The NUC and CVC would do best to beg the government to kindly provide adequate funds for each university's needs. They should be sincere, not servile; honest, not hypocritical; professional, not political. They should be interested in improving the lot of the universities, not in causing more confusion.

Notes

1. Essay written in 1996. The history of the NUC is subsumed in the political configurations of the country. The CVC is, at best, an advisory or, rubber-stamping, arm of the government; at worst, it is a social gathering of university executives, with hardly any influence or usefulness as far as higher education policy is concerned.
2. One of the most striking consequences of Nigeria's dehumanization by the dictatorial regime, is the flight of foreign-funded programs, now finding their way to Ghana, South Africa, and other African countries.

CHAPTER 9

A. BABS FAFUNWA, EX-MINISTER OF EDUCATION[1]

The beauty of *The Guardian* newspaper—which is, indeed, the ugliness of the Nigerian situation—is, that you can dig up past issues and be almost convinced that you are reading the latest number.[2] In addition, past issues help to assess the quality of certain individuals, particularly those whom you once respected and who, unexpectedly, went against principles and honor. As the body politic has evolved (or, rather, kept going round in circles), you still wonder why those revered individuals did what they did, and whether or not they have been able to rehabilitate their dented, or disgraced, images, or whether they just do not care, or notice.

A short while ago, I was engaged in such a review of the past as a means to evaluating the present, when I came across *The Guardian* of February 26, 1994, with a back-page report on the former minister of education and youth development, Aliyu Babatunde Fafunwa. He spoke at the formal presentation of UNESCO's Jan Amos Comenius Medal to him, in recognition of his "longstanding and eminent work in the field of educational research and development." He was the sole African honoree out of five chosen worldwide. In his acceptance speech, Fafunwa made some interesting remarks on education, politics, and economic development: "True, Nigerian education is in bad shape, but it is not collapsing. We simply need to get our priorities right. Education is the best defence of a nation." He recommended that military expenditure be reduced by fifty percent, and the money thus saved be used exclusively for educational purposes. According to him, the Cameroonian skirmishes notwithstanding,[3] Nigeria would likely not be going to war; hence, defense funding should not be a priority. Demobilized soldiers should be retrained to become mass literacy teachers and farmers. Fafunwa further claimed that it was the then state military governors who, unhappy at not "handling the cost," scrapped the National Primary Education Commission (NPEC) whose board was directly in charge of paying school teachers. Now that the board has been reconstituted, Fafunwa said: "I think the country has learnt its lessons." Finally, he appealed to his successor as education minister, Ayu, to sustain his, Fafunwa's, pet project, the mother-tongue languages program. That speech could be considered as the honorable professor-politician's assessment of his national stewardship.

Reading the newspaper report made me think of Fafunwa's character, his contributions, his reputation, and his role in the Nigerian dilemma. I first knew the man when he was still a professor, a devoted intellectual, the legendary *Babs*, the architect of Ife University's renowned faculty of education, and its first dean. To Ife students, and to his colleagues, Babs was neither a Moslem, nor a Christian; neither a military collaborator, nor a political animal. He was simply their own Babs, principled, popular, and professional to the core. Years after his departure from that university,[4] his long shadow still loomed large over the institution, because he was the symbol of excellence, and the originator of the system that gave proper training to our children, the future of our society and culture.

When a friend informed me that Babs had been appointed minister of education, I refused to believe him. It could not be the same Babs whom we all knew; after all, *Aliyu Babatunde* Fafunwa was the new minister's name... Then clarification was made: It was the same man, happy to serve his nation and requesting that, henceforth, he be addressed by his *full* name. That simple metamorphosis in nomenclature proved to be symptomatic of the drastic change in the man's attitude, ideas, and actions. Fafunwa now wanted to be publicly recognized as a Moslem. He had become an apologist for the military, and a (willing?) tool in the hands of the clique whose mission it is to destroy Nigeria's educational system. One would have thought that, after establishing an unassailable reputation in his profession and, given the myriad examples of those preceding him in the corrupting political arena, Fafunwa would have refused to be used in the ministerial mission of destruction. In some people's opinion, however, he deserved the post, and those supporters vowed that he would perform excellently.

They have come to regret their optimism, and to admit that my seemingly pessimistic position was quite realistic. The fact is that, in Nigeria, if you wish to maintain your integrity and dignity, you should not collaborate with unpatriotic, uneducated dictators; for, no matter how solid your expertise, you will not be allowed to apply it. In Fafunwa's case, his being hamstrung was probably coupled with a certain political corruptibility unknown to those of us who had only seen him in the cocoon of academe. Throughout his tenure as minister, he did nothing to rescue the decaying university system, yet one of his chosen subordinates was another Ife University professor who had followed in his footsteps as dean. Fafunwa's evaluation of Nigerian education at his award ceremony, is nothing short of flippant hypocrisy and meaningless verbosity. If an institution is in "bad shape," as he asserted, how can one claim that it is "not collapsing"? Fafunwa should tell the public whether it is now collapsing, or on the upswing. Due to his great performance while in office, he would probably tell us that the latter is true.

With regard to his recommendation on the budget, one wonders why he did not make sure that some action along that line was embarked upon when he was minister. The matter of training demobilized soldiers as mass literacy teachers, is laughable and insulting to the intelligence of Nigerians. In a system where thousands of students in the field are very badly provided for, where thousands of school-children are reduced to the status of street-hawkers and hustlers, where college graduates are without jobs, why not think of taking care of those major problems, instead of expending millions of naira on training chronic illiterates? One might agree with Fafunwa, that ex-soldiers should become farmers although, knowing Nigeria, that might be another opportunity for the lower-cadre men to join their superiors in becoming big-time land-owners, with no interest in helping the country's agricultural productivity.[5]

Fafunwa's statement on the action of military governors,[6] is proof of the professional's irrelevancy and redundancy in the present dispensation. No matter how committed he is, the powers that be would most likely stand in the way of progress and any attempt to resolve the country's nagging problems. Now, when Fafunwa found himself in that situation, what did he do to register his objection? As the expert, as the minister in charge, he ought to have insisted on carrying out his responsibilities, barring which he should have resigned. He has consoled himself with the fact that NPEC has been reconstituted, but he must be dreaming, to think that Nigeria has learnt its lessons. One would like the honorable ex-minister to explain what lessons he personally has in mind.

The appeal made by Fafunwa to his successor, himself now another ex-,[7] must have been out of Fafunwa's passion for Nigerian languages. It remains saddening that an educator of his caliber took up the mantle of minister of education, to promote a program at best peripheral to the needs of a developing country such as Nigeria. Nobody would object to the necessity for a child to be immersed in his mother-tongue; in fact, that was usually the case in the past. However, it would be foolhardy to make such a program the centerpiece of a country's educational policy. Fafunwa, a renowned educator, could, and should, have promoted other ideas in the tottering system which, contrary to his claim, has been depreciating since geniuses, such as Jibril Aminu, emerged in the office of education minister.[8]

Fafunwa was removed from office, quite suddenly and silently. He was like a wet rag used to mop up dirt, and thrown into the garbage-can. This has been the common practice of military regimes. As the Yorubas say, a wife that you meet in the bar will abandon you at the same place. Often enough, important appointments are heard by the appointees on radio and television; naturally, so also is their dismissal. For his part, Fafunwa complained, and begged for the chance to continue in office, but he had to give way to another compromising intellectual, the self-proclaimed socialist, Ayu, who became one more statistic in the ever increasing clan of academic collaborators. Ayu is a younger man; hence, somehow, now that he is out of office, he may have another chance to redeem his image. Not so, Fafunwa, and that is the tragedy. For those of us who remember Babs, not Aliyu, we feel particularly sad and cheated because, being Fafunwa's colleagues, we would like to think solely of the man's excellent contributions to Ife, and elsewhere on the educational landscape. Pity that the ugly has come to taint the beauty of the good. Fafunwa's image as the winner of UNESCO's 1994 award, pales before that of the politician who served as handmaid for the gang trying to lead Nigeria back into a state of ignorance and stupidity. He has been a vocal critic of the military regime regarding the case of Moshood Abiola. It is doubtful whether these efforts would redeem his image as a man of integrity, or resuscitate our dear *Babs*. On a personal level, Fafunwa would do useful service to his people, by advising those that still respect him to think long and hard before deciding to dine with the devil.

Notes

1. Written in 1996, during the period of a heated debate on what would happen to Nigeria in the face of unfolding plans to make Abacha's hold on power a lifetime presidency.
2. In fact, this would go for several other newspapers and magazines, in the five-year period that interests us. Events seem to be repeated, like a broken record, like a replay of the same horror tape.
3. Reference to the yet unresolved altercation between mighty Nigeria and minuscule Cameroons, over oil-rich Bakassi peninsular. Not unexpectedly, France has been giving staunch support to the Cameroons. The whole matter is before the international court at the Hague.
4. Fafunwa left Ife in the mid-seventies.
5. In Nigeria, quite a number of retired military officers become farmers, although nothing in their background has prepared them for this vocation. The question is: How exactly do they come about the very big capital necessary to effect this change of profession? Perhaps the best known among them is the former head of state, Obasanjo.
6. The title has since been changed to *military administrators*, but the role remains the same: to rule the state by decree, not democracy.
7. Another particularity of the Babangida and Abacha regimes, was the constant, sudden change of cabinet and other personnel, a process that often entailed the recycling of what Nigerians call "bad rubbish," that is, the same useless actors in the tragicomedy called governance.
8. Aminu, a Hausa-Fulani, whose meteoric rise up the administrative and political ladders, serves as an excellent example of the North's gigantic position in the scheme of things.

A medical doctor by training, Aminu has been professor, vice-chancellor, executive secretary of the NUC, and minister, first of education and, then, of petroleum. He is now engaged in partisan politics, as he prepares for the new, civilian Nigeria.

CHAPTER 10

OF GARTH BROOKS, THE DREAM TEAM, AND NIGERIA[1]

To all intents and purposes, majority of Nigerians have decided to Americanize everything about themselves and, perhaps, it is some kind of consolation for the millions unable to ride the legendary horse of their various dreams. It need be said that Nigerians are not the only ones caught in the web of "God's own country." From Asia, Africa, the Caribbean, and Latin America, as well as Europe and anywhere, millions converge on *America*, in search of their piece of the paradisiacal pie. What is particular to Nigerians is, that we seem to always choose the most nightmarish of the elusive Dream, and to imitate the worst in the American character. This might not surprise those who believe that the propensity for evil has been an integral part of the geographical entity from the very beginning. And such doomsters would probably win against any argument in opposition to their viewpoint. Be that as it may, let us remember that America, *the U.S. of A.*, has very much to offer, if only one is willing to look and tread carefully. My intention at this point is, to use but a few examples of current events to propose possible areas of imitation, and a means of reassessing and refocusing our lives and society. Since many Nigerians are in love with foreign television (the British Sky network, and the American CNN, or whatever!), we shall refer to events related to the small screen. That action in itself, is symptomatic of the cultural enslavement that is part of our present. Yet, given the facts of incompetence, lack of integrity, and general malaise within the structures of our system, one cannot roundly condemn the *aficionados* of the imported material.

Garth Brooks is a country and western superstar singer honored in early 1996, at the televised American Music Awards ceremony. His was the final award of the night. Brooks had just been chosen as Artiste of the Year, that is, the best of the best. The applause was ear-splitting. The honoree, overwhelmed, stood up slowly, shaking his head in disbelief. He walked over to the other competitors for the music crown, and hugged each of them warmly. He then went up to the podium where he was met by the two celebrities who had just announced his name. He hugged them, too. They stepped aside, leaving him to bask alone in the limelight. Then, he moved to the lectern, clasped the trophy in his two big hands, held it high, very high, paused for a long, long moment as the excited crowd continued to clap and whistle hilariously. They were no doubt expecting the usual speech: an emotion-laden expression of gratitude to God, and all sorts of family and friends; a cocky, chatty reference to some celebrity producer whose proud face is almost simultaneously flashed on the screen; or, indeed, a non-speech of "oh-my-Gods," followed by a few crocodile tears. And, all the while, the speech-maker never lets go of the coveted prize.

Not Garth Brooks of that night, however. All he did was, to stun the audience by refusing to accept the award. He expressed his gratitude to the academy for their interest in music, but objected to the idea that he, or anyone else, was better than the rest. Silence, absolute silence in the jam-packed hall. Brooks bowed and walked briskly back to his seat. Then, as if on cue, everybody, without exception, stood and gave him an ovation the like of which might not be witnessed in another century.

One would hope that those Nigerians privileged to watch the spectacle, recognized the importance of the singer's action. One wonders whether any of them thought of the possibility of such a magnanimous, humble, and human act ever happening in Nigeria. Could it? I can hear a chorus of negative responses rending the air. Nigeria, the land where the selfish, the self-centered, and the shallow-minded grab the spotlight, and claim to be enlightened leaders, and "movers and shakers." Nigeria, the country where the crooked collude with the colonizers to corner the market of wheeling and dealing into which they have dexterously transformed the land of their dream but everyone else's nightmare. Nigeria, the breeding-ground of the best in every sphere of life who are, nonetheless, forced to give way to the worst. In Nigeria, you not only accept an award, you go for it, rush for it, make sure it is yours by all means necessary even, and especially, when you know that you do not deserve it. In Nigeria, you do not accept your mediocrity, you proclaim it as superiority, you denigrate others and, when and if necessary, you destroy them. And, whoever dare attempt to object to your greed and devilishness, you accuse them of lack of patriotism, of a desire to destroy national unity, and to cause disaffection among the peace-loving and law-abiding citizens.

Soon after Garth Brooks had left his award on the podium, another American, head of the navy, committed suicide, rather than continue to be the butt of jokes and doubts about his qualifications.[2] General Buttie saw the matter as one of honor, both personal and professional, an issue that went beyond himself, and engrossed the navy and the nation. His case proves that as Nigeria's leaders love to say, the nation is bigger than any one individual. Once again, the question: Could that happen in Nigeria? Another resounding no! You never resign your appointment, not to talk of killing yourself..., for nothing! You revel in your mediocrity, you boldly dismiss any dissension as the work of disgruntled elements. You make sure that the powers that be hear your empty noise and come to have absolute faith in you as their faithful servant. To you, honor never goes beyond the pocket. Integrity is buried in your bank-account. Patriotism is judged by how much you can lie, to ensure the perpetuation in power of your mentors and benefactors.

Garth Brooks and naval chief Buttie, in their different ways, teach us to see beyond our noses; for, that is the only way to begin to build a nation of which we know nothing right now. Both men are true to the vaunted but misconstrued American Dream. Vaunted because the concept of a nation built on commitment to the community and excellence, and on self-sacrifice, is to be admired. When an American talks of his nation, you can see his eyes light up with pride. Misconstrued, because the very excellence implied in the concept contains the potential for abuse of others' cultures. The American Dream would easily imply that another culture constitutes a Nightmare, with myriad attendant dichotomies, such as Good —Evil, Civilized—Savage, Best—Worst.

It is with these reflections in mind that one is struck by the idea of the Nigerian *Dream Team*, advertisement of which one regularly sees on the Nigerian Television Authority's (NTA) Saturday program, "This Week in the NBA." Note that this is an outdated highlight show of games played in the U.S. professional basketball league. It is probably one of those tapes that American television companies want to throw away, and decide to throw at some "Third World" backwoods, to civilize them. Of course, the enthusiastic Nigerian, addicted to America, cares not a bit, as his eyes are glued to the set showing the awe-inspiring moves by black giants. Now, before anyone thought of the Nigerian version, there was, as stated above, the American Dream. There is also *Hakeem the Dream*, that is Hakeem Olajuwon, the Nigerian-turned-American basketball superstar, whose on-the-court skills make spectators dream of perfection and paradise. Hakeem has been chosen to play in the forthcoming Atlanta games as a member of the American Dream Team III.[3] And we recall that the original super-team, including such extraordinary ball magicians as Magic Johnson and Michael Jordan, was assembled for the 1992 Barcelona Olympics, to avenge the unpalatable defeat of past American teams by the likes of Russia and Yugoslavia, and to avert any future humiliation in a sport the Americans consider as their personal property. The original concept, we must affirm, smacks of the notorious superiority complex of *the Ugly American*, a bad sports person never ready to accept others' quality, and ever ready to downplay every defeat. Quite a number of Americans, and others, remain spiteful of the Dream-Team concept, because the idea of competition and competitiveness has been eschewed. With all these high-flying, sky-walking, dunking Jordans and O'Neills and Pippens, and, yes, Olajuwons, the United States is guaranteed boring, lopsided victories in Olympic basketball. Nonetheless, one still stands to appreciate the excellent skills of the extraordinary athletes. From the original Dream Team, through the second edition (1994 Toronto World Games), to the current group, one notices the clear quality, the ability to entertain us, and the unparalleled teamwork. Even though each player is a superstar, the competition to be on the team, is astonishing. There is a laid-down procedure for picking the team by a knowledgeable, and responsible, committee. The players are well aware of the fact that, to wear the national colors is a matter of pride. Along with that pride comes a sometimes nauseating swagger, almost a contempt for others, etched on those giants' faces as they dunk the ball with authority, and smile slyly with assurance of their supremacy.

Now, here comes Nigeria's Dream Team of football (soccer) players preparing for the Atlanta games. One would want to believe that it is a worthy moniker. After all, Nigeria has been a world-rated team since the 1994 World Cup competition in the United States. But a *dream* team? Who chose the name? Why that name? The team's coach, a Dutch named Bonfrere (good brother!), stated on a Voice of America interview: "I don't know where that's coming from. The Dream Team is a team that has won all its matches, that wins all its matches. But we are still preparing..." So, whoever chose the name must be dreaming.

It is no doubt another attempt to ape America. There is a striking similarity in attitude, a certain feeling of superiority over other teams, but that is where it ends, and then a humbling contrast begins. In the Nigerian example, the superiority complex is ill placed, and uncalled for. While it is true that, individually, Nigerian footballers are highly skilled, they are no Pele, or Romario, or Ronaldo, although their country can boast of an ex-president called Maradona. The country has not been able to forge a *team* from all the great individual talents. And, most troublesome of all, there is no national pride. On the eve of the Atlanta games, our Dream Team remains a *bad dream.* Players are dragging their weary feet back home from their European clubs. They are also asking for their cut of the national cake in foreign exchange, before kicking a ball; and that is important, in a country where the price of everything is calculated in dollars, and pounds sterling, and yen. The football officials are not sure of who will be on the team, since nepotism and other selfish determinants, the least of which are not the whims of Mr. Minister, Mr. Director, and Mr. Head of State, must play a role in such decisions. Yet, officialdom is promising everyone that the team will bring back the gold medal and, in his ignorance, Mr. Head of State is talking of the Cup, perhaps because he is hallucinating about the one in which he takes his regular dose of medicinal whisky.

As Nigerians, we need to desist from the obsession with America. If we must Americanize, let us choose the best of America. Let us create a nation, then nurture it, and then we could begin to beat our chests with pride. Let us cultivate dignity and integrity, then build on it, so that when we inform people that we are Nigerians, they would respect us as responsible and serious-minded people who stand for something, and with something to offer. Let us also know the value of honor. If we dream, let us do so realistically, with the understanding that only honest, hard work, together, as a team, would lead us to success. And I do have a dream, in the vein of the great American dreamer, Martin Luther King, Jr., that one day, Nigeria will have a good government, truly interested in our people's welfare, in justice, in education, in health, and in social services, and in development. Not a sham of a government determined to destroy everything, obsessed with power, absolutely, until death sweeps away its heart and soul. When will my dream come true?

AFTER WORD (1998)

It has been two years since the Atlanta games. Yes, Nigeria did win the gold, and some did believe that The Dream Team was worth its name, in those gold medals dangling from the necks of the young soccer artists who stunned the world. Yet, the reader should not fall prey to the euphoria of one moment in heaven, because the reality, earth, is a mixture of laughter and tears, and it is only consistent, hard work that could guarantee something close to the bliss of a dream, sometimes.

With the Atlanta victory, The Dream Team was projected to stay put at the top, without working hard, indeed, without working at all. Members cashed in on their gold medals with top-heavy contacts with foreign clubs. They bought houses, cars, and jet-planes. They got married to beautiful women from all over the world. They promised to win the France 1998 World Cup. The Nigerian government and football officials lent their expertise in foolishness, and squander mania, disorganization, to the young men's headlong ride towards failure. The team's coach was fired, and foreign replacements came and left, with the one leading the team to France arriving just on the eve of the competition.

True to form, the team progressed negatively in its rather dull matches. It was disgraced out of the competition in the second round, by Denmark, a team that was supposed to be simply a stepping stone to the next opponent, Brazil, the world's number one team which Nigeria was so obsessively dreaming of beating. As an aftermath to the debacle in France, stories emerged, full of accusations, and counter-accusations of lack of professionalism, corruption, bribery, petty thievery, fascism, and plain selfishness. It was alleged that the players had demanded, and obtained, pre-match bonuses for victories that they never won. Officials were accused of pocketing allowances meant for players. The head of state was allegedly angry that certain players of his choice were not fielded on a team that often appeared to be drugged by egoism and greed. Some members vowed never to play ever again, for Nigeria. And, of course, some officials swore never again to invite certain players to represent the great country.

The rumors -yes, everything was, and is, a rumor- have abated. Nobody wants to talk anymore about the dream turned into nightmare. The dream-teamers are enjoying their money, and entertaining their foreign public, while Nigerians are waiting for the next Dream Team, hopefully, to make them laugh and not cry.

Notes

1. Written before the 1996 summer Olympics that took place in Atlanta, Georgia, USA.
2. This tragic event reminds us of Japan, a country with a sense of honor that far outstrips that of the United States.
3. Some have accused the player of being unpatriotic to Nigeria, for becoming an American citizen. In response, Olajuwon might ask them: "But where is the nation?"

CHAPTER 11

YORUBA OBAS[1]

In the original Yoruba culture, before colonialism and neocolonialism came and caused confusion and contradictions in the name of Civilization and Nationalism, the *Oba* was a respected father of his people. He had dignity and integrity. He respected himself. He was a symbol of the very best in the society. He was wise, and one poignant aspect of that wisdom was, that he hardly made his voice heard, directly, that is. He spoke through the elders, and others in his domain. Besides, his voice was not that of an individual; rather, it represented that of the whole community. The *oba* consulted with his people, because he was at one with them. The word, *oba*, has been inadequately rendered into English as, king. The latter, symbolic of a culture with societal hierarchy and dichotomy, immediately conjures the image of a superior being held high by his subjects who are inferior, like servants below the master. Although the *oba* enjoys immense respect as a higher-up, it is not in the sense of absolute superiority. There is, inherent in the institution, a basic element of democracy, in that the oba's respect had to be earned, not taken for granted. Ultimately, his subjects, far from being objects in his control, were active factors in his condition and position, because they had the power of approval and dismissal. The royal families, a small group from which the *oba* was elected, attained their status through their exemplar, their acts of heroism, which set them apart as worthy of playing such a role of leadership in the community. The people accorded the families that singular status, because they deserved it, and they were expected to constantly maintain their dignity. The *oba* was interested in his people's well-being and welfare. In case he failed to live up to expectations, he could be destooled, sent into exile, or, indeed, killed. The institution remained the foundation of Yoruba solidarity, strength, and survival. The *oba* for long remained symbol of Yoruba culture in all its richness and vibrance.

Today, everything has changed, mostly for the worse. I am not saying that we should return to obaship as a system of governance. I realize that, in some ways, the system stood against a certain democracy, the possibility for each citizen to aspire to the highest position, the absence of privileged groups, etc. That notwithstanding, I would have loved to still have in place *obas* with tested traditional qualities, *obas* who respect themselves, and who are able to offer genuine wisdom and leadership to their beleaguered people. In our current trying times, we could really use such wonderful characters.

Let us quickly review the condition of Yorubas in 1996 Nigeria. With the exception of a few, such as Pa Ajasin,[2] one cannot think of any viable, and reliable, Yoruba leader worthy of the name. All we can boast of, are opportunistic politicians playing dirty games, and prepared to sell their people to the highest bidder. Most tragically, our *obas* are as politically bastardized as any other individuals.

Our *obas* see nothing wrong with quarreling in public over innocuous issues. They have become clowns on the comic stage, as each is claiming seniority and superiority. They talk too much. They make stupid comments on every matter being discussed. They are businessmen seeking contracts from any government of the day. Some of them are millionaires traveling all over the world, instead of sitting down with their people to find a way out of the many dilemmas facing us. In recent times, one has witnessed, with disgust, the battle of words between the Ooni of Ife, and the Alaafin of Oyo.[3] As if they and their followers were ignorant of the basic complementarity between culture on one hand, and politics on the other, the two went into battle with no holds barred. As if, in present-day Nigeria, they had anything to gain more than cash for themselves and contempt for their people. As if both of them were not supposed to be symbols of harmony, unity, progress, and cultural sophistication. Now that the government has resolved the power-tussle between the two men by creating a new state, one expects both to give the people some peace.[4] Not so fast, however: There are still the nascent conflicts between the Alaafin and the Soun of Ogbomoso, as well as the emerging rivalry between the Ooni and his counterparts in Osogbo and Ilesa, and any others who might join the fray. I propose that, to solve this whole problem once and for all, a state be created for every deserving *oba*; and we do know that they all are!

One of the most disturbing arguments right now, is brewing in Egbaland,[5] and it shows how some *obas'* foolishness has led us to the abyss of contempt in a country where the Yorubas have played proud roles in its development. His Highness, Oba Dr. Tejuoso, Kabiyesi Osile of Oke-Ona, is embroiled in an ever deepening struggle for superiority with Lipede, the Alake of Egbaland. The most wise Tejuoso, a latecomer to the throne, and an example of the latest vogue among intellectuals and professionals, to add the monarchical crown to their list of laurels (would you say, a ques-tion of inferiority complex?), has written two books to prove that he is not inferior to the Alake and that, to the contrary, his domain's royal father is hierarchically above the latter. Tejuoso has given several interviews, and seizes every occasion to repeat his point.

The Egba Alake Community has shown restraint in discussing the sensitive issue. I read their advertorial in *The Guardian* of June 22, 1996. Even though I am not in a position to assess their histori-cal claims, I cannot help agreeing with the Community, that the Alake has always been recognized as senior *oba,* that, Tejuoso's action and statements show that he is "consumed by an irresistible political ambition," and that his self-conceit has led him into " a state of megalomaniac confusion."

As the post-1993 election drama has been unfolding, one has been dying for the emergence of an elder, such as an *oba*, to offer leadership and proffer useful advice to the Yorubas. The Ooni of Ife seemed to be talking sense when he declared that Abiola, a Yoruba son, had won the free and fair election, and therefore de-served to be Nigeria's president. The traditional ruler actually said something to the effect that, if Abiola was denied his right to rule, the Yorubas would consider secession. Many Yorubas were elated at that speech, but they were proved wrong by His Royal Highness's sudden change of face and pace. His support for Abiola, his "son," proved to be as strong as that of a father abandoning his child to die, and yet proclaiming his unalloyed love for him. The *Oba's* threat was empty talk, perhaps a ploy to garner the government's attention and patronage. Since 1993, Oduduwa's descendant has progressed from one blunder to another, purportedly in order to help keep Nigeria one.

Oba Tejuoso has not only tried to cause chaos in Egbaland; he has also contributed in no small measure to the confusion over the aborted elections. At the mockery of a gathering called the consti-tutional conference of 1995, Tejuoso was a government appointee. By agreeing to participate, he was submitting to the already wide-spread opinion that the institution of *obas* has been demoted to the level of the military's lackeys. Worse still, he went to the capital, Abuja, to disgrace himself and his people: He did not have the courage to pack his royal baggage and return home, after some uncouth member of the conference had booed him for trying to place the contentious presidential election issue on the agenda.

Lately, Tejuoso has claimed that the Egbas have chosen Shonekan, the temporary pretender to the presidency, over Abiola. Were that to be true, the great traditional ruler ought not to be the one to make the pronouncement; rather, he should feel sad at the shameful episode that underscores Yoruba disunity and demise in the Nigerian state. One would, indeed, agree with the Egba Alake Community, that the choice of Shonekan is solely Tejuoso's, and a good sign of his political ambition and desire to be in the government's good books. And, could it be that Shonekan and Tejuoso are both agents of this anti-Abiola, anti-democratic gov-ernment? Babangida put Shonekan on the pedestal as interim head of state; who knows, Tejuoso may be rewarded with his own paper power after the political parties may have buried themselves in the grave being meticulously prepared for them by the dictator's hench-men.

What remains most painful, is the suspicion that Tejuoso may have been deliberately set up to make mince-meat of Yoruba soli-darity. A divided Yoruba nation can never dream of returning to its cherished status as a powerful and progressive people. What is as entertaining as watching a proud family self-destruct in the public arena? One only hopes that, when he is done shouting, our dear royal father will not have dragged down with him into the mud, the whole of Egbaland, and the Yoruba nation. One also hopes that Abiola would stay strong, and keep his dignity and humanity intact, no thanks to the likes of the good doctor hiding under the crown.[6]

Notes

1. Written in 1996, at perhaps the height of anxiety within the Yoruba nation, regarding their participation in the controversial Abacha constitutional conference, and their place in the country.
2. Pa Adekunle Ajasin was leader of NADECO, the anti-military, political association considered by the Abacha regime as number one Enemy. He died in 1997 at the age of 92 years.
3. Ooni of Ife, is seen as the cultural leader of the Yorubas. Ile-Ife, his seat, is described as "the cradle of Yoruba culture," and, indeed, as "the center of the world."

   Alaafin of Oyo, is seen as the political leader, with Oyo as the political center.
4. Ile-Ife and Oyo used to be part of Oyo State. The two traditional rulers never stopped quarreling over the rightful occupant of the chair of the state Council of *Obas*. In 1996, a new state, Osun, was created from the old Oyo State; the Ooni's domain was included in the new creation, while Oyo remained in the old unit.
5. Egba is in Ogun State. It is the home of one of the very first Nigerian groups to obtain Western education. Several major players in the country's unfolding tragedy, hail from there: Abiola, Shonekan, Obasanjo, among others.
6. Tejuoso later suffered the tragedy of his mother's mysterious and gruesome murder by assassins who callously dismembered her. The common belief is, that the atrocity was not unconnected with Tejuoso's political activities.

   Abiola would die in prison, but he did keep his dignity intact. See chapter 21.

CHAPTER 12

ISSUES OF CULTURE
AND POLITICS[1]

When the Nigerian military regime appointed the most recent minister of information and culture, the Honorable Dr. Walter Ofonagoro, senior lecturer at the University of Lagos, it showed the strange vision and insight of the authorities of Africa's most populous and perplexing country. Culture connotes a people's way of life; it derives from their heritage and history; it links the past to the present, and it suffuses a civilization which, in its most global conceptualization, is the practicalization of culture. In general human terms, culture also implies refinement, that is, a state of reasoning humanity that stands in opposition to the instinctive reactivity of animals.

In the African context, certain leaders involved in the independence struggle committed the sacrilegious error of attempting to distinguish between culture and political struggle (the latter, taking cognizance of socio-economic interests). They learnt their lesson too late: Independence came, but exploitation continued. So, in our dear Nigeria, the great leadership has decided to link culture to information, one would hope, in order to give an inclusive definition and experiential determination to culture, to enunciate *our* way of life, to inform *us,* and everyone else, of this way, to educate *us* as to the civilizing force of *our* way. The problem, however, is that no one has clearly defined this *our* culture.

Which is easy to understand, since our country, not a nation, is a conglomeration of cultures. It is left to individuals to make their own definitions and, naturally, those who think they are most competent, are the ones holding political power. Therefore, here comes the great Ofonagoro. At a seminar on "Culture and Education for Peace," held in Kaduna, he advised, indeed, he preached, like Moses bringing down the Word from the mountain top, against destructive elements of culture that tend to institutionalize discrimination, among which he named "the caste system, oppression of widows and denial of property rights to women." (*The Guardian,* June 29, 1996: 3) He said that our nation-state must be based on "pluralism and mutual agreement." He insisted on the evolution of "a peaceful, dynamic, and prosperous industrial state that will lead the world in the twenty-first century." Most significantly, he declared with a scowl capable of knocking dead any dissenter: "Our model of a nation-state cannot come from Europe. It can only bring us chaos and disaster. That is why we shall not accept any interference or dictation!"

There goes the honorable minister rambling and ranting about every and any issue concerning the non-existing nation-state. He condemns the caste system. Question: Which people practice that in Nigeria? And the oppression of widows and women without property-rights, would that be an all-inclusive, Nigerian problem? Ofonagoro spoke in Kaduna.[2] More appropriately, he ought to go from there to other areas of the country, and repeat the speech from the mountain top, in those places where only the first son has all the rights to property; where women run the risk of being treated like second-class citizens; where children hardly have any respect for their parents; where husbands walk majestically in front of their wives who follow them in all submissive humility.

Ofonagoro, excellent choice for his ministerial post, has proven that, for him and his masters, culture is extended to include politics, and information is misconstrued as propaganda. This political propaganda is well exhibited in that Kaduna speech. The very title of the seminar, is suggestive of a political agenda: Everything in Nigeria today is geared towards *peace*, with other items simultaneously implied, such as, *unity, cooperation, compromise,* and *dialogue*, and they all come together in the most patriotic of words in the Nigerian dictionary, *Democracy*. Thus, cultural issues are always conceived as an integral part of the government's programs, not in the normal sense of openness, and mutual tolerance, and understanding; not as harmony through acceptance of the various nationalities' distinctions and differences, but in the exclusively Nigerian sense of coercion based on the rulers' agenda for absolute power. The minister of information deliberately misinforms all and sundry, hiding the political face behind a mask of meaningless culture. Over and beyond the woman question, Ofonagoro's objective is, to repeat what we have already heard too many times, that we must reject Euro-America's idea of democracy, and cultivate our own "home-grown" model. Mr. Minister, great visionary that he is, dreams of an industrial Nigeria that will lead the world in the next century, yes, the very one around the corner. Normally, one would ask how a country unable to produce a functional pin, a country known for its culture of confusion and contradictions, a country caught in the paws of a horde of pillagers, a country rated among the poorest on the face of the earth -its extraordinary potential notwithstanding-, would suddenly become a super-power.[3] But, remember, this is an abnormal country. There are always miracles, always the magic wand that could be maneuvered by wondrous symbols of perfection, such as dear Mr. Minister, so that, overnight, Nigeria could become whatever it wished. Our leaders have said so, and we are duty bound to believe them.

At the Kaduna seminar, Ofonagoro was ably supported by the state administrator, a military man, who added other cultural notions to the minister's already weighty proposals. He decried the spate of armed robberies, assassinations, "and the use of bad language on our leaders and elders." Regarding the violent acts of robbers and assassins, one notes that the government to which the gentle officer belongs, has categorically stated that no political motivation is involved in the systematic elimination of the government's critics, and that the insecurity of lives cannot be linked to state governance. Hence, the government is above board, and above the people, the very people who are considered as bad children when they refuse to follow their marvelous parents and therefore deserve a thorough beating. Yet, we all know better. We know that the government itself consists of an army of armed robbers and assassins. We know that its agents are themselves disrespectful. We know that they are bad functionaries unworthy of any respect, because they have forgotten the first law of culture, that the leaders and their associates must respect the led whose opinions, well-being, and way of life they must protect and promote.

To the minds of the minister and the military administrator, Nigerian culture would best be defined as *collaboration* with the current dictatorship. It is in that vein that Ofonagoro berates foreigners for trying to "interfere," or "dictate," and the administrator condemns "all those tendencies and activities which seek to promote foreign cultural values at the expense of our indigenous culture." Now, maybe given the venue of the seminar, one should understand that subservience and submission to the dominance of the forces of feudalism, must be accepted by the people, but that cannot be true for the whole of Nigeria. For Nigeria to move forward, such distinctions must be made. The big hitch is, that the rulers believe that nobody must moot the idea of distinctions and differences.

Another military administrator, this time in Ogun, a southern and Yoruba state, recently presented a position paper to the Committee for the Devolution of Powers, another official creation apparently meant to engage the population in dialogue, but actually being used to push official opinion down the people's overwhelmed throats. Discussing the essence and necessity of *feudalism*, which he misnamed federalism, the military officer intoned: "The primary position of the federal government is, that the centre should remain inviolable and supreme." (*The Guardian*, June 29, 1996: 7) One need not comment on the contradiction in that assertion. If one understands this Nigerian culture to which the officer has referred, one would realize that it is rigid, reactionary, dictatorial, and demented. Its proponents and representatives are forever angry, forever raging against their Enemy, forever ready to shoot, with their mouths, or their machine-guns.

Belligerent, you might say, and you would be perfectly right. The culture in question is represented not only by the military, but by the fundamentalism regularly seen in the activities of certain religious groups, from the North. For once, Nigeria would appear to be normal: Religion being an aspect of culture, the Islamic fundamentalist is engaged in a continuous struggle, a *jihad*, to prove the supremacy of his religion, and culture. And the government allows the war being waged on other religions and cultures because, even if it is not written in law, this country may well be on its way to becoming a religious (that is, Islamic) state. That would be the only reasonable way to explain some serious occurrences, such as that in which an enraged gang stormed a court in Kaduna and forcibly freed three college students arraigned before the court for cheating at their examinations. In the ensuing melee, some people, including policemen, were murdered. The state administrator set up a committee to reconcile the crusaders, the court, and community, in the spirit of peace and understanding. On another occasion, in Kotangora, fanatics clashed with the police when the former insisted on entering the emir's palace to obtain permission to preach. Death was the result, again. The culture of reconciliation would, naturally, again come into play.

Whether such reconciliation would be meaningful for Nigeria's future, is another matter altogether. In fact, the government does have a National Reconciliation Committee, the members of which have traveled the length and breadth of the country, preaching peace and unity, and dialogue and understanding. As with other bodies, it is taken for granted that the government's position is paramount, unchangeable, uncompromising. The leaders, remember, are elders to be respected, absolutely. And that brings us back to the definition of culture. One would like to propose that, so as to achieve success in its efforts at establishing "a peaceful, dynamic and prosperous state" ready to lead the world in the next century, the Nigerian government should publish a book on culture. It would be the logical follow-up to the excellent one (*June 12 and the Future of Nigerian Democracy)*[4] that serves as cover-up for the government's obstinate refusal to democratize. The next text being proposed by this author, would lay down the ideas already expressed by the honorable minister of information, as well as by other officials of this patriotic regime, who have eminently added the culture of lies to the always growing corpus of Nigerian cultural agenda of confusion, coercion, and corruption.

Notes

1. Written in 1996, on the appointment and performance of a military apologist, Walter Ofonagoro, as Nigeria's minister of information.

The 1986 Nobel laureate for literature, Wole Soyinka, calls Ofonagoro "Abacha's court jester." (Interview in *TELL*, June 3, 1996: 10-19)

2. Kaduna, the traditional nerve-center of socio-political and economic activities in Northern Nigeria. Traditional, because the city was serving those purposes long before the creation of Nigeria's new capital, Abuja, a supposedly central, but truly Northern city.

3. Nigeria used to be among the first thirty in the world, in terms of wealth and income. Lately, it has fallen to the level of the poorest fifteen.

4. Published by the ministry of information, with public funds, this expensive, voluminous text is an example of the wastage common to Nigeria's disaster-riddled rulership. Its title is decidedly contradictory, because democracy does not have a present in Nigeria, how much less, a future.

CHAPTER 13

DEMOCRACY AND THIS CRAZINESS[1]

Our objective here is, to try to understand *Democracy*, as a terminology, and as it should be applicable to any human society, including our dear Nigeria. This exercise -hopefully, not in futility, although out of a certain frustration- has been deemed necessary because, as in other matters, the government and its agents have been trying to deceive themselves by foisting upon the people the notion of particularity, and peculiarity, as if Nigeria were not part of the human community.

Democracy is a form of government in which supreme, absolute, ultimate power is vested in *the people* (note the emphasis) collectively, and is administered by them, or by officials appointed by them. At the center of Democracy are, the common people, the ordinary people, that is the majority. Equality of rights and privileges, in social, political, and legal matters, is a constant. The principle of justice is also central to this form of government. When we talk of rights *and* privileges, we do not distinguish between them as exclusive one of the other, because every citizen in a democracy must enjoy both, equally. Furthermore, every citizen, while enjoying them, must assume responsibilities necessary to nurturing the society as it evolves. Democracy, we must also remember, cannot be viable in a country, that is, a geographical entity without that spirit of unity and commitment transforming it into a nation. Under normal circumstances and in the most natural cases, a nation is a group of people bound together by heritage, tradition, language, and culture. Their commitment is thus a given, a natural disposition. They not only are proud of their past, but are prepared to live together in the present, and to move forward into the future in a state where they feel like free human beings.

We are all aware that Nigeria is an exception to the above rule. Our original national anthem tells us that much: *"Though tribe and tongue may differ,* in brotherhood we stand." That is a statement of fact, a show of sincerity, an affirmation and confirmation of basic differences and, in the second clause, a desire to create brotherhood, that is, to build unity out of disunity. Such a creation is very difficult. It requires total commitment, and concerted efforts by all the different tribes (I prefer to call them nations) to eliminate divergences. One of the essentials of that task is equality which, as stated earlier, is a basic aspect of Democracy. Another essential is freedom of choice: All the ethnic components must be desirous of participating in the process of creating the new nation. They must not be forced into it because, if they are, they will be entering the union without commitment, another *sine qua non* for the viability, the progress, and the development of the new and democratic entity.

When Nigeria's leaders decided to throw out the original national anthem, they were ostensibly trying to eradicate any thought of differences, or division in the country. The new anthem is an affirmation of solidarity, a pledge to a nation, indeed, a command to one and all to be committed to a nation. Unfortunately, however, the architects of this new order, being themselves used to commanding troops that can never say no, failed to understand their folly; for, all they did was, to set the country back from the path of democracy towards an era of dictatorship and demagoguery. The new national anthem is a pretext, a sham. As if ethnic differences could be eliminated by merely refusing to admit them. As if we would become one just because we have been commanded to do so. As if our colonial history, marked by privileges and protection of some sacred cows, and by sectionalism, and by uneven development which kept intact the ethnic differences, never happened.

Those who know Nigerian history must remember that Britain never encouraged unity and harmony between North and South. When independence was granted to the country, it was not, as one would have expected, a prize fought for, and won, through commitment and sacrifice of a united group (a nation); rather, it was a largely tainted trophy awarded to two unequal, disunited groups. One actually had the feeling that the North was reluctant, if not unwilling, to go along, and that the Northerners finally joined on their own terms. If not, how does one comprehend a scenario where those who struggled for freedom ended up being ruled by those others who had preferred to remain foster-children of the colonizer? Of course, many people do not want to discuss the truth, for fear of rocking the boat.

Nonetheless, for Nigeria to even begin to *think* of Democracy, we cannot avoid revisiting the past in order to redress many discrepancies that have brought the country to the edge of an avoidable precipice. First and foremost, we must accept the fact that Nigeria is not at all a nation. It has a chance to be one, but the path that has been trodden to date, will never lead to that ideal. For Nigerians to realize the dream of nationhood, we must sit down as equals, and ask certain questions: Do we wish to become a nation? How should we go about it? This has to be a free choice. No amount of force, or subterfuge, can lead to the desired goal.

Now, let us take for granted that such a discussion has taken place, and the various nationalities have agreed to form a nation called Nigeria. The next step is clear: *The people* must be allowed to choose their leaders and, if any chosen leaders fail to live up to expectations, they will be removed with ignominy and replaced by others duly elected by the people. In the matter of leadership, Democracy does not acclaim the leaders' superiority. It does not allow for self-proclaiming patriarchs treating the people as children, or servants, or slaves. Leaders are there to serve the people, and to represent their interests. Leaders should have superior skills so as to carry out their national responsibilities, but that does not mean that they are superior to others.

Once again, the tragedy of the Nigerian condition is, that historically, our so-called leaders, from colonialism into neocolonialism, have erroneously been seen as superior to the populace. Those who struggled for independence, as well as those who ruled us into our present state of ruin, have been worshiped as heroes and tin-gods, or they have anointed themselves as such. All one needs to do is to scratch a little bit that surface of superiority, to reveal the spuriousness of many a self-proclaimed messiah. In their large numbers, Nigerian leaders are hardly more than opportunists, lynchers, and leeches, who kill or suck people's blood just to attain and retain power. The fathers of the independence struggle, our most revered heroes, are not without culpability in this saga of non-democracy because, in their own period of preparation, they failed to properly lay the groundwork for genuine freedom and unity. A question of haste, or obsession with heroism, or hypocrisy, they won for their compatriots a shallow victory. And the post-independence, civilian and military politicians are certainly worse offenders. A question of megalomaniac messianism, or mindless militarism, or, indeed, murderous materialism, these new masters have disregarded the people who now remain on the periphery as mere observers of a destiny that they themselves should, by right, be determining.

So, when our ear-drums are being battered by the silly sounds of some madness called democracy, we have a right to tell the empty talkers to please slow down, and shut up. What they are calling *home-grown democracy* based on so-called Nigerian peculiarities, is actually camouflaged feudalism that combines the patterns of an old oligarchy with the policy of a military used to giving orders. They just must be told that any free people on the face of the earth, have a right to choose where and how they wish to live, and who should lead them, and how they should be led. There is absolutely nothing peculiar about all that. When, in one breath, the military and civilian politicians spit out banalities about democracy and, in another, threaten to deal drastically with "disgruntled elements" engaged in "unpatriotic activities," they are exhibiting a shameful ignorance of the meaning of Democracy. In all likelihood, they may actually know the meaning, but are refusing to apply it for fear that it would destroy their power, if not they themselves. *Dialogue, reconciliation,* these should not be mere words; concretized in action, they help to create the right atmosphere for real freedom and unity. On the contrary, in Nigeria, those words, and many others, have been stripped of their usual meanings, and now symbolize deceit and decay.

How can Nigeria move forward? How can it, to use the latest linguistic fad, "resolve the political logjam"? Definitely not by insisting on a clearly discriminatory, disunifying, and dehumanizing *status quo*. Not by silencing those who hold views opposed to those held by the undemocratic government. Not by annulling elections. Not by seeking support, and claiming legitimacy, from shallow-minded stooges, and certainly not through useless programs. Nigerians must save themselves from the hell of feudalism and militarism. They must be allowed to choose their leaders who can, and will, make mistakes, and learn from them. The performance of those who bulldozed their way into the fortressed seat of power, is too disgraceful and destructive to warrant wasting our precious time in giving them a millionth chance; it would simply be one chance too many. Let it be repeated, that Democracy is nothing special, or strange.[2] What is strange, is the craziness of cover-ups, of collaboration, of connivance, that is destroying the dream of a nation called Nigeria.

Notes

1. Written in 1996, when the government -out of desperation, according to some- increased its efforts to prove to the Western super-powers that it was leading the country in the direction of the promised land of Democracy.

    In one of his rare moments of "reconciliation," Abacha tried to placate his Western critics by begging for patience. See, Paul Ejime, "No Quick Fix to Nigerian Problems - Abacha," *Africa News Online*, Dec. 3, 1997.
2. See, Claude Ake, "Time For a Democratic Agenda," *TELL*, Aug. 22, 1994: 33-34.

CHAPTER 14

CREATION OF STATES AND LOCAL GOVERNMENT AREAS[1]

Nigerians have long established a culture of agitation for new states and local government areas. It is one of those pointers to the basic incompatibility of the macrocosmic entity itself; in essence, the overall unity of the country has always been in question. Since it is considered unpatriotic to question that unity, the indirect way of dealing with it is, to lie about enhancing it by carving out little corners for every community complaining of marginalization, or discrimination. Maybe not for every community, but for those catching the fancy of the current regime. Nigeria being what it is, a complexity requiring cunning to keep the tenuous bonds from breaking, successive regimes have used the issue of state and local government creation to suit their purposes of, firstly, staying in power and, secondly, diffusing the voices of dissidence.

Rumors have been making the rounds regarding another exercise of geographical fragmentation.[2] We know of the existence of a national committee responsible for making recommendations to the government. Meanwhile, the latter is not bound to implement such recommendations. The committee members are, as usual, among the regime's favorite friends, sons and servants, and are therefore expected to sing songs sweet to the ears of officialdom. The chairman, Arthur Mbanefo, is one of those constants in Nigeria's socio-political equation: On university councils, on various boards, on advisory committees, he is always there to serve every regime well, may it be military or civilian. In fact, his name is synonymous with service, just as is that of Abdurahaman Okene,[3] and, not to forget Joseph Wayas,[4] among others. They all make one understand better the concept of that prominent Hausa-Fulani politician, Maitama Sule, that the same characters must be recycled over and over again, because the Almighty has chosen them to govern and, we make bold to add, because their Almighty has decided that Nigeria must stagnate, and go round in circles!

But, let us delve more into this most national of issues, the creation of states. An advertisers' announcement in *The Guardian* of June 24, 1996, recently caught my eye. Signed by six people "for and on behalf of Ondo State Conference of Chairmen of Local Government," it is an open letter to head of state Abacha "on behalf of the entire people of the Sunshine State," Ondo. After zealously pledging their allegiance to the government and its transitional program [to democracy, as they claim], after commending the regime for its measures to "sanitise the economy [and to] enthrone and sustain accountability in the key public sector," the signatories finally address the real issue of interest: They "wholeheartedly endorse the creation of at least one more state from the present Ondo State." Furthermore, in order to maintain "the sacred principles of homogeneity, sense of belonging, cultural and language affinity," they are unequivocally opposed to the excision of any part of Ondo State to join an existing state. They implore Abacha "to consider ONLY the express wishes of the people of Ondo State and not any behind-the-scene manipulation." The signatories then implore the government "as a matter of urgency to come to the aid of all the local governments in Ondo State and bail [them] out of [their] deep financial straits to facilitate the fulfillment of election promises and REALLY and TRULY bring government closer to the grassroots." In conclusion, they promise to identify with the regime's policies and programs, and to promote peace and enhance their state's cordial relationship with the military government, all in "the spirit of political tolerance and peaceful co-existence of all the nationalities in Nigeria."

This last point brings us back to the fact mentioned at the beginning of this discourse, that Nigeria consists of several distinct nationalities. That, however, is far from being the thrust of the Ondo State politicians' propaganda document. Their letter is actually intended to express solidarity with the Abacha regime. The emptiness of it all is too glaring, and too insulting, to ignore. Let us recall that the elections won by those men and women were flawed, fixed, and outrightly fraudulent. Some groups opposed to the regime's policies refused to participate in the so-called non-party vote. Others that participated, so as not to be perceived as anti-reconciliatory (the Nigerian term is, confrontational), had their candidates summarily disqualified by government agents. Most voters saw no sense in casting meaningless votes; the minority that did, were very Nigerian: They sold their votes to the highest bidder, and the whole fraud was perpetrated in the open.[5] The acclaimed winners, including the signatories of the open letter under discussion here, are saying nothing on behalf of their people; they are representing their personal interests, and those of their masters at the capital, city overwhelmed by Arab structures, Abuja.

That is the only way to appreciate the encomiums showered on the head of state, and his transitional program which transcends common sense and insists on staying in transit on its destination to doom, instead of heading, as it should, non-stop, to freedom, and equality, and justice. As regards the economy, the objective of sanitization appears excellent; unfortunately, charity has not begun at home. Accountability must start from the highest level. On the contrary, Nigeria's rulers remain above the law. The noise over the Failed Banks Tribunal[6] is quite comical, because the beneficiaries of that process are still the privileged handful, the same people oppressing the masses, in short, the masters who organize the armed robbery through which millions and billions in cash are sent into foreign accounts.

The question of state creation is no less fraught with the selfish attitude of those fawning, fraudulent letter-writers.[7] Since they were not democratically elected, they have no right to speak for the people. They have endorsed the creation of *at least one more state* in their section of the country. Their endorsement is deliberately ambiguous. Firstly, it is well known that there is a great deal of agitation for the creation of Ekiti State as a breakaway unit from the existing Ondo State. Secondly, there is the desire for some other form of creation. The ambiguity would therefore serve the purposes of both parties. All in all, a new state would create jobs for the boys and girls, both at the state and local government levels.

Meanwhile, our patriotic scribblers are ignoring a very important factor to which they themselves have referred in their plea to the government, precisely, lack of finances. Every time a new state, or a new local government, is created, money has to be provided by the government. A new infrastructure has to be put in place, beginning with the establishment of a new capital. In a country where infrastructures and funds are already inadequate in the existing divisions, it is stupid to keep creating new units. When those Ondo State copy-writers cry to the government for funds, they do so, not out of their interest in communal development, but as big-spenders reeling from the bribery of the electorate that they undertook during the unfair election. Thus, the pre-vote debt is to be recovered from public funds. These men and women, committed to themselves and their friends and families, will bring government to the grassroots, by taking ten percent from big, not-to-be-fulfilled contracts, and spreading round opportunities for perquisites.

The concluding section of the open letter under review, is disturbing, to say the least; for, it attempts to undermine the high quality of integrity and justice for which Ondo State citizens used to be known. Those chairmen would want the military regime to know that Ondo citizens are not the abhorred "disgruntled elements" who are always causing confusion and slowing down the transition train. They would want to be recognized as peaceful people, cordial, tolerant, and interested in harmonious existence with their Nigerian brothers and sisters. There, again, the missive-mongers reveal their deceitful character, because we all know that, among all Yoruba states,[8] Ondo indigenes have stood firm in their refusal to compromise and collude with those desperately trying to bury the symbolic act of June 12, 1993 presidential elections. No doubt that many readers of the open-letter will denounce the so-called chairmen for their lack of integrity.

In the final analysis, the clamor for new states may be seen as unpatriotic, a possibility that the loud purveyors of pseudo-patriotism are too ignorant to imagine. A sign of geographical fragmentation, state-creation also indicates polarization of the people whose unity, so claims the government, must be absolute. Yet -and this is one of Nigeria's many dilemmas- all such acts of lack of patriotism are reminders of the reality the leadership is trying to wish away. When we have the courage to face the facts of our lack of unity, or unifying factors, we may be able to think of how to establish a foundation upon which to build a nation. For Ondo, sunshine would no longer be a useless dream, but a possibility, and a continuous movement away from the shadows. As at now, creation of states is nothing more than a process that exacerbates existing divisions, divergences, and dissensions.

Notes

1. Written in 1995-96.
2. The government seems to encourage the agitation for new divisions, as it promises to help fulfill almost every group's aspiration for local autonomy.
3. Okene, a reactionary octogenarian from the North, who has been like a recurring decimal in the power structure.
4. Wayas, a second republic (1979-83) senator known for his anti-people positions, and with a great deal of influence in official circles.
5. Throughout Abacha's dictatorship, fraud was an everyday event; the very air was polluted by fraud. It would be useful to analyze the elections (appropriately dubbed, *selections,* by critics) of that regime, as well as those conducted by the preceding Babangida administration.
6. One of the many ostensibly well intentioned actions of the Abacha regime, that tribunal turned out to be a diversion from the trail of the real robbers, and a means of silencing the regime's Southern critics. 1998 update: The tribunal has not yet been disbanded. Only recently, some bank executives detained for months without trial, went on hunger strike, to protest their oppression within a system where corruption among their accusers and prosecutors, is the order of the day.
7. The citizens of Ondo State, in the Yoruba region, have had the dubious reputation of writing petitions to every incoming governor or administrator, to complain against rivals for various coveted public posts.
8. There are five states, officially recognized as Yoruba, in Nigeria: Lagos, Ogun, Ondo, Oyo, and Osun. (Ekiti State, created after the agitation of the writers of this letter and others, now makes the number, six.)

CHAPTER 15

REFLECTIONS ON KUDIRAT ABIOLA, AND OTHER MATTERS[1]

I drove past the spot where M.K.O. Abiola's wife, Kudirat, was gunned down several hours after the event on Thursday, June 4, 1996, unaware that such a tragedy had occurred. Other motorists and myself were routinely stopped and harassed and fleeced by the very efficient, dirty police and military men manning the checkpoint across the road from the Seven-Up factory on the outskirts of Lagos. After learning of the sad event, I returned there on the following day, this time through the Lagos island end, almost to the Ibadan Expressway,[2] making a u-turn up to the road past the factory, making another turn back through the checkpoint[3] down the road heading towards Gbagada Expressway. I noticed the police station in the vicinity, as well as the fierce-looking, heavily armed police and military officers at the former toll-gate. The following questions kept nagging me: How come the conspicuous car, a custom-made, tinted-glass Peugeot, carrying the assassination squad was never stopped at the checkpoint, particularly since, as the Abiola driver had stated, the Peugeot had doubled up the victim's vehicle even before the killers executed their deadly act? How come no attempt was made by the ever so vigilant and efficient security agents, to pursue the assassins' car? How come none of the officers could even describe the vehicle or its occupants? How come the policemen in the station a stone's throw away, went about their business of harassing innocent people, and did nothing during the rowdy, dramatic moments of mayhem and murder? How come?

Now, the equally efficient investigators are vowing to root out the killers. They have not considered it necessary to question those manning the posts in the vicinity of the murder. For a while, they even claimed ignorance of the whereabouts of Kudirat's aide who was in the car with her, and was interrogated by their very colleagues on his hospital bed. They have offered one million naira to anyone able to give information leading to the arrest of the criminals. Talk of criminals wishing to catch criminals! As further proof of their seriousness of purpose, they have been spending most precious time visiting Abiola's family, begging them to assist in fishing out poor Kudirat's killers. You never know, maybe Abiola himself is behind the deed. Just as well: The man should be charged with treason and murder!

Such is the depth of the sickness in this land, that the most tragic event makes you laugh hilariously for fear of going crazy, or committing murder, or suicide. The Kudirat case has led to a spate of spurious praise-singing, all so nauseating that one wonders why those excellent qualities the woman portrayed these past two years, did not lead to the resolution of the problem that must have made her murderers decide to dispatch her to her Maker. In other words, if all those hypocrites making silly speeches, filling the pages of the condolence register with empty words, and now calling on the military regime whose servants they are, to release her husband, if all those shameless men hailing Kudirat as an Amazon for standing firm on principle, for unflinchingly demanding justice, if they truly believed in her, why wait until her death to voice such an opinion? Why did the government of the day send what it called a high-powered delegation, to mourn the death of a woman whose murder it could have prevented by simply following the path of reason and logic, and freeing her husband to play the political role to which he had been elected by the people of Nigeria? Talk of medicine after death. What we are witnessing is actually worse: It is, rather, poison applied to a corpse.

The pronouncements of this regime's operatives lead to only one conclusion, that the government either has a hand in the heinous crime, or has a guilt complex consequential to its policy that permits the snuffing out of innocent souls considered to be enemies for refusing to resign themselves to enslavement in their motherland. The very fact that anyone—and many people at home and abroad belong to this category—feels that the government is guilty of killing its perceived opponents, is in itself proof of its bad performance. In addition, the line of defense taken by certain prominent individuals, shows the shallowness of those supposedly leading the country.

Nigeria's ambassador in Washington, Kazaure, tells CNN that Lagos, which he describes as a uniquely insane metropolis, lacks security and, because it is such an endemically crime-prone city, it easily afforded Kudirat's killers an opportunity to eliminate her. That explanation implies that Lagosians are symbols of the "South-West" (an official coinage for the Yoruba region), that area of Nigeria inhabited by rowdy, unpatriotic anarchists. Information minister, Ofonagoro, goes further to blame the growing violence in Lagos on the loss of security incurred when the federal capital, and ministers and their security aides, were moved to Abuja. The minister then assures everyone that the government, in its magnanimity, has arranged to implement a special security plan for the former capital. Poor, but fortunate, Lagos! To believe Ofonagoro, one must go prostrating oneself in gratitude before the greatest rulership that Nigeria ever had, for such quick, and concerted decision to save innocent Lagosians. Which, unfortunately, can do nothing to bring back Kudirat Abiola, or to bring the weight of justice upon her killers.

Yet, in truth, Kazaure, the political ambassador who plucked the plum position in Washington because of his ethnic background, knows full well that he is lying through his teeth, just as he has always done since the annulled 1993 elections. In like fashion, Ofonagoro is fabricating tall tales to cover up the truth. Both gentlemen, as well as their comrades in injustice and retrogression, are advised to respect the dead by simply desisting from lying, or by telling their master to realize that what goes up must come down; that nemesis always catches up with everyone, including the seemingly untouchable; that Nigeria, as every dictator is quick to declare, is bigger and more important than anyone. Ultimately, every dictator must meet his demise: Remember our dear, dead brother, Sergeant Doe.

In the meantime, the likes of Ofonagoro will most likely continue to lie to try to convince nobody but themselves, that they are the best thing that ever happened to this unfortunate country. Indeed, it would appear that it is Nigeria's destiny to be ruled by the worst of its citizens. If not, how does one explain the presence of so many prostitutes, and pimps, and parasites in power? As I said, one had better learn to enjoy the endless joke called government, or else, one would kill or be killed. When Akinyele,[4] a no-rank traditional chief of a section of his home town, claims to be visiting the presidential palace, to plead for Abiola's release in response to the people's wish, whom does he think he is fooling but himself? When Belgore, multi-millionaire justice, absents himself from court in the disgraceful case of the Abiola intra-family squabble,[5] in order, as we are told, to attend the opening ceremony of an induction course for new judges, whom does he think he is deceiving but himself? And, when the government announces, with all flamboyance and frivolity, that Abiola is being moved from one detention center to another, so as to protect him from possible assassination, whom are they trying to impress but their own unscrupulous selves?

Leave it to the great minister of mis-information to have the last word in this scenario fit for the worst melodramatic horror movie. In his opinion, Kudirat Abiola would probably have been better off, if she had been detained by the most humanitarian regime in the world. Of course, this most enlightened and progressive man (call him another *democrat*), has to be right. I would like to propose, with all humility, that all Nigerians be kept in detention for their own protection. A far-fetched idea? Not really, because, already, living in some parts of the country is almost tantamount to being confined in a detention camp.

Notes

1. Written in 1996, after the gruesome assassination of Abiola's wife, Kudirat. The murder has not been solved until now. Others, murdered mysteriously, include: Dele Giwa, and Alfred Rewane.
2. These are all areas around Ikeja, the Lagos State capital, where police security is a constant presence.
3. Police and military checkpoints are a prominent, more or less permanent fixture on Lagos roads, on the highways, and in other southern cities. On a stretch of fifty miles, one could be stopped a dozen times.

4. Alex Akinyele, once a public relations officer at Nigerian Customs (which, according to stories, he used as a launching pad for his transformation into a multi-millionaire), soared to the national limelight as a military apologist. He went from ministerial appointments to chair the infamous National Reconciliation Committee (NARECON). The only visible reconciliation accomplished by him and his colleagues, was between money and their bank accounts. Providence also effected another reconciliation, between the master's death, and Akinyele's deflated ego, when Abacha's successor dissolved the redundant committee.

5. See chapter 16.

CHAPTER 16

ABIOLA'S FAMILY[1]

As Nigeria continues to stumble along the road to development, or destruction -it all depends on whose viewpoint is being considered-, one fact stands out: the confusion in Abiola's family. That family's condition may actually be worse, because everything points to the likelihood that those men and women are what we call average Nigerians, that is, cowardly, selfish, material-minded, seemingly apolitical but truly the opposite, in the sense of singing the right tune in order to profit economically, and thoroughly patriotic as pawns in the game of self-preservation and perpetuation organized by the grand masters in the capital city. Events following the assassination of Kudirat Abiola, would easily lead one to these conclusions.

Before her sudden, and speedy elimination, Kudirat had become one more victim of harassment in the hands of those holding the poor country in bondage. Everyone with a brain knew exactly why: Unlike many others echoing their master's voice by calling for compromise, dialogue, and connivance as the best way forward, the woman kept insisting on her husband's right to justice. In Nigeria, if you insist on your right, you are adjudged to be confrontational. Since the military and their brothers and sisters from the North have been chosen by the Almighty to rule the country forever,[2] it makes sense that, if you are oppressed, battered, butchered, or whatever, it is your duty to beg the oppressors who are simply acting out their God-given right. You must not resist, because Allah has decided the condition to which you must resign yourself. Maybe that is why Kudirat's submissive family did not deem it necessary to cry out on her behalf while she was still alive.

Maybe another reason would be more pertinent: They were convinced she was being confrontational or, worse still, over-ambitious, obsessed with first-ladyship (as Abiola's most senior wife), and the power deriving from the position. Now, as far as the first-ladyship is concerned, let us agree that, in the Nigerian context, particularly in the performance of those two namesakes who followed each other in proving their care for the Nigerian Woman and Family by piling up billions, there is reason to fear, or envy, Kudirat's potential. Which does not mean that she was into anything unheard of, or beyond her right. For, whether the Abiolas or all of us like it or not, she was the man's senior wife and, therefore, in charge of the household, and his affairs, while he remained in jail. Kudirat proved her mettle during the 1993 election campaign. Her husband never has any reason to doubt her competence. The very fact that, throughout his ongoing travails, she was the ONLY member of his family with enough courage to speak out, and to refuse to veer from the path of justice and fair play, shows that Kudirat was a superior human being.

Before she was killed, Kudirat was embroiled in a quarrel with Abiola's first son, Kola, over the choice of attorneys. The case was, and still is, in court.[3] The two lawyers are, G.K.O. Ajayi, and F.R.A. Williams, both of them well respected in the profession. Kudirat stuck with Ajayi, the one handling the case from the beginning, while Kola preferred Williams who, according to him and Falomo, Abiola's personal doctor,[4] has been chosen as replacement by Abiola himself. This last piece of information or, let us say, clarification of near- (now, total, with Kudirat's passing) unanimity, is contained in a full-page advertorial by the family, published in several newspapers on June 16, 1996. The signatories are, Alhaji Mubashiru Abiola, the detainee's junior brother, and Alhaji Adio Kassim, a close family friend. It is useful to make a comprehensive analysis of the published statement.

Firstly, the family members express their gratitude to the federal military government, "for sending a high powered delegation to express heart-felt sympathies over the death of Alhaja Kudirat Abiola." Then, they thank many other bodies and individuals, including the Diplomatic Corps, Pro-Democracy Groups, Student Organizations, and the Nigerian Public. They go on and on about the efforts initiated by Kudirat to reconcile herself with "Abiola's instructions to Kola." In a nutshell, the advertorial smacks of cowardliness, connivance, and complicity. Do the signatories, and others in the Abiola household, honestly believe that this government is really interested in finding the killers of their beloved wife and mother? One would say that it serves them right, that Nigeria's most efficient detectives have started arresting anyone bearing the Abiola name, or any resemblance to him, and torturing them, in order to extract the lie of guilt out of their sick souls. And one would like to hear from Mubashiru and Kola, and the rest when, after their foolish statement, why the very competent government agents would have finally failed to bring to book any real culprit.[5]

The fact is, that Abiola's family is telling the public that they were never party to Kudirat's confrontational standpoint; that, contrary to Abiola's instructions that she and the other two wives[6] work together, she, overtly ambitious and overbearing, seized power and went on a mad rampage, basically to hug the limelight and be perceived as a political heroine *a la Winnie Mandela.*

They would like to have us castigate her further as an irresponsible wife and mother. Witness the interview allegedly given by Bisi, the new senior wife, to the newspaper, *Thisday,* in which she expressed notions diametrically opposed to those for which the late Kudirat bravely stood, and sacrificed her life. Bisi emphasizes her roles as wife and mother of five children. She says that she is not at all interested in politics, and that she is not ready to face the military "moving train" that would obliterate any fool standing in its way. Yet, we do know that Bisi spent a great deal of time overseas, and that she and the other surviving wife, Doyin, have been so silent that, without Kudirat's vocal position, many would have wondered whether Abiola's family (elders, wives, children, all of them) had not disappeared from the face of the earth. Kudirat, we cannot forget, was the senior wife. By making mention of Abiola's instructions to the three wives, the family is guilty of shameless hypocrisy: Are they not all Moslems versed in the tradition of polygamy? Or, since when have all wives become equal in the matter of responsibility? Besides, is this family so naive as not to recognize Kudirat's great achievement, for the whole of Nigeria, by being a principled revolutionary who laid down her life in the struggle for justice? If the family has absolute belief in Abiola's *unwritten* instructions passed to Kola and others, how come they have none in the *written* directives given to Kudirat and her own group? Could it be that she is being vilified because of her womanhood? Or, that, as a forceful, fearless, and imposing figure, she had stepped on some toes within the family?

Why did Kola Abiola speak out on his father's incarceration, and what did he have to say? He spoke out for the same reason now being proffered by the family, that they all miss Abiola, the family's head and bread-winner, and the symbol of economic success. In short, Kola's *love of money*, not for his father, would be the main concern. Kola said that his father had suffered enough, and that he should forget his political mandate and return to his family and business. Kola, the little boy with the golden spoon in his mouth, the privileged one, the one who has never suffered one single day in his life, is now faced with the scary possibility of bankruptcy and an uncertain future. That uncertainty has been reduced by sheer good fortune: Kola, once arrested and incarcerated for days, was finally released, but not until after the good government had put the fear of Abacha in his materialist mind.

It is so sad and sickening, the unfolding tragedy being subconsciously abetted by Abiola's family. With regard to the two attorneys in question, rumors of collaboration are flying all over the place. It is common knowledge that Williams is a "government man," an accomplice in many an oppressive policy-decision, including the very issue for which Abiola is being punished. Williams, the political lawyer, is opposed by Ajayi, the consummate professional who has not even been paid a penny for his two-year service to Abiola. No wonder Pa Ajasin, the revered Yoruba leader, refused to help in the process of debasing the Abiola case from a *cause celebre* to a charade of disgraceful horse-trading.

One cannot help comparing Kola to his younger sister, Hafsat (Kudirat's daughter), who has promptly assumed the mantle vacated by her departed mother. In contrast to the man without direction blinded by the glow of money, the young woman has shown courage, love, and faith in her family. She is thus the true daughter of her parents, not a bastard. In addition, her firm belief in her father's mandate reveals her as a heroine, the quintessence of Nigeria's youths who are capable of saving the poor country, and proof that, perhaps, all is not lost after all.

One must believe that Abiola's family-members are tired of suffering financial and material hardship. They are ready to beg, to lick boots, to do anything ordered by their masters in power, to obtain Abiola's release, even if it means welcoming back home a vegetable. What a grave error! They need to be told to wake up and be human. Abiola wants to be the president of Nigeria, not patriarch of a shameless family. Many people, including his dear, courageous wife, have died for that popular cause. Many others, including millions of Nigerians, are looking up to him to stay strong, to be their hero, even while they themselves remain cowards. And that is not uncommon, because real heroes and leaders are extraordinary beings symbolizing the best in their community. If Abiola's family cannot understand that, let them, "in the name of the Almighty God and Allah" (and we are quoting their advertorial), please shut up. Enough is enough.

Notes

1. Written in 1996, after Kudirat Abiola's assassination, and the ensuing confusion in and outside the family. See chapter 15.
2. The opinion of Maitama Sule, former federal minister. Other Hausa-Fulani patriots have supported this position.
3. After Abiola's death, the several court cases by, or about, him came to their natural death. It would be interesting to study how, in the Abiola matter, the Nigerian government stalled, and forestalled, the legal process with politics, and arrant brutish power.
4. The actions of this doctor would also make for useful analysis of the complexities of Nigerian politics and the professions. Could Falomo have been a government agent, or was he really devoted to his professional duty and to the cause of the man whom he loudly called his bosom friend even as he proudly called himself the friend of the man's enemies?
5. As at now, in late 1998, not a single person has been charged with Kudirat's murder.

6. Mrs. Bisi and Dr. Doyin Abiola. It is not a secret that Abiola had many wives. Before his death, one of them had been bought over by the Abacha regime: She said that everyone should forget about the elections for which her husband was detained; that, as true patriots, people should work with the regime. The family immediately disowned her. The overall effects of polygamy on Abiola's struggle, would provide invaluable understanding of the Nigerian realities.

CHAPTER 17

WOMEN IN NIGERIA[1]

In the generality of African culture, Woman has always been considered essential, primary, and all-important to our lives. Without woman, the world would be devoid of humanity. The concept of *Mother Africa* expresses this notion. Woman is our all in all, our beginning, and our end. Ironically, that image of the omnipresent and the omnipotent (no idea of having woman replace the Almighty, however) giving force to human presence and potential, especially in the persona of Mother, also entails the possibility of neglect: A most reliable Presence, the African woman is too often taken for granted, neglected, indeed, negated by forces of oppression that have continued to garner strength since the earlier epochs of our enslavement. Woman's dilemma has been made more complex by the very fact of her humanity. She is always expected to be the epitome of love and loyalty.

Our culture, centered upon the community, has not encouraged social engagement and struggle in the individualistic, and centrifugal fashion of the West; hence, gender issues have been less pronounced here. Yet, given the evolution of our society towards Westernization, it is impossible to avoid viewpoints emanating from the Western model. Another aspect of our colonized condition is, how to live our lives and cultivate our culture as a viable originality while adapting to the inevitable, invading forces of the Imperialists. The choice is very difficult, in large measure, due to the tantalizing material benefits of Capitalism that preaches *individual* hard work yielding immeasurable wealth to the worker, and making him or her an excellent specimen in society. With all this in mind, one sees the real dangers of mis-evolution of the African woman in the new millennium.

In the case of Nigeria, the dangers are quite frightening, what with the corruption, and contradictions dogging the country at every level. One notes the mushrooming of feminist-oriented organizations, and the growing number of studies on women as an oppressed group. Remarkably, and expectedly, there is a palpable similarity between the opinions and agendas of some of these organizations and those in the avant-garde of feminist movements in Euro-America. It is an open secret that funds used by many an NGO come from those "civilized" countries. Researchers working on the currently popular subject of women's issues, have inundated us with very detailed statistics. International agencies are falling over one another to fund such investigation in our *Third World*[2] where, in the considered opinion of the West, women are traditionally victims *par excellence*. And there are data galore to support this view. Women constitute a shade over 50% of Nigeria's population. The proportion of female heads of households is 11% in urban, and 14% in rural areas. Women in polygamous families have greater responsibilities for their children's welfare and education than in monogamous families. "Women constitute the majority of the poor, the unemployed and the socially disadvantaged in Nigeria, and they are the hardest hit by the current economic recession." (Georgina Ngeri-Nwagha, UNICEF Project Officer, in *The Guardian*, July 1, 1996: 27)

Women are marginalized in the modern labor force. In the public sector, only 1% are in the top bureaucratic level. Women are minimally employed in the formal economy. Women's work is given low priority and quality, and women petty traders have low income and high attrition rates. Forced early marriages are widespread. There is a high rate of pre- and post-natal mortality. More males than females are enrolled in schools. The issue of "genital mutilation" (female circumcision), has become a question of murder. The United Nations Development Program (UNDP) supplies many of these statistics. University departments, such as Ibadan's Women Research and Documentation Centre, are also deeply involved in analyzing what has been called gender disparity. Of course, statistics do not lie; nonetheless, they do not tell the whole story. They can be manipulated, by *experts,* just as the colonizers used to do the colonized bourgeoisie, and as the present-day political power-mongers do the unfortunate people.

In a culture centered *on Community,* that is, the collectivity of the people, it would be quite confusing and contradictory, to lay too much emphasis on sex and gender as determinants of developmental process and progression. Moreover, in a culture focusing on humanity, that is, the all-inclusiveness of the contributions of various sections of society, it would be unacceptable to break down figures along those same lines that would cause cleavage and encourage already existing weaknesses in the society. For instance, when the researcher mentions polygamy—a heresy worthy of condemnation to hell, in the eyes of the *civilized* Westerners[3]—, and woman's responsibilities therein, he or she ought to be careful to note that, firstly, the concept of marriage is different in African culture and the West; secondly, it is neither unusual, nor strange, to have African women heading households; thirdly, polygamy, a way of life and an institution prevalent in traditional non-materialistic settings, is more common in the rural than in urban areas.

Regarding the level of poverty, while it may be unacceptable to have such a low percentage of women in the public sector, it should be noted that the sector itself is not at all privileged as far as economic and financial status, or expectations, are concerned. It is wrong to believe that the market woman and the petty trader, for example, are poorer than the civil servant or, indeed, the university professor. Women in the informal private sector enjoy power over their product. Witness a scene in the market-place where a seller of rice and beans is shocked to learn that a professor earns about 8,000 naira per month ($1 = 80 naira).[4] She can earn as much in one day! Briefly, employment in the formal sector may be a bane, not a boon. And, in this age of rationalization of positions and retrenchment of workers, women in the private sector would perhaps count themselves lucky not to be in the shoes of men, and women, shackled to a system that can suddenly put them out to pasture like some haggard, worn out cattle. We must concede the fact that bureaucrats do have the opportunity to spend -and steal-millions and billions, to make and break policy, in short, to be in control. Yet, that advantaged group hardly adds up to one percent of the total population and, surprisingly enough (only to the outsider, one daresay) women are included in that number.

With regards to the figures on the mortality rate of pregnant women and new mothers, this is but one aspect of Nigeria's tragic and disgraceful health system. The traumatizing tales of pre- and post-natal deaths go hand in hand with the harrowing sight of carcasses of destitutes lying in the streets and being pounced upon by dogs and vultures; forlorn figures of patients too poor to purchase simple prescriptions and reduced to using fake drugs and consulting charlatans; hospitals, deserted by doctors scampering off to the greener pastures of Saudi Arabia, become home for those abandoned to die or, better still, serving as half-way houses to the ultimate freedom of the grave.

The practice of "genital mutilation" cannot be rightly transformed into a feminist crusade outside of the very real and valid ethos within which women have thrived for centuries. Such "horror" has to be viewed and understood in conjunction with others, such as facial marks, male circumcision, piercing of the nose, ears and lips, to name but a few. And, lest we forget, female circumcision has to be understood from inside a culture not obsessed with sex. Contrary to the horrifying pictures of women being scarred forever and being exposed to possible death, female circumcision is also considered as a source of beauty and a symbol of humanhood, and womanhood, in many a traditional community. The bottom line is, that the practice is not a matter of life and death, and can be stopped without any problem once the people are well informed. Unfortuantely, the false notion being spread about the practice is, that the West, always civilized, always superior, is engaging in another mission to save poor African women from savagery.

In essence, researchers, including, and especially Africans, ought to understand and explain the cultural roots, as well as the nuances, of women's condition, that is if they are really interested in working for positive evolution of humanity. They should attempt to make an all-inclusive, not exclusivist, analysis because, without such orientation, they run the risk of either condemning women to the very marginalization of which they are complaining; or, worse still, raising them to a level of false superiority now occupied by those sacred cows who do not care about the people's destiny. In the Nigerian example, not a few women and "womanists" appear to be treading the path of confusion laid out by the "missionaries" from abroad. Women leaders and women's organizations are often elitist, and *modern*, either in the extremist sense of militant feminism, or in the reactionary vein of the autocratic, ego-tripping establishment.

The National Council of Women's Societies (NCMS), the government-imposed umbrella body for the 400 women's associations in Nigeria, is said to be almost forty years old. Its leadership is perpetually reactionary, which is perhaps to be expected, since the individuals are women close to the corridors of political power, and in the Western-oriented professions. The official task of NCWS is of Amazonian proportions: "Apart from giving central leadership and uniting these organizations, the NCWS was also expected to give them ideological direction and define parameters for involving women in national life and development." (*National Concord*, July 3, 1996: 11) Due to this presumptuous posture on the part of the founding mothers and fathers, the NCWS has failed woefully in its gargantuan quest for harmony and unity (a badly camouflaged desire for control) in the disunited society. The leaders, *women of timber and caliber*,[5] tin-goddesses matching in character their men full of talk but not much substance, usually are lacking in intellectual sophistication, and popular social orientation. The ideological direction propagated and promoted by these NCWS *madams*,[6] leads only to the harem or the brothel dominated by the big men, revered and rewarded for their mastery over womanhood with a brood of children, or—for the material-minded women—bulging bank accounts at home and abroad.

Nigerian female intellectuals are usually criticizing those female leaders for their retrogressive programs. Which, however, has not stopped some of these academic geniuses from serving as their servile surrogates in the name of nationhood and, naturally, womanhood. I remember the story of a female professor employed as director of Bureau for Women Affairs by one of the patriotic military regimes. The knowledgeable, self-opinionated feminist was consumed by the desire to transform her patriarchal society into a progressive, feminine-friendly nation; hence, her tendency to seize every occasion to make incendiary statements against "the neocolonialist masters and feudal overlords." That habit finally drew the ire of her mistress, the all-powerful First Lady and Commandress-

145

in-Chief who, very late on one very cold night, phoned the eminent professor to command her to never forget who was in charge, and to therefore make sure to obtain official permission for every word coming out of her venom-coated mouth, or else she would be summarily dealt with. The nonplussed professor could not sleep a wink that night. She had no peace of mind until she was safely on the plane taking her into exile.

She ought to have learnt her lesson from the experience of another professor, older and more respected than she, who, as chairperson of a women's group, was invited to a meeting with the same First Lady, only to be tongue -lashed and disgraced in the presence of baffled press representatives. The lesson: Nigeria's First Ladies are prolongations of their patriotic men; they are *dictatresses* inebriated with a false superiority complex, backed by the supreme power of the bullet. When these Eminent Ladies talk of women's issues, they simply mean that all Nigerian women should jump to it when they, the *commandresses*, bark out orders. Hardly ever interested in women's struggle, they are committed to what they call *family values*, that is, firstly, to the oppression of the rest of us by them and their husbands; secondly, to the privileges of a corps of bourgeois associates who, offered financial support, stand ready to proclaim women's rights at internal and external gatherings; and, thirdly, to the perpetuation of women's submission to feudalism. Hence, in some sectors of this very diversified country, children are married off to rich old men. Girls are advised, indeed, goaded, to marry early as a matter of socio-religious duty, even before giving any thought (precisely, an after-thought) to their education, because their lives' meaning is found only in marriage and motherhood. So, when the government continues to waste public funds on encouraging these child-brides to go to school, one can only laugh at their hypocrisy. The fact is, that education, Western education, is considered irrelevant by those steering those girls towards the harem.

As an intellectual myself, I am most concerned about the actions of the privileged women mentioned above. The leaders of the NCWS are mostly suspect in their activities on behalf of Nigerian women. In a recent interview, a former president of the council, Laila Dogonyaro, wife of an ex-military strongman, exposed the reactionary agenda of which many a family-oriented patriot would be proud. Not for her the fiery feminism of the followers of the setting sun. She believes that women must willingly defer to the supreme authority of men: "I don't believe in that women's liberation attitude... In the first place, the whole being of every woman in this world depends on the man." (*National Concord*, July 3, 1996: 12) She believes firmly in marriage, the only institution that accords women societal respect. According to her, woman's "respect lies in the man; so how can she fight that person who has the power to strip her of her self-worth, especially in the African set-up?" Dogonyaro advocates cooperation between men and women, to sensitize everyone to the role and importance of women in society. The problem with her viewpoint is, that once man's supremacy is accepted, or taken for granted, it means that any objective achieved by woman can only be those sanctioned by him. Since woman must be married in order to attain the position of respect, control by man would only remain more or less absolute, and forever. When Dogonyaro refers to "the African set-up," she reduces Africa to the narrow, religion-centered culture of a section that is being imposed as a national configuration. It is true that, generally, marriage is strongly encouraged in many African societies, but not for the sole reason of garnering respect for woman; rather, it is seen as the coming together of a man and a woman, to continue a line of humanity, and to direct the offspring towards lives marked by responsibility and productivity which are essential to the society's survival. Viewed in that light, marriage would offer woman feeedom, not enslavement; the occasion to cooperate with man as comrade, not to be coopted as a copycat, or a thoughtless collaborator. In addition, given the flexibility of some African cultures, this definition of marriage would include relationships not formalized in the Western or Arab sense. Thus, woman would always maintain her self-worth, recognized as such by man, and devoid of any limitations of external or self-imposed inferiority complex.

As president of the NCWS, Dogonyaro promoted programs purporting to favor all Nigerian women. On the contrary, she readily worked against many women. Programs, such as the Better Life for Rural Women, apart from helping the Nigerian First Lady and her coterie of multifarious materialists amass wealth comparable to that of the First Gentleman's male associates, constituted a source of confusion and trauma for many women. Rural women were brought into the cities to celebrate in a manner reminiscent of the farcical cultural shows of colonial times. It was all pomp and pageantry, with women flying in planes, lodged in five-star hotels, and intimidated by gorgeously attired goddesses and gadgets, serving as constant reminders of the irreductible distance betweem them and these modern *madams*. Instead of better life, the wasteful programs underscored most Nigerian women's *bitter* life, as well as the *bastardized* existence of rich women. All the tales about women's economic empowerment, were mostly window dressing for realizing the personal ambitions of the leading lights, easily recognized by their light skin attained through hereditary, or artificial cleansing.

As a result of the recommendation by the NCWS, the government has established a ministry of women affairs. The minister is a woman, which is the only achievement to which women can refer as a sign of progress. The new office is duplicated in each state, and that may be counted as additional victory. Meanwhile, the new First Gentleman (Abacha) and his First Lady, Myriam, have appointed a new NCWS president and executive, and established a new program for women. Better Life has been replaced by *Family Support*. At least, one might say that this is a more appropriate name, one that enunciates the government's belief in women's subservience to men, with respect and dignity being accorded to him. However, it is another name for profligacy, opportunism, squandermania, power-mongering, by women, with men's support. Trust Nigerians to absorb the new name into their highly imaginative socio-linguistic universe. When you want a bribe in Nigeria, when you want to be rewarded for doing a favor that should normally be free service rendered as part of your official duties, when you want to coax some money out of the poor citizens, or some crumbs out of the pockets of the filthy rich oppressors, when you want to take your cut out of the national cake to satisfy your hunger or your greed, you simply ask your understanding client for your *family support*. More often than not, in the society of the corrupt and the corruptible, you will receive a handshake of a folded money-bill, symbol of real support—you might say, reciprocity and complementarity—between the oppressors and the oppressed which, in the very imaginative setting, translates from the support given by the government, the lords and masters, to women, their obedient servants. One more interesting note: the NCWS has a patron, a man who is well respected by the ruling class, and an ex-vice-president, Alex Ekweme.

To the credit of Nigerian women, there are associations considerably more progressive than the NCWS. Two of them have been capturing headlines in the current political debate. The older Women in Nigeria (WIN), appears to be more intellectually oriented, while the younger Women Empowerment Movement (WEM), is more involved in practical matters. Both have shown a high level of autonomy and originality, which would enhance their relevance and competence in addressing women's, and other, issues. Nonetheless, one's reservation about their ability to optimize their potential, arises from Nigeria's patently unprogressive terrain, as well as women's sometimes unclear objectives and methodologies. For instance, WEM, interested in women's participation in the "new" politics being midwifed by the National Electoral Commission of Nigeria, (NECON),[7] proposed statutory female representation (40% of offices at all levels) in the political associations vying for registration as parties. Rather than accede to that proposal, NECON has simply required each association to identify the place of women, and youths, in its constitution and manifesto. Though dissatisfied, WEM has thanked NECON for this act of *generosity*, and urged the political associations to appoint one woman out of every three state conveners. WEM would like to realize the goals laid out by the post-Beijing Political Awareness Summit, held in Lagos in June 1996, to ensure that political parties and candidates address themselves to women's issues; to raise the awareness of female politicians, and voters, and to encourage the emergence of women role models for younger women committed to promoting their involvement in the political process. WEM's efforts are commendable but, within the political context, they may be doomed to failure, because NECON has not aroused any positive feelings in this observer. Similar to its predecessors, the National Electoral Commission (NEC) and Federal Electoral Commission (FEDECO), it has deliberately set out almost impossible guidelines, apparently meant to make the process collapse so that, as usual, the military politicians could continue to rule without a mandate, *ad infinitum*. By approaching NECON at all, WEM has tacitly approved of a transitional program that deliberately sidetracks basic issues on Nigeria's present and future. In other words, WEM is indirectly collaborating in a flawed process, which does not augur well for Nigerian women. NECON's action in regards of gender requirements for political parties, would be logical since it is an organ of a reactionary regime representing the interests of a male-dominated political system. One wonders why NECON has required information on the place of "women and youths" in the parties' manifestos. Could it be that both women and youths are viewed as immature, incapable of fending for themselves, and therefore in need of patriarchal protection? Or, could it be a matter of recognizing their potential for new ideas that would lead Nigeria away from the precipice?[8]

WEM's reference to the Beijing conference, and the Lagos summit, raises another question: What did Nigerian women achieve in the Beijing extravaganza of 1995? The conference confirmed what some of us have often affirmed, that the conditions and circumstances of African women are to be distinguished from those of others, especially their Western counterparts, who are too often hell-bent on imposing their *civilized*, first-world agenda upon their so-called unfortunate and helpless sisters from the third world. In the case of Nigeria, its delegation, led by the First Lady, could hardly be faulted for any conscious, or conscientious, attempts to represent the generality of Nigerian women. The elites and *socialites* in that delegation are interspersed with some serious-minded individuals, such as members of WIN and WEM. Nevertheless, it would be difficult, if not impossible, to really address women's issues without a certain commitment at the center, and without involving women at the grassroots in the deliberations. WEM has not done that. The organization would need to draw up a policy geared towards genuine coalescing of women across classes, and communities, not only to resolve women's particular problems, but also to actualize women's concrete contributions to the country's political process and socio-economic development. WEM is to be applauded for calling for the emergence of women role models, because the present crop of female politicians, and other public figures, share with their male counterparts all the qualities of corruption that are preventing the transformation of Nigeria into a veritable nation.

WIN has shown maturity and courage by distancing itself from the questionable political process. It has called for a resolution of the crisis caused by the annuled 1993 presidential elections, as a forerunner to any other action meant to move the country forward: Political prisoners, including Abiola, should be released unconditionally and open discussions should be held about the country's future (that is, genuine dialogue should take place). WIN has also recommended that the government accede to the request for better conditions of service, and for infrastructural improvement by university academics. This is refreshing because, unlike the general malaise and resignation of Nigerian parents, here are women (wives, workers, and mothers) rejecting the popular *siddon-look*[9] attitude and standing up to be counted. WIN's radicalism, or revolutionary position, bodes well for Nigerian women. If its members persist as a pressure group, whatever they achieve would be authentic and long lasting. Ideally, both WIN and WEM should join hands. The former would provide the right attitude; the latter, the right action, for the good of Nigerian women, and everyone else.

Meanwhile, some women are dutifully following the men on the path of sycophancy, as they take the ever available crumbs thrown down by a regime desperate for the stamp of legitimacy, however fragile, or fraudulent. One of such shameless groups is the Ogoni Women's Forum, which lays claim to fame because it was founded in the volatile, anti-Abacha region and the home of the assassinated environmentalist, Saro-Wiwa. These unscrupulous women have been bought by the authorities to storm the presidential palace, to express solidarity for Saro-Wiwa's murderers. On the heels of that solidarity march in July 1996, the First Lady of the current Warlord, hosted a West African First Ladies Peace Summit, to prove that all the wars in the region are but unreal nightmares, and that we are living in a hevean on earth.[10]

Finally, the reactionary ideology dominating the landscape notwithstanding, one remains impressed by women's willingness, thanks to the tenets of our culture, to cooperate with men, and to see beyond the individualistic, disintegrating tendencies of a gender-based struggle. WIN and WEM prove that women should not be, are not, servants to men. They attest to the necessity for an exchange of views, and for working together, to realize women's objectives in a society that respects all human beings. This is being emphasized in seminars, such as the one on "Capacity Building in Women in Development" (Lagos, June 1996), in which both female and male participants told one another certain hard truths. For example, some people were astonished to learn that, in several ways, women are more anti-women than men; more men than women would like to have a woman president; women professionals engage in bitter competition to keep other women from occupying a position of authority, in order to prove their superiority and uniqueness. The seminar thus reminded everyone that man is not woman's enemy and that, while it is important to eliminate all aspects of gender disparities from society, the objective is not to attain privileges, but to make available opportunities to assume one's humanity. And this cannot be clearer in any other country than Nigeria, with its conundrum of contradictions and conflicts combining to create a complexity of dehumanizing conditions. The lack of progressiveness among elite women, is no doubt a symptom of the country's myriad problems posed by a group of men comfortable in their status as overlords and willing and able to invite and accommodate both men and women as collaborators. One would, indeed, be elated at the coming of a woman courageous enough to face all the country's problems, and to proffer practical solutions.

Needless to say, these problems include many that are particular to women, and lack of equality in the workplace is one of the most disgusting. As with other aspects of Nigerian life, it is a struggle against a shamelessly conservative, neocolonial system. To take but one example, the legal profession: There are only three female Senior Advocates of Nigeria (SAN), in a profession dominated by men and, specifically, conservative men. Single mothers are known to have been denied appointment as judges. The gender plight must, however, be considered hand in hand with the ideological; for, there are also prominent male attorneys who are denied honor because they are radical and non-conformist.[11] In brief, once again, Nigerian women's status combines the limiting factor of gender with the limitless condition of humanity.

Notes

1. The ideas for this 1996 discourse arose out of the growing popularity of the "woman question" in Nigeria, especially in the aftermath of the Beijing conference to which Nigeria's then First Lady, Maryam Abacha, led a large delegation.

2. One has never ceased to wonder at the concept of *Third World*. To think of how universally accepted this misnomer has become, is to capture the depth of the psychological-political-economic-human hole in which our culture lies buried, forever(?)...

3. You must not be husband to two wives simultaneously, but you are free to divorce, and marry, as many times as you wish. Besides, you may, from time to time, fall prey to the human weakness of adultery, as long as you keep it secret.

4. In late 1998, the Nigerian government decided to increase salaries in the public service by as much as 600 percent. This clearly shows how badly paid civil servants have been over the years. Now, this latest action cannot but be viewed as another example of the confusion, and strange logic, embedded in the Nigerian system. Such an astronomical increment would exacerbate inflation, and further diminish the value of the country's currency.

5. Words that are often used to describe pompous personalities with not much serious quality to their character. Their caliber is, at best, quartered in mediocrity.

6. *Madam*, a thoroughly Nigerian terminology, used to address, or describe, a certain kind of woman. It implies a mixture of (less) respect and (more) derision. Think, for instance, of *cash madam*, a rich woman with either no class, or no integrity as to how she acquires, or spends, her money.

   Fela Anikulapo-Kuti, arguably Africa's greatest musician, calls the modern woman, *lady*: She prefers this word to *woman* (Fela's song, "Lady"). Such is the sophisticated Nigerian woman, who would do anything to prove that she is in a class by herself, and the superior of men.

7. With Abacha's death, NECON and other government creations, have been disbanded as a sham, the shame of an entrapped country, and symbol of the regime's agenda of perpetual power.

8. One's misgivings about NECON have been proven right: With Abacha's death, the commission has been swept away into oblivion. The new regime has appointed what it touts as an *independent* body to organize elections between December 1998 and May 1999. One

can only hope that this latest gang will act accordingly, and without taking orders from anyone. A tall order for a Nigerian commission, one daresay.

On the matter of women's participation in the complex debate over Nigeria's destiny, there has been a proliferation of women's groups, particularly NGOs, in the past few years. They are taking due advantage of the easy money coming from the United Nations and other organizations. Women Empowerment Movement, Women for Democracy and Leadership, 100 Group Network, Centre for Women for Independence, and Gender and DevelopmentＡction, these are some of the many organs dealing with women's issues.

9. *Siddon look*, a popular expression in pidgin English, coined by a former civilian governor of Oyo State and frontline politician, Bola Ige. Sit down and look, that is, waiting and watching, not with indifference, but with absolute interest, to see what will happen. Implied is the conviction that nothing good is expected from the events being played out in the public arena, because the players are crooks.

10. This new body has been given sanction by the post-Abacha regime, with the head of state's wife having attended a meeting in Accra, Ghana, in July 1998.

11. To become a Senior Advocate, one must pass the litmus test of excellence in the profession, supposedly. In reality, the committee in charge of the process, is influenced by the powers that be. Radical lawyers, such as Gani Fawehinmi, are regularly left out of the list of new SANs. Besides, the travails of the Nigerian Bar Association (NBA) also indicates the sad state of affairs in the legal profession. The Abacha regime stymied the association's relevance by infiltrating its ranks, and creating a dichotomy between government supporters and the opposition.

It need be mentioned that women are making headway in the legal profession; the NBA's current president is a woman.

CHAPTER 18

THE QUESTION OF SANCTIONS[1]

Sanctions constitute a form of punishment by other, influential countries against a country considered a bad egg by the international community. No matter what form they take, sanctions express the idea that the country is so bad that it needs to be ostracized, to be made to suffer, so that it may be compelled to change its policies and activities, particularly its actions and attitudes towards humanity. The very consideration of sanctions is a sign that a country is a pariah, a beast among human nations, a savage among the civilized, a symbol of the very worst in the human soul.

Nigeria is under consideration for sanctions in 1996, a few years removed from the new millennium. Interestingly, the country's leaders and sympathizers refuse to acknowledge that something is seriously wrong, that it is unusual to even think of sanctions in any setting, system, or state free of crimes against its own, or other, people. Were the leadership in a condition of openness to reality, and not suffering from a case of self-inflicted delusion of absolute righteousness, they would sit down, examine their conscience and their society, and do what is necessary to remove the stains for which their critics are now calling for sanctions. It would, indeed, be un-Nigerian to accept one's failings and crimes; far from it, the criminal must continue to crave the indulgence of his critics for patience, understanding, and appreciation of peculiarities that would translate acts of savagery as quintessential show of civilization in the Nigerian context.

It is tragic and traumatizing that Nigeria, a country that prides itself in having led the anti-apartheid struggle by spending billions of dollars and by insisting on sanctions against the apartheid regime, is now trying to convince the very countries that brought South Africa down to its knees and back from the brink, that sanctions should not be applied against Nigeria. The most ludicrous reason being given is, that the mass of the people would suffer most. One's response to that opinion is, that the people are already living in hell, experiencing hell, already down, and almost out; hence, sanctions will not worsen their condition. Maybe, in the short run, hell would expose and exaggerate its highlights of death and disease; however, in the long run, those tragic details would lose their impact, and hope and happiness and good health would be restored. The renegade regime would end up feeling the heat and rediscover its forgotten humanity. It is a mere cop-out to claim that sanctions would not help the people. South Africa's apartheid masters said the same thing but, soon enough, they were compelled to reconsider.

Is Nigeria any different? The officer and gentleman whose name used to be synonymous with anti-apartheid campaign at the United Nations, Joseph Garba, a retired military general and Nigeria's former permanent representative to the United Nations, has joined the bandwagon of the no-sanction apologists. In his opinion, Nigeria would overcome sanctions, because it has peculiar endowments and socio-economic qualities. (*Punch,* June 26, 1996:21) Garba says that sanctions will simply not work. He believes that Europe and the United States of America are just bluffing. Such pomposity and optimism are not unexpected; for, Garba symbolizes the sickness of a society ruined by an irresponsible ruling class suffering from delusion of grandeur, among other ego-ballooning maladies. Like others before and after him, Garba became an icon, a guru of Nigerian diplomacy simply by being in the vanguard of a successful coup-plot and thereby transforming from a man of the machine-gun to that of the microphone making propaganda about democracy as practiced by dictators. So, Joe Garba cannot, in all honesty, call for sanctions against a country to whose conditions he has eminently contributed. He is on the money about Nigeria's natural endowments, but he should be informed that these most patriotic regimes have squandered those endowments. The problem is, that the patriots do not seem to live in the same country as the oppressed, impoverished millions. Garba is no exception. He would claim that democratization is going on in a country where any dissenting voice is temporarily, or permanently, silenced. He would flaunt Nigeria's petro-dollars and its astonishing development even as billions are disappearing in meaningless, uncompleted projects, and people are unable to eat one single meal a day. He would proclaim success for a regime continuing the process of destroying education, labor, health, social services, economy, politics, and everything else concerning development in a modern world. And he is right to do so, because he is another excellent candidate for president!

Other politicians are proving to be as two-faced as Garba. After the hue and cry over the annulled 1993 elections, they have settled down, they have been "settled,"[2] and they have seen reason: Better to collaborate with the monster than to be condemned to the cooler. A class of shameless chameleons, they have perfected the art of maneuvering and manipulating everything and everybody. Facts and fiction; masks and faces; resemblance and contradictions, everything becomes harmonized in the hands of the expert analysts and actors in the comedy called the politics of life. The government knows those characters for what they are; hence, whenever problems arise, politicians are entrusted with the task of fronts men and women ready to fool their people and the whole world. Not surprising, therefore, that the classless political class is echoing the reactionary refrain, that sanctions will not work, that the government is committed to making life better, that this hell is truly a transition to heaven. And you can see them posturing and pumping up their fat chests with pride, as they pretend to be reflecting on people's condition, whereas they are only reflecting their benefactors' image.

The United Nations fact-finding mission to Nigeria submitted its report some weeks ago. Many people were displeased with the pass mark given to the regime for the so-called transition program. Instead of sanctions, the group recommends further delay, to give the patriotic regime a chance to show its hand. Right on time, a few decrees have been amended and, to coincide with the meeting with the Commonwealth Ministerial Action Group (CMAG), some detainees have been released. A political ploy? Even a child would wonder why, all of a sudden, the same regime that has been seizing any perceived opponents, or their wives, or children, or parents, in case the targeted enemies manage to escape—and keeping them without trial, incommunicado in secret cells as long as it wishes-, is so easily disposed to releasing them at this time. A political ploy? No! The patriotic politicians would respond in unison. Interviewed, almost all of them are thanking the government for its generosity and concern, and encouraging more of such actions. Before the Commonwealth encounter, or, a contest of wits, in which Nigeria, ever the wily giant, stands to win, some observers were certain that the CMAG members would refuse to be impressed by that exhibitionism of releasing detainees. Well, they were wrong: Britain, the clog in the wheel of Nigeria's progress, the lethal thorn in its soul, has continued to beat the drum of compromise. In the same Marlborough House where they granted independence, that passport to neocolonialism, they negotiated another season of oppression for the unfortunate people of Nigeria. And the politicians are hailing the wisdom of it all. And they are pointing to the registration of political parties as one striking sign of the journey towards the democratic paradise. And some of them are saying that Nigeria has done absolutely nothing wrong to warrant sanctions. And, so as to show more concerted solidarity, those men and women, paid to participate in the unconstitutional conference, gathered again at the capital, for their anniversary celebration where they, most logically, praised the regime for its excellence and its "wisdom to settle for dialogue rather than confrontation and fanning the flame of hatred." (*The Guardian*, June 28, 1996: 4)[3]

Meanwhile, the voices of truth continue to speak out on behalf of the millions being victimized but unable, and unwilling, to revolt. Concerning the release of detainees, the Committee for the Defence of Human Rights (CD-HR) informs us on the phantom list of the few released people: Some have, indeed, not been released; some, released earlier through legal pressure, have been included as beneficiaries of this unprecedented magnanimity; some, though released, are not frontliners in the democratic struggle. And, as this is being written, new detainees are being arrested. Besides, those released now may be re-arrested tomorrow, that is if they are not eliminated by "armed robbers" interested only in taking their lives, but not their property. And, how come no one is questioning the torture and trauma undergone by the detainees? Abiola, the symbol of the struggle, and the main reason for the unfolding dance of death, or, hopefully, of redemption, is not even being mentioned by the Nigerian government: As they say, June 12, 1993, is dead! The CD-HR rightly castigates the regime for its "official double-speak and gross insincerity" (*The Guardian*, June 27, 1996: 1), qualities which have served it well since the 1994 announcement that Shonekan, the interim pseudo-head of state, had resigned when, in actuality, he had been removed with ignominy by the man who had spent too many years of national self-service as best man, and had been patiently scheming to become the bridegroom, and to give Nigeria, the plum bride, the kiss of doom.

The decision of the visiting CMAG delegation not to recommend sanctions, must have been viewed as a foregone conclusion with the presence of a Togolese as chairman. Togo is under the vice-grip of another dictator, Eyadema, the master coup-plotter-killer, the epitome of military-civilian complementarity, the best and only life-president that Togo will ever have, and Nigeria's best friend.[4] Why, then, one might ask, did the United Nations do that to Nigeria? Why do all those foreign countries continue to fall prey to the government's bold-faced lies? For one thing, Nigeria's potential may be too frightfully great to be allowed to blossom. Imagine a Nigeria, rich with all sorts of resources, well organized, genuinely united, focused, responsibly assuming its destiny, and committed to development and progress. Imagine! For Euro-America, such a veritable giant would be a big threat to their imperialistic agenda. Imagine! Nigeria could be the basis of a pan-Africa, a world power in its own right. Imagine! And a black nation at that. Imagine!

For another thing, Nigeria's native masters are boosting the economy of places such as Britain, with all those billions stashed away in their bank-vaults.[5] And we know that the United States is the major buyer of Nigerian oil. One can therefore appreciate the over all selfish slow-footing in efforts to bring about change. At the end of the recent CMAG meeting with Nigeria's delegation, the Commonwealth spokesman declared: "The Commonwealth wants to hear from *the wider spectrum, if possible from the Nigerian society* (emphasis mine) before it makes a decision."[6] Apparently, the loud pronouncements of human rights' activists in the country, are neither loud nor convincing enough.[7] Apparently, the statistics of those clamped into detention without any given reason, without trial, and under abominable conditions, apparently, that is not enough proof of abuse. Apparently, the exiles, among them a Nobel laureate (Soyinka), and the man who, in 1956, demanded independence for Nigeria (Enahoro) in the very building where the delegates and their collaborators were playing football with the country's fate, apparently, those exiles and others that would, in a sane society, have been honored and properly utilized for national development, apparently, they are all talking nonsense, or talking to deaf and mute people. For, you need to spend but one day in Nigeria, among the people, to realize how depressed and desperate they are as a result of oppression and abject poverty, with no hope for respite in the near future.[8] Apart from the members of the regime and their beneficiaries, that is, the civilians chosen to sing their praises, and desperate to hang on to their blood money, apart from this accursed handful, the vast majority in Nigeria remain victims of torture and betrayal. Here we are on the eve of a new century, in Africa's biggest, and richest, country, yet nothing functions. No rights, no freedom, no hope. And Nigeria is pushing a puzzle-ridden peace in Liberia, and spending billions to aid other countries' dictators, and to even promote coups.[9]

The message from that Commonwealth spokesman would appear to be, that Nigerians must resolve their own problems, themselves. They should stop relying on outsiders to come and free them; they have to do it themselves. Fair enough, and a necessary reminder, because in all cases where sanctions were imposed, the internal struggle, *by the people themselves*, was already in full flight. South Africa was burning before sanctions were reluctantly implemented. The people, conscious and committed to the cause of freedom and equality in their motherland, refused to resign themselves to a fate of endless enslavement. At every opportunity, they protested, they marched, they made a point, no matter how small, in the name of their humanity. Sharpeville, Soweto, these are symbols of that struggle against apartheid. Many, including women, and children, were killed by government goons, but the people were not deterred, realizing as they did that death is the ultimate sacrifice in the fight for freedom, and that a life of slavery is no life at all.

In Nigeria, people are seemingly too cowardly, too selfish, to care. Too selfish to understand that oppression is a shared condition to be overcome by communal action. And they, indeed, we all, are too corruptible to say no to the forces leading us into decadence. When the dictator's troops hit the streets, everyone runs for cover. When the forces of destruction attack the educational system and the lecturers go on strike in protest, parents and students beg the lecturers to please return to the classroom, and to implore the government, not to desist from its destructive policies, but to kindly engage the lecturers in *dialogue,* that is, force them to listen to its monologue of commands and threats. When the military regime democratically imprisons innocent citizens for daring to demand their basic human rights, the public begs the criminals to forgive their innocent victims. When those in power have their critics eliminated, there is collaborating quiet in the land. "I cannot come and die for nothing, o!" Such is the refrain among the law-abiding citizens. Yet, people are dead in the brain and in the soul and, without action, the place will be full of dead bodies ready to be dragged into a mass grave.

Would that mean that sanctions would be useless, as apologists of the reactionary regime are telling the world? Absolutely not. Sanctions will become inevitable when the people begin to protest, together. Sanctions will be effective when the victims themselves begin to stand up to their oppressors. Finally, in the Nigerian context, if and since so many people are scared of mass suffering consequential to an oil embargo by the international community, there are other sanctions: Freeze all individual foreign accounts owned by those in power; send back home all family-members of the regime, and their collaborators, including their children enrolled in universities; impose total embargo on travel outside Africa; and expel Nigeria from the United Nations, and the Commonwealth. We shall then see how the great messiahs would survive.[10]

Notes

1. Written in 1996. Predictably enough, Nigeria, with her alluring oil-wealth, has been able to avoid serious sanctions by the oil-guzzling, international powers. With Abacha's death on June 8, 1998, evaporated any threat of such an unbecoming punishment.

2. *Settlement,* another Nigerian terminology, describing the corrupt habit of paying off anyone in sight, in order to continue perpetrating evil in the society.

3. The sycophancy of that dishonest class culminated in the five political parties' decision to draft Abacha as the sole candidate for the presidency in early 1998. [The unfolding farce was suddenly aborted by his death in June.]

4. One of the means used by the Abacha regime to solidify its stranglehold on power, was its forceful friendship with other West African regimes, whose bills it paid, whose wars it fought, and whose allegiance it thus purchased with impunity.

5. Interesting that, in post-Abacha 1998, Britain was very aggressive in its efforts to renew economic ties with Nigeria. Thus, British Airways placed new, wide-body, 400-seater jumbo jets on the London-Lagos route. On the contrary, Nigeria Airways has remained in a funk, with no planes to fly the lucrative route. Its befuddled chairman tried to fool the public by propounding the theory, that most world airlines now lease planes instead of purchasing them. To that foolishness, the British are probably responding with a guffaw, as they carry their booty to the bank, and plan to earn more millions by leasing planes to Nigeria.

6. Note that, during the Nigerian crisis, both the Commonwealth's suspension of Nigeria, and the European Union's several acts of condemnation, constituted only hot air, posing no danger at all to the rampaging dictatorship.

7. The post-Abacha regime, led by General Abubakar, has released many, but not all, political prisoners. Many bothersome questions remain unanswered. One notes, for example, the recently announced death of the journalist, Bagauda Kaltho: According to the police, he was killed in 1996, while trying to plant a bomb at a hotel in Kaduna, Northern Nigeria. But the authorities had kept silent over the "fact," and had said nothing to the many demands over the man's whereabouts. The general belief is, that he was arrested at that time, and tortured to death. The Abubakar regime has declared its acceptance of the police report, thus closing the case, forever...

8. Hope came with Abacha's death, although some doubt whether real change is in the offing. That hope was suddenly smashed to smithereens by the death of Abiola.

9. One would never know how many billions of dollars have been spent in Liberia, and Sierra Leone.

10. Events of the second half 1998 put to rest all the debate over sanctions. The West must be happy to return to the rich oil-fields, and for

the opportunity to obtain other large pieces of the Nigerian pie. The privatization policy is being implemented, and Nigerians do not have the cash to buy the big, public-owned businesses, parastatals, banks, etc. So, the free market will be open to Euro-Americans and their local partners. One might say, that the neocolonial enterprise will continue apace.

CHAPTER 19

RECONCILING IRRECONCILABLES?[1]

One remains confused about the exact meaning, thrust, and goals of the suddenly popular—and, of course, patriotic—exercise called *reconciliation*. Lest people get carried away by groundless zeal, it is of the essence to remind everyone of certain facts, as well as an estimation of what it takes to achieve the tall order of genuine reconciliation.

Firstly, the facts, briefly: Nigeria, from the very beginning, has been a conglomeration of incompatible parts superficially forced into a sham unit (not even union), to the advantage of the exploiting master, Great Britain. That incompatibility has remained the bane of a country abundantly blessed with diverse resources. Historians would be quick to inform us that, in 1960, Nigeria became an independent *nation*. But, every honest person knows that there is no nation here, absolutely. Yes, there could have been, when activist leaders from the South, notwithstanding their own experience and preparation through self-government, stretched out (down, one could actually say) a brotherly hand to the unwilling, ill-prepared North to join the *independa* train, and to, indeed, be at the helm of power. Yes, there could have been a nation, if the power-mongering, new masters, and self-chosen leaders, had ever tried to seek accommodation and understanding of their compatriots whom they have always treated as their inferiors.

Now, suddenly—and many of us are relieved and simply overwhelmed by the turn of events—we are being told by the day's rulers that reconciliation has begun, with regional consultations coordinated by military service chiefs. To buttress its point, the regime has released some political prisoners, most notably a former head of state, Obasanjo. Day by day, one reads of various views on what is called *the way forward*. Those expressing these views are also as various in their identities. A truly democratic process, some would tell us. At least, the present actions have impressed many at home and, especially, abroad.

In order to assess these current attempts at reconciliation *a la nigeriane*, let us emphasize the meaning of the word. Reconciliation declares the presence of conflict, victimization, deep problems that have made enemies of brothers and sisters, situations that have witnessed the activities of one group, the oppressors, lording it over the others, the slaves and servants. Most likely, the architects of the Nigerian scenario chose the word because they would like to imitate, and take advantage of, the happenings in South Africa. That is exactly why one must view the process with suspicion. Unlike the Nigerian example, South Africa is a model to be envied and emulated. There, one sees qualities, such as honesty, dignity, respect for human life, in short, a willingness to accept blame, and to make amends. On the contrary, Nigeria is a bundle of dishonesty, fraud, selfishness, in short, an unwillingness to face facts, and to build a meaningful society.

When South Africa decided to dismantle the apartheid machine, Nelson Mandela was released to form a government of national unity. Then president de Klerk agreed to work with him. Whites recognized the rights of Blacks to rule. The apartheid regime accepted its acts of bestiality and, through concrete actions, apologized for them, and made it possible for Blacks to begin to live as human beings. The Archbishop Tutu-led Truth and Reconciliation Commission, in session several years after Blacks came to power, is proof that, for it to be authentic, reconciliation must entail avowal of guilt, as well as readiness to redress wrongs, willingly, gradually if necessary, and fully. South Africa also teaches us that reconciliation refuses to respect sacred cows, that nobody deserves immunity. That is why former president Botha, epitome of the worst in that country's tragic history, has been compelled to confess his sins, and to seek pardon, barring which he must face the consequences before the law of the land.[2]

Back to Nigeria. The circumstances and the concrete evidence, do not encourage optimism, except the kind emanating from a population that has been so battered that it is prepared to hope in the face of hopelessness. Imagine a drowning swimmer marooned in the middle of a shark-infested ocean, grabbing at a suddenly floating straw, in the hope that his life will be saved. Many questions must be asked of the managers of the Nigerian process of reconciliation. Have the victimizers, and the victims, been identified? The guilty and the innocent? The essentials of the problem that must be resolved? What are the real issues? Are people prepared to be honest and truthful, and not hypocritical and truthless? Do Nigerians want to build a nation on a solid foundation once and for all, or are they trying to construct a skyscraper on quicksand, and to keep playing the same old games, so that tyranny may continue to prevail?

Any serious-minded person would wonder whether the current exercise is meant to bring about real reconciliation, that is, if it is supposed to be a springboard towards genuine unity, the roots of a nation, and the beginning of democracy for a country that has spent all of its thirty-eight years drifting towards the abyss. In spite of the hopeful words and actions of the new head of state, this observer dares to add a dissenting voice, to tone down the euphoria, so that everyone may slow down and think seriously of the situation. One is concerned, not because one is unpatriotic, not because one is a hard-core pessimist; but, specifically, because one is interested in seeing Nigeria prosper, and its people free, and because one would like to witness the birth of a real nation, not the *countion,* or the pseudo-nation, to which everyone has been forced to attach their destiny, even as they are being more and more dehumanized.

More questions. Why has the government not said that simple, straightforward word, *sorry,* for all the glaring and gory iniquities perpetrated against the poor, innocent people of the country? Why does one keep hearing the same old, suffocating songs full of lies and licence to maim and murder, from the same, soulless singers pretending to be patriots? Why does the government insist on making a hero of one of the most contemptible villains ever to misrule the sad country? Why does it allow those very instruments of oppression, and murder, those very stone-hearted yesmen and women willing to do everything inhuman to prolong their master's reign of terror, why does the government allow such reprehensible figures to continue to claim knowledge of *the way forward*? Why? Reconciliation, the genuine article, demands that criminals be identified and dealt with; or, at least, they must not be allowed to contribute their sick notions to a country still suffering from the effects of their murderous agendas.

When the new government—and one might wonder about how new a wine can be, when the same old product is simply poured into an old but newly branded bottle—invites all and sundry to present ideas; when the same government uses the same functionaries, the state administrators,[3] to compile lists of invitees for the dialogue; when the same old system of governance is retained, with a few cosmetic changes (for example, dismissal of special advisers, and release of some detainees "for health reasons," and as implementation of the decision already taken by the late dictator), then one has many reasons to fear that this reconciliation thing could be another ruse in the loaded bag of tricks used by tyrants to cling on to power.

After reading the tales of horror recounted by several released political detainees,[4] one is convinced that the government has a lot of explaining, and atonement, to do, not to forget reparations to those individuals and their families. Worse, still, is the fact that other victims, as innocent as the ones released, are being kept in the cells hardly fit for Ramadan rams. As it is, the government feels no remorse, no reason to retrace its steps. And, Nigerians, poor, sad, and silly Nigerians, are praising the Lord and showering the new leadership with encomiums, while foreign governments and international public figures are rushing to ally themselves with the democratically-minded regime. And one senses that something is just not right in all this. Something is wrong when those who have been tortured, and remain marginalized, begin to thank their tormentors. Something is wrong when foreign masters are jumping into their jets and heading for a place very recently classified as a universal pariah. Something is awfully wrong when, all of a sudden, hell is supposed to have been transformed into heaven. Just to take a look at the home front: It would be instructive to provide data on those heading all of Nigeria's military units, ministries, parastatals, the judiciary, the diplomatic corps, etc.[5] And one notes that, as the vaunted reconciliation continues, the UN and

Commonwealth Secretaries-General have visited Nigeria. They held a meeting with the government, represented by, among others, the ambassadors to South Africa and the United States, and the permanent representative to the UN. All three are Hausa-Fulani, and Moslem. To their number may be added others of the same origins, like the ambassadors to Great Britain, and France. And one might note that the federal capital, Abuja, symbol of the nation, is perfectly a Northern enclave, always under the thumb of a Northern minister. And the Law School, the professional institution where newly graduated lawyers are licenced, has been moved to Abuja, in addition to a second stock market, and the Nigerian Ports Authority, while Lagos, the former, now out-of-favor capital, is reeling under the hammer of deliberate dismemberment, like a misbehaving servant made to starve for refusing to obey his master. And, yes, Nigeria, a secular state, is still a member of the Organization of Islamic Conference. And the government has just replaced the dreaded national security adviser, Gwarzo, a Hausa-Fulani, with another; oh, yes, with a twist: The new one served in the 70s in the regime of Obasanjo, a Southerner who, one cannot forget, worked very well with the Northerners. Would mere talk deal with all these glaring cases of discrimination? If, as it does, reconciliation entails making amends and righting wrongs, Nigeria does have a very long way to travel, far beyond wooing the international community with cosmetic changes.

Both the Secretaries-General of the UN (Annan of Ghana), and of the Commonwealth (Anyaoku of Nigeria), finished their marathon discussions with the government, "a broad spectrum" of the population, interest groups (excluding the main opposition group, NADECO), and, finally, Abiola. One might consider all that to be great for pan-Africanism; great for democracy, too. What is not at all great, what, indeed, is most depressing, is Kofi Annan's reported statement that Abiola had assured him that he would not insist on his presidential mandate, and that he just wanted to get on with his life. Talk of dictatorship disguised as democracy! It is tragic that African sons and daughters are being used by foreign purveyors of *dictocracy* to perpetrate the rape of freedom, a sin that, supposedly, those very masters have been condemning in the Nigerian setting. For example, how democratic is it, to ask a man incarcerated and held incommunicado for four years, to decide on not just his personal life, but on the fate of millions of his people? How democratic is it, to keep the man away from his associates and advisers, from the realities of the lives of those who freely chose him as their president? What a democracy, this crazy way of subtly forcing the man into submission! What a democracy, this subterfuge! What a reconciliation, this hypocrisy promoted by a rulership intent upon shoving its absolutist agenda down the throat of a man heroic and patriotic enough to repel, for four long years, the temptation to be selfish and short-sighted! Annan claimed that the government of Nigeria would release political prisoners, including Abiola, at the time chosen by the *militocrats*, after Abiola might have been adequately reduced to another common prostitute called politician. One can only hope that, for Abiola's and the people's sake, that process will fail.

The unfolding mess reminds one of Obasanjo's 1994 statement in Harare (before he himself became an unwilling guest of the murderous regime), to the effect that Abiola was not the messiah that Nigeria needed. One also recalls the lack of commitment of Abiola's eldest son when, oblivious to the fact that his father had become a symbol of ideals far superior to the personal needs of wealthy brats, he, the son, threw dignity and self-pride to the wind in a naive attempt to have his father set free. Could it therefore be true that, after all, Abiola is just another opportunist and power-monger, committed only to his self-aggrandizement, and unprepared to be Nigeria's Mandela? Could it be true that he just wants to get on with his life? Let us hope not, for the sake of his assassinated wife, Kudirat, and Rewane, and the innumerable nameless ones who have made the ultimate sacrifice so that, for once, Nigerians may be free.

On the other hand, could it be that the UN Secretary-General has been used by the government to pursue its own purpose of deception and confusion? Already, Nigerian newspapers are giving different interpretations to what Annan said, and to what he said Abiola said. By the way, what did Annan himself say? And, what exactly is the government's position? So, one may be pessimistic, or realistic, enough to expect the Nigerian ball of confusion to come alive again, soonest. You know the old game of deception, arguments, leading to a place we call Chaos. And the military, ever more adept than anyone else in its ability to confuse people, may have succeeded in weathering the whirlwind that was threatening to sweep it back to its rightful abode in the barracks, with Abacha's death. The one glimmer of hope lies in Abiola, a free Abiola, who will tell the public his own story. For now, whoever had any doubt must be reassured, that Nigeria is not South Africa, even though it spent its billions to spearhead the latter's struggle for freedom.

What has happened to Abiola is but one example of a long history of oppression in Nigeria, a country where one nationality keeps trampling upon all others. How, then, do you reconcile diametrically opposed cultures, principles, and peoples, when those on one side (the self-proclaimed owners of the land), refuse to allow an honest, open discussion of the differences and inequalities? How do you reconcile, when the dictators want to dictate, absolutely, forever? Rumors persist that Abiola is being urged, through all sorts of pressure, to forget, and forgive, so that the country may "move forward." This observer says, so that the established positions may be maintained, so that the manipulators of Nigeria's fate may continue to ride their slaves and servants indiscriminately. One keeps hearing various voices of that unique Nigerian wisdom (read: foolishness), advising Abiola to help us find peace, that he is just another victim of annulment; that many events have overtaken the election that he is supposed to have won; that there are now five political parties working hard to implement democracy, and that anyone insisting on a revisit of the 1993 exercise is unpatriotic.

The response to such talk is, that reconciliation must affirm that Abiola is symbol of the aggrieved millions who have been deprived of a chance to be free, and to prosper. As stated by Beko Ransome-Kuti, a pro-democracy activist recently freed from prison where he was serving a twenty-five-year term for a coup he knew nothing about: "We don't want an olive branch, we want repentance." The government must do the right thing: Apologize to Abiola, and to the whole of the Nigerian people. Macrocosmically, Nigerians must be allowed to discuss and decide their destiny. They must be free to choose, free to act, free to do as they wish, with themselves; indeed, free to define what Nigeria means to them.

And I can hear someone say that it is a very tall order. Which is reason enough for that question: How do you reconcile irreconcilables?

Notes

1. Written in 1998, after Abacha's, but before Abiola's, death.
2. Botha remained defiant to the end. He was convicted and given a suspended sentence, due to his old age and deteriorating health.
3. The post-Abacha regime made some changes in state administrators: Some were moved to other states; some, back to the "barracks," at times to other assignments, including political postings. Among those retained in the position, are those whom the people adjudge to be incompetent and insensitive, and most corrupt.
4. See, for example, *TELL*, August 10, 1998: 4-10.
5. One such analysis shows that Northerners are in charge of almost everything. See, *TEMPO*, July 23, 1998: 9.

CHAPTER 20

THE YORUBA FACTOR[1]

With the sudden death of M.K.O. Abiola, now may be the most appropriate moment to assess the Yoruba factor in Nigeria. Questions that interest us, include the following: How important is the Yoruba nation to Nigeria? How have the Yorubas contributed to Nigerian independence, and post-independence? Are Yorubas essentially tribalists, or nationalists (that is, *Nigerian* nationalists)? How does one evaluate the performance of Yoruba leaders in Nigerian history? And, finally, what does the present mean, and the future portend, for the Yorubas? In order to address these issues, one need refer to the fact that, at Abiola's death, there is a chorus of voices, both Yoruba and otherwise, criticizing the Yoruba (so-called) leaders for the Yoruba marginalization in current Nigeria and, indeed, for the tragedy that befell Abiola in the hands of a regime that literally ran over any obstacle to its objective of perpetual domination.

One essential point which the reader must always bear in mind: Nigeria is *not* a nation. At best, it is a conglomeration of nations and sub-nations, with a strong, and strong-armed center determined to maintain the artificial geographical entity—a country—created by the British adventurers. In truth, every Nigerian is a tribalist because, due to the non-existence of a nation, and the non-encouragement of the qualities of community, each person has been compelled to link his basic instincts and interests to the unit (named tribe) that remains most real to him. Those governing Nigeria have been, and are, guilty of helping to create and nurture this state of non-nation. They have never acted in the spirit of selflessness, of harmonization, of consciousness, required to arouse in the people that sense of oneness, and readiness to sacrifice individual wishes and needs for the good of the larger community.

Having noted that, one must add that, in Nigerian history, the Yorubas have actually contributed as much as any other nation, to the existence, and survival, of the country called Nigeria. In other words, they are among the most detribalized Nigerians or, to use the misnomer, the most *nationalistic* of all. Let us begin by contemplating the character and contributions of each of the acclaimed leaders of the Hausa-Fulani, Igbo, and Yoruba, the three major ethnic nationalities in the country. Ahmadu Bello, the Sardauna of Sokoto, was a hard-core believer in his ethnic group's superiority, not to forget his faith in the supremacy of their religion, Islam. At Nigeria's independence in 1960, Bello and his followers insisted that, in order to join the independence train, they must be the drivers; they must be in control, in the seat of power. That requirement was all the more galling because, during the struggle against the British colonizers, the North refused to participate and, while the East and the West were undergoing the political apprenticeship of self-government, the North remained an appendage or, the foster-child, of the lily-white Queen. Most significant of all was the fact that, after forcing the hands of both the British and the accommodating activists from the East and West, Bello was too proud to journey down to Lagos to rule; he therefore sent down his surrogate, Tafawa Balewa. Throughout his life, Bello did nothing to promote the idea of a Nigerian nation. He could not see beyond his oligarchic nose, as he firmly implemented his program of "One North, One People." When he and his underlings thought of the south, it was in terms of conquest. In the spirit of Uthman dan Fodio, he had the notion of a *jihad* through which his people would subjugate and rule over the vast land mass, from the edges of the Sahara to the shores of the Atlantic. Everyone following events in Nigeria would recall the eye-opening remarks by one of Bello's kinsmen, Maitama Sule, a former federal minister who, at a book launch in 1993, propounded the following bizarre essentialist thesis as an explanation of the North's monopoly of power: "Everyone has a gift from God. The northerners are endowed by God with leadership qualities. The Yoruba man knows how to earn a living and has diplomatic qualities. The Igbo is gifted in commerce, trade and technological innovation. God so created us individually for a purpose and with different gifts." (*TELL*, Nov. 14, 1994: 13) Sule went further to praise Bello's foresight in encouraging Northern young men to enlist in the army, a fact that would explain how the military has been used to attain the said monopoly. It is not by coincidence that the military has ruled Nigeria for thirty out of thirty-eight years of independence, and almost all the heads of state have been Hausa-Fulani. If only the great Bello had planned for the young men and women of his nation to obtain other professional training besides the military (particularly, Western education, without which no country can adequately participate in the process of modern development), perhaps his people would not have been so desperate to cling to political power. Today, Hausa-Fulani leaders shamelessly state that they must rule (or, misrule), because the other nations have cornered socio-economic power. They, the self-chosen leaders, seem to have conceded the non-political areas to their more Westernized rivals. They would appear also to be disinterested in developing necessary skills to compete therein. Witness the systematic debilitation of education, industry, judiciary, and every other aspect of development. The North is simply underdeveloped, thanks to Bello and those coming after him.

With regards to the Igbos, Nnamdi Azikiwe, their highly reputed leader, did struggle for Nigerian independence.[2] In post-independence Nigeria, he also promoted non-ethnic ideals, which made him a big name in the Yoruba West, for instance. However, in the overall history of Nigeria, Zik remained leader of the Igbos; in fact, he lost that position during the tragic era of the Biafran war (1967-70), to the military ego-tripper, Odumegwu Ojukwu. If Zik had been more committed to Nigeria, perhaps the civil war could have been avoided. On the other hand, his firm support for the Igbo cause might indeed, have led to a different outcome of the tragic encounter. Of course, this is mere speculation, a hindsight, academic exercise. In reality, no right-thinking Igbos could have been expected to commit themselves to a life of genocide choreographed by a blood-thirsty hegemony hypocritically declaring its commitment to a non-existing nation. In his later life, Zik was best known as a self-proclaimed prospective political bride, thus confirming his, and his people's, status as secondary players in the country's power-game.

Now, to Obafemi Awolowo, the acclaimed leader of the Yorubas who, by his role in the Biafran war, single-handedly frustrated the Igbos' secessionist agenda and helped keep Nigeria intact as a geographical entity. An honest assessment of his life proves that Awo was the most Nigerian of the three leaders, both positively and otherwise. Besides the civil war, he had been at the forefront of the independence struggle. Until today, many Igbos are still seething from what they consider as Awo's betrayal of their cause which, in their opinion, would have definitively resolved the problem of Hausa-Fulani domination.[3] Note that Awo did engage in a game of semantics, regarding Igbo secession. Thus, he exhibited the legendary Nigerian (or Yoruba) characteristic of political slyness which would later backfire on him and his people. Meanwhile, Awo it was who spoke out on the minority nations' rights, a fact much appreciated by the likes of the late Ken Saro-Wiwa, the Ogoni leader. Awo's position on the subject was first expressed in 1947 (*Path to Nigerian Freedom*, London: Faber & Faber). No other majority (that is, Hausa-Fulani, Igbo, and Yoruba) leader ever addressed the issue. It is also noteworthy that the Western Region, home of the Yorubas, was the very first to be fragmented, with the creation of the Mid-West. Rivers State, carved out of the Eastern Region during the civil war crisis, came into being, not out of the Gowon regime's magnanimity, or its appreciation of the minorities' protest against Igbo domination, but as a political and military ploy, to prevent the Igbos from laying their hands on the rich oil-fields.

Just as Awolowo had a chance to spearhead the dissolution of centripetal Nigeria, so also did another Yoruba, Olusegun Obasanjo, upon whom was thrust the Nigerian headship by the assassination of the incumbent, Muritala Mohammed, in a failed coup. Everyone has asserted that Obasanjo worked assiduously for Nigeria. He left office as the only military leader who, till date, has willingly organized and implemented a transition to civilian rule. He handed over the reins of power to a "democratically elected" president in 1979. Nonetheless, several questions may be asked of this "eminent personality," an epithet that Obasanjo garnered as a member of that unique group of internationally respected leaders chosen by the United Nations to dialogue with the South African government, during those dark days of apartheid. And the questions arise from one's perception as a Yoruba who recognizes the facts of Hausa-Fulani domination, and the shameful roles that Yoruba leaders have often played in sustaining it. For example, why did Obasanjo refuse to stand by justice and fair-play in the 1979 elections, when it was crystal clear that the vote had been rigged in favor of Shagari, the Hausa-Fulani, against Awolowo, the Yoruba? Why did Obasanjo declare that the better candidate did not necessarily have to win? Reports were, that he, Obasanjo, actually vowed not to pass the baton to Awolowo. Was that due to Obasanjo's efforts to prove (to whom?) that he was not a tribalist? Later on, after the 1993 presidential elections, Obasanjo again had the unique opportunity to stand up for justice. He stated that Babangida, the *Maradona* of Nigeria, was wrong to have annulled the free and fair elections, won by Abiola, a Yoruba. However, instead of using his immense stature to ensure that the winner was duly installed in office, Obasanjo started dancing like another shameless, parochial yo-yo. Full of himself as some superior God-sent, he told the world that Abiola was not the messiah that Nigeria needed.

It is interesting that, after his failure to do the right thing, Obasanjo himself came to suffer the dire consequences, when the devilish dictator, Abacha, roped him into a concocted coup plot and nearly succeeded in sending him to his death. One recalls that many people in Nigeria, Yorubas in particular, did not shed one single tear for the beleaguered Obasanjo; in fact, the consensus was, that he got what he deserved! Before we take a look at the new, "born-again," 1998 Obasanjo, let us add the saga of another Yoruba leader, Abacha's ex-lieutenant on the Aso Rock, Oladipo Diya. The story of the coup for which he and a slew of subordinates, both military and civilian, were sentenced to death, with the commutation to twenty-five years in prison, is now part of the extraordinary lore of lies and mob-lynching tactics of Nigeria's evil men. Diya was once a very vocal, anti-Babangida-self-perpetuating, military general. He had built for himself a reputation for professionalism, probity, and fair play. He had a chance to have justice done to Abiola and the Nigerian people; unfortunately, he refused to do so. He became Abacha's handmaid in oppressing and suppressing the voice of democracy, a resounding, pan-Nigerian voice which, however, the oppressors deliberately reduced (a figment of their imagination, but one successfully sold to many a non-Yoruba, by a well oiled propaganda machine) to that of "the tribalists from the South-West." Diya reached the nadir of bastardization when in late 1997, at the burial ceremony of Adekunle Ajasin, one of the Yorubas' most revered leaders, he renamed the leading pro-democracy group, NADECO, as *AGBAKO,* a Yoruba descriptive for an evil, destructive, and retrogressive body, that is, in his opinion, a group of rabble-rousers intent upon preventing his government from making progress to nowhere but a dead end! Diya disgraced his own ancestry, to the pleasure of his master at the capital; he therefore lost the respect of his people. When Abacha decided to deal a death-blow to his ever faithful servant, Diya, as well as the two other Yoruba praise-singing, General Adisa and Olanrewaju, no one sent any condolence message.

Back to Obasanjo, the born-again Baptist recently saved from the path of perdition. It is noteworthy that, in his several speeches, besides praising the Lord and preaching His Word, and confirming what we all already know about Abacha's devilishness and lack of qualifications as a leader, Obasanjo said not a word about Abiola. Yes, he referred to the necessity for justice and for resolving the issues arising from the 1993 elections, but he refrained from making any direct reference to Abiola. Yes, he said something about releasing political detainees, but it is left to the public to interpret that to include the man who had won the presidential elections hands down.

Obasanjo's latest assertions and activities, appear to be a logical continuation of his past, pro-Nigerian posture. Babangida, Abacha's predecessor, and the one that really started the work of total dictatorship over Nigerian lives and livelihood; Babangida, the one that annulled the elections and began the season of murder and misery, was a visitor to Obasanjo's house at Abeokuta. The public was informed that they discussed how to move the nation forward! Other players in the ongoing game of gangsterism called governance, have also met with Obasanjo. There was even talk of his having been approached to head another interim government, *a la Shonekan.* Shonekan, another Yoruba whose hands are red with the blood of the suffering masses, and who is always ready to be used by the Hausa-Fulani clique. Shonekan, Babangida's messenger of the madness called interim government. Shonekan, first flushed down the drain like stinking feces by Abacha, when the latter seized power in November 1993 (see, Olusegun Adeniyi, "Sunset for Shonekan," *African Concord International*, Nov. 29, 1993: 12-17), and later brought back by him into the dimmed and doomed limelight of collaboration and surrogacy, as chair of the blind contraption called *Vision 2010*. In the same boat with Shonekan may be placed other Yoruba prostitutes incessantly climbed and stepped upon by yesterday's and today's plantation masters. They include so-called traditional rulers, such as Sijuade, Ooni of Ife, who has the unique talent to sleep with the lion and the lamb, simultaneously; Tejuoso, from Egbaland, a professional (medical doctor) probably enticed by the many perquisites offered by the real rulers to the prostitutes in the gilded palaces; Aladesanmi, from Ekiti, a colorless newcomer hidden in the backwoods, but eager to make a name (and, yes, a lot of money) as a so-called nationalist.[5] To that royal list may be added other names, no less royal in their readiness to serve the rapists ruling Nigeria. Olumilua, Olajumoke, Babatope, Jakande, Arisekola, Oyelese, and Adedibu, to mention but a few, are all Yoruba politicians who, in various ways, have contributed brilliantly to the entrenchment of injustice and misrule, as they continue to collaborate with their proud people's enslavers.

Many people would insist that the Nigerian crisis must be blamed on the Yorubas, and they would be right, to a certain extent. The above analysis of the country's political past and present, indicates that Yoruba actors in the tragic drama have not been tribalists. Would that be a commendable characteristic, or not? To be a non-tribalist would be enviable if there were a nation, that is, if there were, across the board, a consciousness of an entity where all are equal; where all enjoy the same rights and, therefore, have the same responsibilities; where there are no double, or multiple, standards. That would be a nation to live and die for. Unfortunately, given the non-existence of a nation, Yorubas have only collaborated against the best interests of their own people. The tragedy of it all is that, if some of the Yorubas had been committed to the Yoruba nation, they might have consequently helped the larger unit, Nigeria, much more positively than they have done to date. Take, for instance, Awolowo's standpoint in pushing for independence of the Nigerian macrocosm, instead of the smaller, more realistic, ethnic unit, either solely for the Yorubas, or for the South. A smaller, independent country would have had the essentials of a nation. If, later, the North had wanted to come on board, there would have been specific conditions and ground rules for the formation of a new, bigger nation. Another example: If Obasanjo had stood on the side of justice in 1979, Awolowo—the man whom the con artist, Babangida, called "the best president Nigeria never had"—would have had a chance to rule. A third possibility: If Obasanjo, again, had stood firm in that season of tyranny in 1993, Abiola would have actualized the most popular mandate in the history of the country, and Nigerians would have had been the better off for it.

One of Obasanjo's most publicized activities upon his release from jail, was an international tour, to personally thank those who, according to him, spearheaded the clamor for his release. Many Nigerians wonder why the urgency, when there are many more important matters to be discussed and resolved at home. One is not even convinced of the influence wielded by those Westerners whom Obasanjo has gone to thank: Had Abacha still been alive, Obasanjo would most likely have continued to rot in jail. Obasanjo's action must be understood within the context of his self-evaluation. He has always insisted that he is not a Yoruba leader. He is a bigger fish, far worthier than the small waters of Ogun River, in his native Abeokuta, and more deserving of, and better suited for, the vast oceans of the Atlantic, and the Pacific. He has proudly declared: "I see myself as a national leader, a continental leader and, by the grace of God, a world leader. I doubt if I would receive as much international support and acclaim if I had been a leader of one ethnic group." (*Sunday Punch*, August 2, 1998: 8) Pomposity? Delusion of grandeur? Genuine self-appraisal? Note that, as long as Nigeria remains a cauldron of conflicts and a center of sociopolitical confusion, and the Yoruba nation remains internally colonized and divided, Obasanjo's cherished international fame will remain a huge fraud.

Another Yoruba son, Fela Anikulapo-Kuti, no doubt the most revolutionary and relevant musician on the Nigerian scene, spent a whole lifetime fighting for the people's freedom and rights. He was constantly at odds against the Obasanjo regime. He revealed the horrible side to the man who now claims to be an evangelist. As head of state, Obasanjo created the infamous Ita Oko detention camp on the Atlantic. The crocodile-infested island served as prison for anyone deemed dangerous by the government. It was the inspiration for the late Ken Saro-Wiwa's novel, *Prisoners of Jebs* (1988). Besides being discouraged by crocodiles from trying to swim to safety, the prisoners fell easy prey to mosquitoes as big as cannibals hungry for human blood. Obasanjo's well publicized action of passing the baton of governance to a democratically-elected president in 1979, has hidden another fact, that he sat silent, and satisfied, as a collaborator in heinous crimes does, when the country's attorney-general, Akinjide, concocted the mathematical magic of finding the correct figure for twelve two-thirds of nineteen: Obasanjo's brilliant regime had not thought of how to resolve such a complication, when it decided to base the election results on percentages of states won by each candidate. To most observers, Akinjide's "genius" was used to railroad Awolowo's candidacy. Just as he used the strong arm to put down political opponents, Obasanjo made sure to use "unknown soldiers," that is, faceless, and brainless, gun-toting robots, to wipe out anyone standing in his way. That was the fate of Fela's octogenarian mother, Mrs. Funlayo Ransome-Kuti, who, during the government's gestapo-like attack on her son's residence, "Kalakuta Republic," was thrown down from a four-storey building, and died some days after. Fela's abode was burnt to the ground. His property was destroyed. No one paid him any compensation. His tragedy is recounted in the song, "Unknown Soldier," one of his innumerable classics on the corruption and confusion named Nigeria.

Let us be clear on this point, that the idea of calling upon Yorubas to act as Yorubas, in support of the Yoruba struggle, is not a call for tribalism in the negative, xenophobic sense. In each of the examples given above, as in innumerable others, it is a matter of demanding accountability from those who have been in a position of authority, and have been unjust towards their brothers and sisters. After all, it is only natural for human beings to show faith in their family, before considering foreigners. What is inimical, and uncalled for, is any attempt to show discrimination on the simple, and simplistic, ground of shared ethnicity, or culture, rather than proven qualities.

In Nigeria, it is common knowledge that blatant ethnocentrism has, indeed, propelled the actions of the Hausa-Fulani, [nation in particular,] and the Igbo to a lesser extent. One hears of instances where a Yoruba person in charge would be extra careful not to be seen to act in favor of other Yorubas; whereas, an Igbo, in a similar situation, would not hesitate to fill the ranks with his brothers and sisters. It may also be said that the Hausa-Fulani are not only particularly guilty of such bias, but are also the biggest beneficiaries, since they have long controlled the center. Think of the anachronism called *federal character*.[7]

A story that I recently heard, may further clarify the Yoruba character: If there is War, the Igbo would rush out headlong, his matchet raised high above his head, in readiness for a fight to the finish. On the contrary, the Yoruba would ask where War is coming from, and then run in the opposite direction, his matchet held down, hidden behind him. He would be patient, work out a strategy of attack, minimize the energy expended and, when the time is right, get behind War and cut off its head. As for the Hausa-Fulani, he would push forward his cattle to take the first hit or, if possible, engage others to fight for him. At an opportune moment, he would use his bow and arrow to hit War right on the money, through the heart. One would only like to note here, that what the Yorubas might call wisdom, could be construed by others as cowardliness. Furthermore, in real life, time is of the essence. War, that implacable enemy, attacks its quarry relentlessly, until he surrenders. And, yes, War has developed other arms besides matchets and guns, such as, Money. There is no gainsaying that certain Yorubas have become slaves to Money; yet, materialism is supposed to run counter to our culture.

What, you may ask, has all this got to do with Nigeria's destiny, and, indeed, the departed Abiola? Note that Abiola himself was Yoruba. Just as significant, nonetheless, is the fact that he was no doubt among the most zealously dedicated to the ideal Nigeria, the nation of some people's dreams, and of others' nightmares. In his actions and attitudes, Abiola made sure to do unto others as he would they do unto him. He spent his billions of naira and dollars to build and develop minds and institutions all across the country, and beyond. He was involved in meaningful projects concerning Nigerians, and other Africans. He was committed to the struggles of Africans the world over, an example of which was his efforts to obtain reparations for Euro-American enslavement of Africans. Now that he is dead, everyone, including his avowed enemies, everyone is showering praises upon him for all those unrecognized, exemplary qualities.

The Yoruba factor in the Abiola, nay, the Nigerian tragedy, derived from what was, and what should, and could, have been. Obasanjo and other Yorubas played roles in robbing the people of the services of the great man. If only they had seen the necessity for ethnic solidarity as springboard for the realization of a Nigerian dream, perhaps Abiola would have become president, to the benefit of all Nigerians. But, how about Abiola himself? What would have happened had he been a Yoruba nationalist? Certainly, he would not have attained the glory encapsulated in his election victory, and more humanly exhibited in the goodwill he enjoyed in places as diverse as the United States, and Cuba, and South Africa. On the other hand, perhaps he would have used his talents on behalf of the Yorubas, the current victims of recidivist neocolonialists trying to pocket our destiny.

Many stories have been told about Abiola's past, about a period when he was best friends with Babangida whom he helped to ascend to the seat of power; also about how Abiola was a major player in the agenda of foiling Awolowo's presidential ambitions. If those stories are true, they would fit into the complex, and confusing terrain called Nigeria, as well as the no less complicated character of the Yorubas. The saving grace, for Abiola, would be his overwhelmingly genuine philanthropy, and humanism. Obasanjo was a beneficiary of his many good deeds: When the former was hustling for support in his quest for the post of UN Secretary-general, Abiola went to Wole Soyinka, another Yoruba with immense international connections, and begged him to help Obasanjo. Patriotism, or nationalism. Abiola was a believer, absolutely. His error, as was Awolowo's at another level, was in failing to realize that nationalism would forever remain meaningless, and self-defeating, without a real nation.

The current, foaming-at-the-mouth, born-again democrats must be reminded that the idea, as well as the ideal, remain embedded in Yoruba culture and civilization. Indeed, the existence of freedom, in all its ramifications, partially explains the visible lack of cohesion pervading the Yoruba nation. Those who may like to jump up to challenge this position, are reminded that Yoruba system of government was the one African way used by most diasporan slave societies; and the culture has aided the survival of the slaves' descendants in their new homes. Back in Nigeria, an excellent example of the culture's democratic soul may be found in the universities. At Obafemi Awolowo University, a non-Yoruba can become anything he or she wants to be. Go to Nsukka (Igbo), or Ahmadu Bello (Hausa-Fulani), and find out how far a non-ethnic person can go, or how many of them there are in the establishment. Note that, in such an exercise, Ibadan would stand out as a broad-based university, due to its status as the oldest (1948). But, there, too, you may ask whether that would still be true were Ibadan, say, Abuja. All in all, it is a matter for reflection, whether the Yoruba ethos of freedom of expression, liberalism, accommodation of others, multiplicity of views, has not mitigated against the nation's survival as an equal in the Nigerian multinational country. In regards of Abiola, the politician, it can be rightly claimed that he will for years to come be the epitome of democracy in a country kept on a leash by dictators. It cannot be overemphasized that Abiola was not a Yoruba candidate. He won the presidential polls across the length and breadth of Nigeria.[8] Even though his was a Moslem-Moslem ticket,[9] African traditional-religion adherents, Christians, Moslems, everyone, voted for him.

Still on the issue of religion, the Yorubas have proven their democratic ethos. They are found across the whole religious spectrum, without discrimination against any sect. One makes bold to state that it is that open-mindedness in which was subsumed Abiola's adaptability, and his final success which shocked his enemies into the decision to block his path to the presidency. No doubt that, had he become president, he would not have tried to Islamize the country. Ironically, his enemies, and those nay sayers deriding him as a Yoruba candidate, and the Yorubas as tribalists, the same people have been competing to find words to describe his patriotism, and pan-Africanism, naturally, to pursue their personal agendas.

It would be useful to examine what exactly happened during the truly horrible five-year period after the 1993 elections, specifically regarding the actions of so-called prominent Nigerians, those whom Wole Soyinka calls *supranationalists* (see, *The Open Sore of a Continent,* New York: Oxford University Press, 1996: 40). The Nobel laureate, in his usually brilliant fashion, comments on the conspiratorial efforts of those non-nationalists, to label those fighting for Abiola's mandate as "Yoruba tribalists." I totally agree with Soyinka that, were that to even be true, that is, if some Yoruba individuals "wish to take a special pride in lancing such a long-festering though hidden boil, there is nothing to be astonished at in this, and certainly it is hardly the place of the cheats, the hege-monic minority, to take them to task over their euphoria." (48) Furthermore, as Soyinka again affirms with absolute confidence, the Yoruba nation "has always been the spearhead of nationalist struggle, from colonial times." No other individual symbolizes this fact better than Soyinka himself. During the civil war, he singlehandedly stood up to the hypocritical federal government of General Gowon, as he revealed the regime's sectionalist pogrom against the Igbos. For his efforts, Soyinka was imprisoned for over two years (see, his prison notes, *The Man Died,* 1972). His commitment to democracy and justice, in the current situation, led him into exile. There is no doubt that he is an activist *par excellence*, whose commitment has never been restricted to his Yoruba nation. Indeed, if one were to concede to anyone the claim to leadership beyond the confines of his nation, and extending to the whole world, one would easily consent to Soyinka's candidacy, far more authentic, and earned through action, than the spurious declarations of an Obasanjo. Soyinka's forthrightness in his support for Abiola, is the direct opposite to Obasanjo's self-serving moves to maintain relevance and, as many believe, help his design to return to the presidential palace.

To crown his earthly existence, Abiola, that is the man caged in the captial, taught us all a lesson in democracy and patriotism, by refusing to fall into the government's trap to negotiate away his mandate with foreign messengers. The lesson: If we are truly an independent country, if we are not servants of the West, we must endeavor to solve our problems by genuine dialogue, and in an honest fashion. We must stop trying to sweep, and keep, the deep, persistent dirt under the carpet. We must realize that foreign powers are mainly interested in exploiting Nigeria's riches, and not in establishing democracy. And, as for us, Yorubas, without cleaning up the home front, (think of fraticidal skirmishes and self-defeating politics), we shall never find our feet in a *one Nigeria*.

Notes

1.   Written in 1998, after Abiola's death.
2.   For more on Azikiwe and Awolowo, see, chapter 3.
3.   For a discussion of the politics of the civil war, see, Ken Saro-Wiwa, *On A Darkling Plain*, London: Saros International Publishers, 1989.
4.   *Vision 2010*, one of Abacha's loudest, and least laudable, creations; an almost 200-member body mandated to project a vision of Nigeria in the year 2010, ostensibly the end of the Abacha reign.
5.   See chapter 11 on the character of Yoruba *obas*. Aladesanmi served as spokesman for the traditional rulers who had been invited to the capital by head of state Abacha, who showed them a video of the Diya coup plot. Stories abound on how many brown envelopes stuffed with hard currency also passed into the royal fathers' pockets.
6.   As the latest transition to civilian rule unfolds, Obasanjo is being touted as a presidential candidate, although he keeps denying any interest in the office. Interestingly, his candidacy is being promoted especially by Northern politicians who have stated that he is the one Southerner to whom they would gladly defer. In short, he is still their man, as he used to be in the past. It is also significant that the Yorubas have shown no desire to have him as their, or Nigeria's, leader. See, "The Abeokuta Deal," *TEMPO*, Sept. 17, 1998; Tajudeen A. Raheem, "Encounter with General Obasanjo," *The Ghanaian Independent*, August 6, 1998. In the latter article, the author recounts Obasanjo's anger at being questioned over his lukewarm attitude towards the Abiola tragedy. In addition, he points out Obasanjo's misconception of Abacha as just an aberration, a mad man, rather than a product of the traditional colonial army to which Obasanjo himself belonged. This notion brings to mind the sanctimonious attitude of Europeans who would say that Hitler was a unique villain, a devil in a culture of saints.

7. *Federal character*, an official policy based on the necessity to give every nation a chance to participate in, and benefit from, the system. Invariably, the least developed sections have benefited most, to the detriment of the most developed. Such anomalies would have been easy to overlook, had there been an effort on the part of those obtaining a free ride, to improve their professional training and competence, as one would find in a place like the United States with its affirmative action on behalf of the long deprived African Americans.

8. Abiola was the only Nigerian who could boast of owning chieftaincy titles from every part of the country. His *Concord* newspaper outfit was the only one with titles in several Nigerian languages.

9. His vice-president, Baba Kingibe, became one of the collaborators used by Abacha to *rubbish* (a Nigerian coinage) Abiola's bid for office. From 1993 to 1998, Kingibe was a constant in the cabinet. He is still playing politics, in an attempt to remain relevant.

CHAPTER 21

THEY KILLED OUR OWN MANDELA[1]

I was visiting Lagos, and was just lazing around on Tuesday, July 7, 1998, anxiously awaiting the arrival of night, and the 8 o'clock kick-off of the World Cup semi-final match between Brazil and the Netherlands. Then, suddenly, shockingly, the afternoon sun set; night arrived too soon; darkness covered the whole Nigerian space. A passer-by in an expensive car shouted out of his window, that CNN had announced the death of Moshood Kashimawo Olawale Abiola, one of the most detribalized and philanthropic Nigerians ever. Of course, nobody, not the least myself, took the carrier of bad news seriously. You know, Nigerians and their knack for rumor-mongering. Maybe the Lexus-cruising liar, after a wild moment doing drugs, just wanted to start something as wild as his own outrageous manners. Maybe he had heard the tall tale somewhere, and decided to spread the hogwash. Maybe, indeed, the government started the rumor, to "fly a kite," as they say, in order to gauge public opinion, and Abiola's popularity, all in preparation for their imminent announcement that, upon his release, the man must remain dead to decisions on the country's destiny. A myriad of *maybes* converged on my mind, insisting that the story was a blatant lie. Besides, since Nigeria itself, a country built on quicksand, is a big, black rumor, I convinced myself that Abiola was alive and well, and preparing to come out of the government's gulag to fulfill the dream of millions of people for a free, civilized, buoyant, and prosperous society. I could not resist a gentle smile at the thought of the unique Nigerian art of rumor-mongering. A country that was a gigantic fabrication from the start, cannot but be a fertile ground for rumors. Successive regimes have encouraged the culture, by regularly refusing to tell the public the truth, to offer simple information, preferring, instead, to whet people's appetite with snippets of truncated information, and to sit back and enjoy the hearty manipulations by the very imaginative public. In certain cases, it must be that officialdom itself, either is ignorant of the truth, or loves to use the rumor machine to draw up a policy. For whatever it was worth, I simply refused to face the fact of Abiola's demise.

After my initial resistance, I returned to my room to switch on the match-box of a television set given to me as a privilege by the guest-house management. One can usually access three channels: the 24-hour- service AIT, with its series of stale, second-hand music videos; DBN, a more or less carbon-copy of the former, for less than a full day; and the various forms of the government propaganda organ, NTA, *No Truth Available*.[2] The first two channels were busy with their usual music fare, while the NTA stations were yet to open. When, at last, they did, there was nothing special, or unusual, in their programming format. So, no news flash, no breaking news anywhere. I strolled back outside and found a small group of people engaged in a heated discussion, this time with an air of certainty that Abiola was dead. I learnt that AIT had flashed the news. Maybe I had missed the special minute while checking out other channels. Maybe, again, the cruel lie was just gaining ground among our people. I hurried back inside and sat before the screen, to watch AIT. Barely five minutes later, there it was, the announcement, the fact that I had been refusing to acknowledge.

Events surrounding this latest tragedy speak volumes on the sad society in which our people are trying desperately to survive. We are told that Abiola suffered a fatal cardiac arrest during discussions with a United States delegation invited by Nigeria's latest military regime, to help resolve the self-imposed political problem. This delegation came only days after the United Nations and Commonwealth Secretaries-General had each met with Abiola on the same issue. From their statements to the press, it seemed that the two gentlemen were brought to Nigeria specifically to convince Abiola to give up the popular struggle and to forget his presidential mandate. One can only imagine the heavy dose of pressure of which those international civil servants, and sons of Africa, were messengers. However, it was also patent that the two of them did not succeed in their mission. Hence, the need for the American delegation to pile on more pressure on Abiola. The government has tried to absolve itself of the man's death by allowing foreign pathologists to perform an autopsy on the body. The later have provided a preliminary report confirming that he died "from natural causes."[3]

History is replete with such civilized tactics. You wear down your victim psychologically by painting before him a picture of negativities that you promise to transform into one of positivities, if only he agrees to accede to your request or, rather, your veiled threat, or order, that he abandon every element of principles, self-respect, and human dignity, so that he may survive as your slave! In Abiola's case, they must have informed him that he was living in the past; that his associates had all but abandoned the common cause, and that they were simply interested in having him remain in detention so that he might never learn of their iniquities during his absence; that his business empire was in tatters, and that his family was in disarray. They, his jailers, were therefore his only hope for salvation and rehabilitation. If only he would give an undertaking to get out and go home in peace, they, the magnanimous, magnificent magic makers, would grant him his total freedom, and help him to rebuild his ruined existence.

The pertinent questions that the government must answer are: Why was Abiola not released before that infamous cardiac arrest? Why all the negotiations with the so-called international community? Why did they not bring him out, in person, for everyone to see him alive, even if only for one final second? Why did Emeka Anyaoku, the Commonwealth Secretary-General, pull out those pictures of Abiola, and to prove what?[4] We do know why they did not want Abiola to be free. Because they were afraid of him; of what he symbolized; of his impact on their lives, and on everyone's; of the truth that, willy-nilly, must triumph in the corrupt country held hostage by self-imposed, bad rulers. Because, with Abiola alive and back in the midst of his people, they would run the risk of losing their stranglehold on power, at least, in those sections of the country where people refuse to succumb to feudal enslavement as the will of Allah.

The press conference given after Abiola's death, by the UN Secretary-General, Kofi Annan, was quite interesting. The eminent public servant offered his condolences to the deceased's family, but not to Nigerians. For a man of such reputation, for the one man saddled with the responsibility of bringing together almost all of the world's countries, Annan ought to know much better. He ought to realize that Abiola's death is a blow, particularly, to the dreams of Nigeria's poor, shackled millions; for, Abiola was, and remains, a man of his people, much more than father of his blood family. He represented the only hope for the millions dehumanized and marginalized by the concerted actions of an oligarchy of self-chosen messiahs intent upon keeping everyone under their militarized boots, forever. Abiola, Annan and others should know, is symbol of the people's deferred dreams. It has now come to light that, contrary to what the Secretary-General told the public, Abiola never hinted that he was ready to renounce his mandate. In a letter sent out to the pro-democracy community just before his passing, the pillar of pan-Africanism stated categorically that Annan had not told the whole story.[5]

For his part, Jesse Jackson, the American president's special envoy to Africa, has described Abiola as Nigeria's Mandela which, obviously, is an appropriate, thought-provoking trope. Yet, it comes as a surprise from Jackson, an African American preacher-politician who has been a supporter of Abiola's jailers. (See chapter 1) If and since Jackson knew of the man's talents, how come he did nothing to ensure that Abiola was installed as Nigeria's president? How come Jackson and others, black like us, and supposedly our diasporan brothers and sisters, kept urging their government to exercise patience with the terror machinery in Nigeria? Like Jackson, Nigeria's United Nations Permanent Representative, Gambari, has spoken on Abiola's death. In his opinion, with both Abacha and Abiola gone, Nigeria can now "move forward." He would like to forget that, while Abacha represented an evil that must be extracted from the country's soul, Abiola symbolized, and still does, the soul that, for one painfully short month, stood a chance of being cleansed and ready to thrive in its glory.

Gambari and others in the Nigerian power-house, would be mistaken to breathe a sigh of relief at Abiola's death. As events continue to unfold, one will see exactly how they intend to "move forward." One suspects that, with Abiola physically out of the way, they would gleefully tell the public that the nagging issue of June 12, 1993 is no longer relevant; that people must "look forward" to better days; that all Nigerians must "work together to establish an enduring democracy, and to maintain the unity and integrity of our fatherland, because we have no other country but Nigeria," or something to that effect, using their unique language of deceit to cover up their obsession with power. Nonetheless, one is certain that it is too late to cover up. The pain of Abiola's death, and the bare-faced process utilized by his jailers, should have opened the eyes of all right thinking Nigerians, that is, those being oppressed and repressed in a country that they built with their blood and sweat.

Abiola, Nigeria's own Mandela, would have given us a chance to finally discuss and determine our destiny; a chance to rule, as per our right, not as a result of the largesse of some masters whose interests we must represent, or support; a chance to develop those immense, God-given resources that the self-appointed leaders have been systematically squandering; and a chance to live, and survive, happily here at home, instead of trying to run away from the concentration camp called Nigeria.

Our challenge is, to engage now in the struggle for freedom. That would be the wish of our own dear Mandela. That is the only way that Nigerians can leave behind this engulfing, suffocating darkness. No amount of murders can stop the realization of the dream of freedom. Already, "keepers of the peace," the armed operatives of the people's oppressors, have killed many protesters demanding an explanation of Abiola's death. According to the anti-Yoruba propaganda, the battle-ground is limited to that region they call "the South-West," an euphemism for the Yoruba nation. Radio and television stations have been condemning what they perceive as violent acts of Yoruba tribalists against Hausa. The idea, one suspects, is to show up Yorubas as disgruntled and unpatriotic xenophobes who are overreacting to their kinsman's death. In the meantime, nothing has been said about those Hausas in Lagos who took it upon themselves to attack Yorubas without any provocation.

The sooner we all realize that the Abiola factor is not at all a Yoruba affair, the better for all Nigerians; the better we would be able to begin to think of how to forge a nation, at all, if anyone is interested in so doing. Nigeria may yet benefit from Fate's hand. Abiola's published letter to his pro-democracy associates should be carefully read by the present "government of reconciliation."[6] By Abiola's death, they have not only tried to shave our head in our absence, but to cut it off. Unfortunately for them, we, the people, are still alive. So as to make restitution, and to restore some hope to Nigeria, the rulers should heed Abiola's final words, and "correct once and for all the tragic mistake of purporting to abort a pregnancy after the baby has been born."

Notes

1. Written the week after Abiola's death on July 7, 1998.
2. AIT, African Independent Television, is a grandly inaugurated outfit that is now reported to be making desperate efforts to survive because of incompetent management. If it goes under, it will follow in the footsteps of other Nigerian big, but hollow, enterprises. The Nigerian Television Authority, with stations all over the country, is known for its incompetence, and bold-faced lies on behalf of the government of the day which, invariably, uses the public television, radio, and newspapers, as if they were the personal property of those in power.
3. Since then, a final report has been announced, with no contradictory information. That, as many of us expected, has not cleared the controversy.

   For an example of facts about Abiola's condition, and lack of medical attention, see, Eunice Imianvan, "Death at The Door," *TELL*, Sept. 19, 1994: 24.
4. The only "living" image of Abiola that Nigerians had the privilege to see, after 1994, was that of him in two pictures purportedly taken with Anyaoku and the new Nigerian second-in-command, Akhigbe, days before his death. The pictures were shown to the press by Anyaoku. Abiola, once robust, and full of life, looked pale, like a ghost floating in the over-sized *agbada* attire, as he stood between the two men who seemed to be propping him up. Yet, he had that usual, broad smile on his face, which made the spectacle exceedingly sad.

5. In a bizarre move, the government had allowed Abiola's family to visit him, for the first time in some three years, on the eve of his death. Although the reason might forever remain a mystery, it turned out to be a providential act: Abiola seized the opportunity to send out his last letters, to family and friends, thus clarifying several major points, including his firm commitment to the democratic struggle.
   See, "The Last Statement," *The Guardian*, July 11, 1998: 12. The edition includes several useful articles on Abiola's final days on earth.

6. See, chapter 19. Remarkably, as dust has settled upon Abiola's grave, the government is no longer enthused about the matter of "reconciliation." Violence has abated; therefore, no more need for sweet talk. Has the fire been doused definitively, or would there be a fire next time?

CHAPTER 22

OF RELIGION, VIOLENCE, AND DEATH[1]

One is struck by the various ways in which Nigerians reacted to the sudden death of M.K.O. Abiola on July 7, 1998. Before discussing the two reactions that mainly concern us here, let us quickly dismiss the sea of words invading and inundating one's senses almost to the point of nausea, or amnesia: Even the most implacable of the man's enemies, with a few, all-hating exceptions, has had something nice to say, as if they were ignorant of his exemplar, or, of his existence, before his demise. But, we probably should modify our point of concern, because one of the two reactions of interest does have to do with words: Prayers, Preaching, Praises, all directed towards, or deriving from, Allah, or God, always the Merciful, and the Almighty.[2]

The first reaction, logically attributable to religious faith, is, that Abiola's death is "the will of Allah," and should therefore be accepted with humility and obedience, since the believer is called upon to be in total submission to the omnipotent, and omnipresent, and omniscient God. A corollary to the oft-repeated expression of submission is, that the annulment of the June 1993 presidential elections is "an act of God." This reminds us that, in those long, desperate days of speculations and fervent prayers in the face of dictator Babangida's Maradonic magic, he made famous, or infamous, the very religious exclamation, *Insha Allah* (by the grace of Allah!). Those of us who recognized the irreligious character of a man too willing to declare his piety and reverence before the Almighty, quickly saw through Babangida's mask to reveal his political ambition and diabolical designs. Interestingly, on the contrary, many Nigerians believed him, just as many do not dispute the readiness to always blame Allah, or God, for every sin committed by human beings.

One cannot but note the usage of the two words, *Allah* and *God*, in the Nigerian setting. The former belongs to the Moslems; the latter, to the Christians. It would be interesting to carry out a modest research project, to find out how often, in what context, and by whom, each of these two words has been used in the years 1985-1998, that is, from the advent of the Babangida brigandage to the demise of his surrogate, successor and, ultimately, superior in the fine art of oppression, suppression, and destruction, Abacha. In all probability, the researcher would come away with, at best, inconclusive results; at worst, with confusion, which might be in line with the country's past and present. Precisely, he or she might find that, on one hand, Moslems call on Allah, while Christians evoke the name of God. On the other hand, it might also be true that, under certain circumstances, avowed Christians would adduce events to Allah, while their Moslem counterparts would refer to God. Besides, it might be true that Moslems would be less likely to exchange names (not *foreign exchange!*),[3] and more likely to evoke the Almighty. This last point, one daresay, stands a chance of being one of the most clear-cut discoveries of the research, simply because those in power, or walking in its corridors, have been Moslems, and their friends and followers. This fact becomes significant when one considers another fact -pity that it has been reduced to another fiction, by the ungodly act of men-, that Nigeria is a secular state. The secular status was ostensibly written into the Constitution, to prevent the kinds of unholy wars that have devastated many potentially prosperous lands, and to encourage the spirit of oneness in a country with overwhelmingly natural divergences. Events of post-independence Nigeria have led one to question not only the wisdom of creating this octopus of a state, but also the honesty of expecting it to operate on a non-religious basis. For one thing, the colonizers who created the unwieldy country, were fully aware of the depth of religious faith and fervor among the many nationalities, even if they wanted the whole world to believe that they were savages worshiping trees and beasts, and the devil. For another, their own experiences must have taught the masters the basic lesson (call it Religion 101), that you cannot merge fire with water. And there lies the irony, or the essentially contradictory foundation of the Nigerian entity: Britain, the Christian master, became much closer to the Moslem North than to the multi-religious South. With regards to the aforementioned faith existing among the various nationalities, one may forgive the "civilized" master for finding it impossible that the "savages" could ever have a viable religion in the depths of their jungle. And, any Nigerians wishing to contest and condemn this comment as the author's unwarranted derision, may wish to remember that, by their very attitude of shame and civilized sanctimoniousness towards their ancestral religions, they have given the master the right to demand that they pay him homage for giving them salvation, and redemption from their savagery.[4]

Perhaps as one more cynical aspect of its colonialist adventurism, Britain, at home, succeeded in reducing to a minimum any conflict between Church and State, but did nothing to establish such a policy in its Nigerian colony. It used to subtly stoke the fire of conflict through its infamous divide-and-rule tactics. That brings to mind the nagging question: Why did a supposedly civilized nation insist on amalgamating the glaringly opposed parts that became the geographical giant of Africa? Britain must have known that, by and large, the different nations have inculcated religion into their cultural essence. Therefore, the very idea of separating State from Religion must have been seen to be impractical under prevailing circumstances. For peoples who are wont to submit themselves and everything to their various forms of the Almighty, it would be natural that the imported notion of governance would constitute an imposing mountain. One cannot overemphasize the fact that the two religions now looming large in the people's lives, were important pieces of the colonial machine, as they are of the exploiting imperialist monsters. Understandably, the British would want Nigerians to continue to look up to Allah and God, while they, the predators, are busy grabbing everything on the ground and underground. Britain would stay on the sideline, watch, and laugh at the two combating armies of the Almighty's children (or servants? or slaves?) going for each other's jugular, in an attempt to win the best place in the life hereafter. Meanwhile,

Britain, and its European allies, as well as its once rebellious off-spring in the wild West, are working hard to maintain their cosy positions in the here and now.

The history of Islam and Christianity is dotted with acts of violence, in spite of the docility, and defeatism, projected by the pious postures mentioned earlier. *Jihad* and *crusade* are not figments of anyone's imagination. They occurred and, from time to time, Nigeria has witnessed their contemporary manifestations. It is pertinent to note that, of the two religions in question, Islam seems to be the more aggressive, the more violently fundamentalist in its acts and attitudes. One only needs to say the word, *Maitatsine*,[5] to make some Southerners living in the North, and even in the South, run for cover. At the highest level, those governing the country, Moslem Hausa-Fulanis, aided by military might and fire-power, have not only tried to Islamize the country, but also visit various types of violence on the people.

Poor Nigerian Christians! They have hardly had any opportunity to breathe what they would probably call the purifying air of their faith into the corridors of power. The stop-over regime headed by Obasanjo, Southerner and Christian (1976-1979), was too short-lived to qualify for evaluation along religious lines. Nonetheless, one notes that the man was surrounded by mostly Northern Moslems. In a post-mortem to their tenure, Obasanjo's deputy, Yar'Adua, declared that they, the eagle-eyed overseers from the North, and not Obasanjo, ruled Nigeria. Perhaps if Obasanjo had been "born-again" then, he would have performed differently. For now, we are only sure of a behavioral pattern among Moslem rulers, and the facts of their rulership are as palatable as a plate of poison.

Think, for instance, of a presidential palace constructed with a beautiful mosque in the complex, but no church. Think of ministers and university vice-chancellors appointed by the almighty head of state, according to their religious credentials. In several cases, appointees have dumped their normal names, to emphasize the Moslem nomenclature, with a threat to prosecute anyone who makes the mistake of addressing them by their former, *pagan* names.[6] Think of the government's decision to join the Organization of Islamic Conference (OIC), a group of solely Islamic countries, with the membership announcement being made by none other than the

Sultan of Sokoto, president of Nigeria's Islamic association, but—
hopefully—not of Nigeria.[7] Think of a so-called secular state where
the government gets involved in pilgrimage matters: While it is
true that it organizes journeys for both Christians and Moslems,
everything points to the bias towards the latter. Think of a secular
state where non-Hausa-Fulanis, and non-Moslems, change both
religion and ethnic background, to be on the right side of the track,
on that route that leads to material heaven and away from the hell
reserved for *kaferis* (pagans).

Perhaps by mere coincidence, during these recent years of
Abiola's, and Nigeria's, agony, a former head of state, Gowon,
came up with a new concept: He organized *Nigeria Prays,* an association of religious faithful, to pray for Nigeria. For this most patriotic effort, Gowon has been traveling across the country, leading large and small groups in prayer. Prayers of confession, and for
forgiveness. Prayers of atonement, and for wisdom to live in peace
and unity. From his Abuja fortress, Abacha complemented Gowon's
work with his own call to every religious sect to congregate at the
capital, to pray for him so that he could make the correct choice
between self-succession and "stepping aside." The Gowon-Abacha
politics of prayers is no doubt one of the glorious novelties of today's
Nigeria. It shows once again that religion and politics are insepa-
rable in the secular state. It also shows how the most hypocritical,
indeed, the farthest removed from the fear of God, are the most
likely to claim closeness to Him. Gowon led Nigeria in the civil
war against Biafra. He won the war, as well as the vast wealth
accruing from the gushing oil-fields of the delta. Thus faced with
the unique problem of how to spend the money, the visibly excited, enraptured ruler went about squandering the booty. He even
postponed his announced exit date from office, so as to do as much
damage as possible to the country's treasury. Given those past actions, Gowon does indeed need to pray. Unfortunately for Nigeria,
his prayers cannot reconstruct what he destroyed; they cannot resuscitate the lives lost during a civil war that broke out largely as a
result of the power tussle between him, Gowon, and Ojukwu.
Prayers cannot bring back to the oppressed people the lost years of
hope for true freedom and prosperity.

In 1966, Gowon was planted on the executive seat by the Northern military. In what turned out to be one of those tricks for which

successive dictators have come to be known, he set up an ad-hoc constitutional conference to which every Region submitted a proposal on how to govern the country. When he learnt that everyone opted for a loose federation, Gowon, in his wisdom, suspended the exercise. However, what was not completed in 1966 has not been forgotten by those kept in servitude. Gowon would do better, he would be much more of a religious, God-fearing soul, to advise the current regime in Abuja to constitute another conference to table the matter. The 1966 proposals must still be available somewhere (*The Daily Times* carried them verbatim). Gowon could then go down on his knees, and remain there in fervent prayer, until the country has agreed upon a system of government in which every nationality will have autonomy to decide its destiny. God, being a good God, a God of justice, will definitely accede to that prayer.

Death has already announced God's verdict on the prayers held in Abuja for the Abacha-for-president bid. Scholars of politics and religion and psychology, will enjoy analyzing the minds and manners, as well as the principles and habits, of both the man, the marabouts, the priests, and the public engaged in those political prayers. Reports mentioned the vast amount of money stuffed into the hollows of holy books; the controversies consequential to the self-serving exercise; the ridicule visited upon Religion, and Allah, and God, by those spineless slaves summoned to prayer by the devil himself. Significantly, it is the religious shepherds that misled their flock. In essence, if leaders, in every sphere of human existence and endeavor, act responsibly by doing the right thing, their followers will emulate them. If, on the contrary, the leadership is ungodly, the led may wake up one day, revolt, and visit their wrath upon them.

When Abiola died, the masses reacted with physical violence. Officialdom immediately tagged them all as hoodlums and miscreants, worthless *area boys*[8] glad to seize the occasion opportunity to loot and murder, as a natural manifestation of their shady and shallow character. A perspicacious and honest observer would disagree with that assessment. Violence is manifested in many forms. Words and looks can kill. A seemingly harmless body language can be murderous. An attitude of indifference, or refusal to admit a person's existence, can constitute a violent condemnation to death. In other words, to engage in acts of violence, one does not have to be armed to the teeth, like the ubiquitous, uniformed armed robbers ripping off unprotected drivers at Nigeria's checkpoints, in the name of law enforcement and protection of human lives and property. To commit a crime of violence, one only needs the authority to play god, and the callousness of men with hearts of stone, like those Hitlerian goons who visited psychological murder on Abiola for four years. Imagine a man controlling billions of naira and dollars, reduced to a penniless prisoner. Imagine a man whose very existence was built on the company of family and friends, condemned to solitude. Imagine a man who enjoyed worldwide respect and love, constantly mocked and threatened by uncouth warders. Imagine a human being born to bask in sunshine, confined to the darkness of a dingy cell that they locked, and then threw away the key. Such psychological terrorism, interspersed with its physical side-kicks, must have contributed in no small measure to Abiola's death.[9]

So, it is farcical to read all those official condemnations of the masses' violence after Abiola's death. The presumptuous and pompous vilification only makes one reflect more deeply on official hypocrisy. Some of those who went burning and stealing everything before them on that tragic day, were opportunists. That is nothing unheard of; in fact, it is to be expected in a society where the vast majority are dispossessed by a mindless minority of highway robbers. For example, in the United States, reputedly the most developed nation in the world, racial riots have always brought out the beast in many a normally law-abiding citizen. In spite of the racism embedded in the system, the American government does not simply dismiss such violence as the madness of a few animals. It is human and humble enough to confess that America is not yet the heaven on earth that people dream about. It accepts that there is work yet to be done, and sets about doing it, even if, at times, half-heartedly.

In the Nigerian context, the rampaging crowds, those conscious of the lethal wound inflicted on their hopes for final freedom and economic salvation, carefully chose their targets: the political prostitutes who sold their own souls, and mortgaged the people's destiny, for brown envelopes stuffed with foreign currency. This well reasoned outrage proves that those people's acts of violence are a reflection of the inhuman conditions to which they have been subjected by bandits claiming to be national leaders. Their violence is precisely a counter-violence to a culture marked by cruelty and criminality. One is not surprised that Nigerian officialdom has refused to see the logic behind that reaction to Abiola's death. After all, this is a government that can do no wrong; one that kills and asks the people to applaud; one that condemns innocent people to death, and expects them to beg to be killed, kindly; one that offers amnesty to those whom it has wrongly incarcerated, and demands to be praised for its magnanimity. A government committed to its people would pay attention to such details as those of the violence visited upon the shameless collaborators who were brought to book by the angry populace. Their action must be contrasted to the jubilation that welcomed another death, that of the erstwhile dictator, Abacha, exactly one month before Abiola's. At that moment of ecstasy, peace reigned supreme, not pandemonium. Happiness, not sadness. Harmony, not disharmony. The community of the oppressed felt the air of freedom descend upon them, like manna from on high; they felt uplifted from hell to heaven, instantly. They felt a sense of relief that the symbol of violence had been extracted from his fortress, finally. By reminding us that Abiola was a man of peace, a man of humility who never resorted to, nor encouraged violence, the government has only called attention to its own intrinsic violence, as represented by all those years of murder. The military are masters of violence. Witness the draconian decrees, the heavy-handedness in dealing with citizens, the tendency to threaten, even as they talk of reconciliation. If there is a culture of violence, it has been introduced and nurtured by the military. Coupled with the culture of religious polarization, exemplified by Islam, this mode of governance has almost dealt a death-blow to any dreams of freedom and development in a modern world.

For Nigeria not to die, for it to metamorphose into a nation, the rulers would do well to examine the content and context of both Religion and Violence in the polity. They would have to accept the guilt of having done everything to Islamize a multi-religious state which, according to the constitution, is supposed to be run outside the prejudice-prone scope of any religion. They would have to admit that, in today's world, no people want to be ruled by force; no nation can be built, or survive, upon the commandment of military generals who, by their profession, are commissioned to protect the people, not to pulverize and pauperize them. They would have to understand that democracy is, foreign to the laws governing their obey-and-never-complain establishment. They cannot escape the fact that any people suffering from slavery, thus victims of violence, have always been compelled to utilize counter-violence to free themselves from the shackles that have relegated them to the status of two-legged animals.

At Abiola's burial, Nigerian students took charge, decisively, and violently. Their firm action overshadowed the vacillations of certain members of the Abiola family who have been known to compromise, and to collude with the military regime. The students screened all the guests who came to pay their final respects to the fallen hero. They turned back several individuals, while they carried others shoulder-high and demanded that they address the mammoth crowd, to pay homage to Abiola. Most importantly, those young men and women refused to allow anyone in uniform to enter the Abiola compound. For their part, the military and police, decked out in their combat gear and apparently ready for war with their plethora of weapons, and perhaps wishing to scare one and all with their armored tanks, gave the impression that the whole area was in a state of siege. A discerning eye could see, nonetheless, that those dogs of war were themselves the scared ones; for, the unarmed students represented the might of the Nigerian masses, standing firm against oppression, making a statement of rejection of the repressive forces that have tried to transform a free country into a police state. For once, the uniformed men were under the control of the youths, symbols of a future that still remains uncharted and unclear. That scene at Abiola's house was a singular triumph of the people's will. Using the yardstick of commitment to the cause of those whom Frantz Fanon calls "the wretched of the earth," they sifted, as it were, the wheat from the chaff; the good from the bad; the democrats from the despots. That resistance, that revolutionary act, was not, can never be, a peaceful process.

Death often results from such actions. It is only the death of individuals, however. Like Abiola, everybody will die. But some deaths are meaningful, just as others are meaningless. The former constitute a sacrifice, a symbol, paving the way for the people who must fight for their liberation. The latter, analogous to the death of a rabid dog, are applauded by the people who are happy that the earth is rid of beasts devoid of human feelings and worthy ambitions. Did God, or Allah, kill Abiola? Should we sit down, docile, defeated, convinced that it is His Will? Should we not do anything about it? In order to adequately answer these questions, it may be useful to think of our ancestors' religion, the one that the modern masters made us throw into the Atlantic, as they achieved their civilizing mission. Useful memory it would be, because the two imposed religions have, besides serving the invaders well, become, in the lives of the conquered acolytes, instruments of suppression of personal, God-given will, and an easy means of shirking responsibilities and warding off accountability. *Ifa*, Yoruba religion, tells us that God gives each human being freedom to live and survive in this world. It all depends on one's choice of *ori*, head, not just the visible, physical body-part, but the invisible, essential destiny. There are millions of *ori* in Ajala's compound. Ajala, the keeper, is an excellent but capricious molder who is often absent from his post. Hence, quite often, some impatient and careless person just picks a head and comes to earth. If they are unfortunate, they may pick a useless one; if fortunate, they may pick an intelligent, even exceptional one. Therefore, whatever happens to us on earth, especially, the tragic events, cannot be blamed on Olodumare, God. And Abiola, which *ori* did he pick, or obtain from Ajala?

Abiola was a Moslem. He was also versed in Christianity. On the contrary, he knew nothing about Ifa. Of his innumerable chieftaincy titles,[10] the most traditional was that of *Aare Ona Kakanfo* (the supreme warrior), a title that demanded depth of knowledge and authentic adherence to Yoruba ancestral culture, which Abiola lacked.[11] It is said that, during a war Aare leads the way. Invincible he is; he is so powerful that the enemy's bullets simply bounce off his body. He is capable of bringing the enemy to his knees in the twinkle of an eye. Among Aare's many characteristics, is his ability to fashion his fate as much as possible. Now, our fallen supreme warrior was a fake, having bought the title from a greedy *oba*. Abiola reputedly spent some 90% of his vast fortunes of philanthropy in Moslem Northern Nigeria. He was often accused of blatantly neglecting the Yoruba nation. Yet, when the chips were down, when it mattered most, his brothers and sisters in the faith denied him, and his beneficiaries abandoned him. They colluded to kill him, and then blamed it on Allah. If Abiola had learnt the basics of Ifa, he would have been aware of the tragic eventualities that befell him, and forestalled them. But, then, perhaps he chose his *ori*, and his death could not have been avoided. In any case, what is certain is that it is wrong to blame God for human crimes.

Most annoying is the action of the very preachers of the sermon of peace upon Abiola's demise. Those religious pacifists were condemning popular violence; yet, they themselves were waging war on the people, just as they had been doing before, and have not stopped doing. As usual, the army and the police shot and killed anyone who dared stand in the way of officialdom's god, named Gun. As usual, the dastardly murders were downplayed as a necessary aspect of law enforcement. As usual, we shall never know how many lives were lost. As usual, God's name is invoked as cover-up. Murderers probably would love to forget that they, too, will die. And, finally, the truth of any religion is, that God is neither a murderer, nor is He a slave-master. He is neither a permissive nor unprincipled God. He is fair, and stands firmly on the side of justice. He is a loving God, but He never supports, nor encourages, lying and lynching. Surely, He will see to the freedom of the oppressed. Amen.

Notes

1. Written in 1998, after the death of both Abacha and Abiola.
2. Nigerians must be among the most prayerful people in the whole world. And, if the amount of prayers had anything to do with a country's state of affairs, and the quality of the people's lives, then Nigeria should have been the best of the best, an outright paradise on earth.
3. *Foreign exchange*, magical words in Nigeria, and sometimes reason for murder: money, in superior foreign currencies, such as the almighty dollar, the yen, the pound sterling, all recognized and preferred even by the most locally-rooted hobo. Give the Nigerian naira to anyone and, immediately, you will be told the equivalent in dollars, as proof that you have offered but a paltry sum, and that you are too cheap!
4. Nigeria is still suffering from colonial mentality: You are either a Christian, or a Moslem; the third option is, that of being a pagan.

For an excellent commentary on Nigeria, one only needs to listen to the music of Fela Anikulapo-Kuti: tracks, such as "Sorrow, Tears, and Blood" and "Zombie" (on police and military brutality); "ITT" (government and corporate graft); "Colo mentality" (inferiority complex among Nigerians attempting to be "modern").

5. *Maitatsine*, a Moslem sect in Northern Nigeria, known for its violence. Once restricted to the North, it has recently moved as far south as Lagos, on the Atlantic coast. Successive Nigerian regimes have failed to address the problem of religious conflicts.

6. See, for example, chapter 9, on Fafunwa, former minister of education.

7. The Sultan of Sokoto, recognized as spiritual leader of the Hausa-Fulani, also wields immense power in the political arena. The holder of the royal office is considered to be in a position to make and unmake individuals, and policies.

8. *Area boys*, another Nigerian linguistic invention, identifying a gang of irresponsible young men visiting terror upon innocent citizens in their area. The term has come to be used for any persons behaving as such in the public arena, imposing their will on people by brute force, and for no good purpose.

9. Details of Abiola's sufferings during those four years, are now coming out. See, for example, "Abiola: In Open Grave For Four Years," in *TheNews*, Oct. 5, 1998 (published on the Internet by *AfricaNews on Line*).

10. Abiola was honored with many traditional titles across the length and breadth of Nigeria. He himself counted well over three hundred of them.

11. See, chapter 11. The way and manner in which Abiola was given that particular honor, raised the issue of his relationship with the reactionary forces in Nigeria. It was claimed that he bought the title, as he reportedly did several other things. Such criticism, however, would not stain the quality of the commitment of his final years in life.

CHAPTER 23

AFRICAN REALITIES, NIGERIAN NIGHTMARES[1]

How could we not return when this is where the afterbirth was buried for rebirth? Afrika my music.[2]

Often we never moved beyond blackness, beyond the racial aspect of the struggle for national liberation from colonial rule.[3]

No thinking African can escape the pain of the wound in our soul.[4]

To hold a responsible position in an underdeveloped country is to know that in the end everything depends on the education of the masses.[5]

INTRODUCTION: THE AFRICAN BOURGEOIS, FOSTER-CHILD OF THE WEST

My generation can rightly be called, with a certain cynicism, *the generation of Independence*, that group of teenage boys and girls who used to march proudly on Empire Day, the birthday of the almighty king or queen of England, sweating zealously in the scorching tropical sun, singing to the glory of the immortal Empire, and standing tall in our khaki uniforms. That generation also witnessed the hoisting of the national flag in or about 1960. We sang the new song with as much enthusiasm as before. We marched with equal pride. We hailed our patriotic heroes, those extraordinary fighters for freedom who had led us to the promised land, a terrestrial heaven where we would live forever in happiness and harmony and, as a people, stand up to any other nations on earth, including, and in particular, our ex-masters.

The Generation of Independence, fresh out of high school, fresh out of colonialism, was ready to grow up and flourish in free, African nations that we were destined to lead later; for, we had no doubt in our minds that the future belonged to us. Unfortunately for us and for our nations, the ground upon which that destiny was being built was very shaky from the beginning. The definition of freedom and development, the plan and process of progression, and our very education, everything was utterly wrong. In our civilized ignorance, we believed that we were the best. Our own existence and experience were marked by pomposity and paternalism towards others, a superiority complex implanted by the European masters, and gleefully internalized by new masters of a tomorrow's heaven configured in today's hell. My own school aptly named *Government College*, was headed by a white master from the overseas motherland. We were groomed to be truly civilized! Talk civilized, eat civilized, act civilized, live civilized, and die civilized. By the time we left the school to enter the wonderful world of Independence, we had become totally dependent on the ex-colonizer who had conquered and colonized, not only our minds but also our country's immense material wealth. We had succeeded in freeing ourselves of the fantasies and fears of the inferior, ignorant masses living in the villages. We swore on the Bible, or the Koran, to lead them out of the darkness of our ancestral, barbaric customs into the light of Western education and progress. I remember that, whenever I went home on holidays from the boarding-school, my less fortunate friends envied me. They emulated my walk and talk. I was a been-to, the new bourgeois, the black white man. My father was proud of me, especially the day I boarded the big balloon heading abroad for a tenure of fine-tuning of my developing civilized skills. Those of my generation who did not travel abroad, entered the university at home. We were all well on our way to national leadership, or so we believed.

Both the overseas-trained and the home-based intellectuals have since embarked upon the arduous task of living out our vaunted leadership roles. Tragically, we have found that everything has been a big, white lie. Let us make no mistake about it: To be an intellectual is, to be a living lie, or a liar, alienated from the essence of our culture and civilization, consciously or otherwise mimicking the European who made a caricature out of God's creation, a puppet out of a whole people, and machines out of human beings. You went to school, you had to go, in order to be prepared to lead your people. That was the myth; the reality was, so that you could become "better" than others, and make money, and become privileged. That first misunderstanding has led to a life of frustration. However, some did understand, and very quickly, too. Rather than waste their precious time reading big books, they enlisted in the army. Today, they are among the political masters, and we all know that, in Africa, there is no distinction between the so-called political and military classes; they are both twins born of the same corrupt parents. More on that theme later.

We should repeat that the bourgeois, the man or woman "of culture," the professional, the writer, the one that espoused the civilizing mission as a way of contributing something concrete to the community, has reached a cul-de-sac at home. His or her consolation is life in exile, among his original masters and mentors. From out there in the diaspora, he has continued to criticize the robbers and rapists of his poor people.

AFRICAN REALITIES: OF RAPE, ROBBERY, AND REACTION

The exodus out of Africa has become, for quite a number of us, a matter of life and death. Go to any Western embassy in an African capital -Lagos, Dakar, Accra, or Nairobi-, and you will witness the same scenario. Desperate people hell-bent upon running away to greener pastures, they spend a whole night waiting outside the steel walls of the visa office. Dehumanized, they refuse to be defeated in their desire to escape. The Western diplomats are fully aware of the macabre dance; hence, they carry the insults to the extreme and the African government dare not complain even when the nation's officials are treated with ignominy. As if these same Western countries were not over-generous in issuing multiple-entry visas only a few years ago. As if a country such as Britain did not have its doors wide open to us as Commonwealth citizens. As if Independence was not supposed to improve our lot in a world of equally free nations treating one other with dignity.

The farcical irony of being a bourgeois in Africa has probably not struck some of us as we incessantly count our bastardized blessings in our state of marginalization. In many instances, escape abroad is more difficult for us than for entrepreneurs of all shades. The visa-issuing embassies have been known to reject applications by reputable professors and honest individuals, while granting entry documents to prostitutes and cocaine-pushers. Invariably, it is the latter characters who, caught in the act in almighty America, are regarded as representatives of Africa's all-pervasive decadence. Of course, we complain vehemently, not because we love Africa so much, but because those vicious villains are tarnishing our image as civilized individuals. Besides, we howl in anger at their capacity to corner entry-permits to a paradise for which our training qualifies us, and us alone.

Those running away from Africa do so, due to the tragic existential realities ruining any chance for self-survival. It is to be noted that we are not concerned here with right or wrong. I recall my late father lamenting the good, old colonial days, not for the presence of the colonizer, but for the pre-eminence of certain qualities that the old man always attached to traditional society. Then, the community, a concert of proud, dignified, honest, and generous human beings, demanded of the individual adherence to unwritten but well known precepts that showed respect for life, for the individual and communal life, and survival. People used to matter more than property. A rich robber was rebuked and rejected, castigated, and condemned. The leader was expected to live and lead by example, with hardly any excesses. If you committed a crime, you expected to pay the price, not win a prize. Religion, based on respect for humanity and for human life, upon the knowledge that heaven begins from here below, and upon communal survival, was an integral part of our culture. Before my father, dejected and defeated, died in 1989, he had gone worse in his lamentation, as he expressed a wish that the white man should have remained in Nigeria! And I have since heard quite a few others whisper a similar sad song.

Those running away and those wondering why the whites left, see an Africa being raped and robbed by reactionary dictators, an Africa being terrorized by self-proclaimed fathers who have transformed whole countries into their personal property, or prisons. Somalia, Ivory Coast, Kenya, Zaire. And, Nigeria, Uganda, Malawi, Lesotho. Just name them. There are life-presidents galore. We have developed underdevelopment into a cultural and national symbol. We have proven that incompetence and insensitivity, corruption and non-accountability, are truly patriotic qualities essential for good governance. From 1960 to 1994, Africa has seen a series of robbers and rapists at the helm of power. We call all of them *politicians* because, unlike the West, the only distinction between the military and the civilians is the gun. Otherwise, the two pursue power viciously and voraciously, the difference being that one road, the military, is shorter and surer to the cherished destination than the other. In a situation of underdevelopment in countries largely created by colonial scramblers, public office is considered a passport out of poverty into the paradise of power and plenty. Contrary to what my father and others would think, the colonizer went away only to return to cooperate with the patriotic robbers.

As stated earlier, some smart members of our Generation of Independence headed for the military school once they were convinced that the classroom books were too big for their brains. We used to laugh at them for their stupidity, and for their death-wish. However, we soon learnt our lesson; for, in no time at all, they became generals, the gun in one hand and check-books of millions and billions of dollars in the other. Their clique controls the country's politics, threatening to literally terminate the existence of cowardly civilians. In many countries, the military patriots came to replace the latter's cowardice with their outstanding courage. Courage to be crooked, to steal with impunity, and damn the consequences. And the new politicians in uniform proclaimed themselves democrats and saviors. And praise-singers composed poetry for the new fathers of the nation. And collaborators, including once revered kings and chiefs, fell over one another to do the new masters' bidding, all in the name of a sophistry called nationalism.

When I think of Africa, I remember Frantz Fanon's seminal text, *The Wretched of the Earth*. I recently re-read it with some students of mine, and we all were shocked by its relevance and contemporaneousness. Fanon, in 1960, foresaw the realities of the 90s: The leader turns into a dictator, "the most eager worker in the task of mystifying and bewildering the masses." (168) The party (only fools are deceived by the fraud called the multi-party system) helps the regime to keep the people down: "The greatest wealth is surrounded by the greatest poverty and the army and the police constitute the pillars of the regime." (172) Furthermore: "Privileges multiply and corruption triumphs, while morality declines." (171) No wonder Fanon's work has been thrown into the garbage by brilliant modernist scholars, and it has never been known to the illiterate messiahs. For, if we Africans were really serious about shedding the shackles of neocolonialism, we would read, understand, and implement many of Fanon's concepts on revolution. It is a pity that self-preservation and selfishness would not allow us to undertake such a cleansing task. Fanon prescribes the elimination of all privileges, and the holders of privileges are not prepared to let go. And the cleansing must start from the top.

The leader runs the country according to his whims. He is the absolute master; he demands, and obtains, no less; maybe even more. But it does not always work that way. In complex countries, such as Nigeria, His Excellency needs, and easily obtains, the support of surrogates, or partners in the progress towards the total destruction of the people. Like a chameleon, the clique keeps changing the colors of their clothes, but their soul remains the same as ever, shady, selfish, shallow, and rotten to the core. As the drama of neocolonialism unfolds, the dictator and his henchmen act more ridiculously. Drunk and dazed by their power and their billions, they make decrees by the minute, recast the constitution by the second, make new appointments just as fast, and have new money-bills hurriedly printed so as to sop the so-called political class into submission. Gratuitous speeches roll off the presses as easily as the millions spent in prestige projects where the proposal is of greater value than the final product. The speeches are crafted by hordes of Cambridge, or Sorbonne, or Harvard graduates, excellent manipulators of foreign languages. The state of the pseudo-nation becomes more tragic in unison with the dictator's daring devilishness. The praise-singing becomes more deafening; the speeches, more desperately demagogic. Remarkably, the Man-Master-Monster reads everything proudly and loudly, hardly missing a beat, even though he cannot explain the meaning of most of the words, much less translate them into action. Certain cliches recur, reverberating in every capital where lies prevail, where lynching of body and soul is daily perpetrated, where life has lost its meaning.

"This nation," shouts the national savior, "belongs to us all; it's the only nation we have, and we must, and will, salvage it together!" To hear him say it, you would think that he said, *savage*! To any foreign power trying to meddle in the nation's internal affairs, the self-styled Father has a word of warning: "Nobody can love our dear nation more than we do; so, let our detractors leave us alone to fashion our own, authentic African democracy." The multitudes, though disgusted, are nonetheless aroused in their anti-imperialism, and you can actually see some of them with tears of patriotic joy in their eyes! To potential coup-plotters, the Father also has a warning: "We shall not accept any act of indiscipline, and whoever tries to test our resolve will be dealt with with alacrity!" Unknown to him, the messiah is revealing the real reason for his heavy-handedness: If he does not watch his back, another, hungrier traitor is waiting to overthrow him. The most strident call, the most meaningless message echoed across the ill-fated continent, is a repetition of the need to lay down our lives for our nations: "We all must be ready," shouts the great Father, "and I know we are willing and able, to make sacrifices, the ultimate sacrifice, for the good of this great nation of ours, so that our children, as well as their children after them, may not have reason, ever, to curse us tomorrow." Meanwhile, he thinks that people have forgotten that his own sacrifice has been, to save the nation's money abroad, so that his children may study in schools and universities with well structured, and established programs, a far cry from those at home that His Monstrous Majesty the Father of the Nation, sees fit to regularly close down to make sure that the students are not properly educated.

African leaders compete in inventing new, patriotic ways to pulverize the people. One was asked by a foreign journalist -an African dare not ask such a stupid question!- whether it was true that he, the most frugal Father of any nation on the globe, had 250 million dollars to his name. Mr. Life-President was visibly angered by the outrageous allegation. He quickly calmed down, anyway, and humbly confessed to having only 50 million, "by the grace of God Almighty." His brother in patriotism burst into tears when asked by another foreign journalist, why he was allegedly still clinging to power after all of twenty-five years in office. As usual, his enemies, being funded by former colonialists and now imperialists interested in destroying African nations, had been carrying rumors, when they knew well enough that his people had refused to let him step down. Yet another savior of the nation came to power through the barrel of a gun in a bloodless coup in which only the blood of unpatriotic pranksters was shed. He then announced that there would never be another coup in the nation! He invited well meaning compatriots to work with him to establish a true, lasting democracy. The most progressive elements joined him because, if they did not, reactionary riff-raffs would. So began the nation's progress on the road to perdition.

And, then, there is Nigeria.

THE PAIN OF NEOCOLONIALISM:
THE NIGERIAN EXAMPLE

When the eminent Nigerian writer, Chinua Achebe, referred some twenty years ago to "the pain of the wound in our soul," he was addressing the tragedy of colonialism, but probably also the growing wound inflicted upon the people by the new, insensitive leadership. It is necessary to all the details of the 1993 farce called Nigeria's democratization process. The incubus is yet an imposing menace, and there are many people convinced that we are witnessing the beginning of the end of a country blessed with everything leading to greatness, but never able nor willing to harness them for the construction of a livable society. The bitter truth is, that Nigeria was never meant to be a success. From Britain's divide-and-rule policy through the sham independence, to a post-independence that has turned out to be a patch-work of contradictory and conflicting entities, with one group, the least prepared to rule a country patterned after the West, determined to hold onto power indefinitely, Nigeria's fate may lie in the dung-heap of history.

The death of the dream of becoming, or of the myth of being, Africa's giant is all the more painful when one compares the country to its neighbors, where Nigeria is hated more than death itself, while it keeps extending to them the generous hand of the Big Brother.[6] It is often claimed that Nigeria's problem is lack of leadership. One cannot but agree. Yet, one must modify that statement to include the problem posed by a followership of fools, a bastardized bourgeoisie without depth or direction, and a community that has simply lost its dignity. Reading Fanon again, I find myself disagreeing with him in his assessment of the mass of the people who, according to him, "slowly awaken to the unutterable treason of their leaders." (*The Wretched of the Earth:* 167) Fanon is right in stating that Africa will be saved only when power is given back to the people, or when the people themselves snatch it. The problem lies in the people's lack of consciousness, and will to act; in their ready collaboration with the bourgeoisie; in their resignation to oppression; and in their willingness to grant rightness and power of god, to a criminal leadership. The leaders' lack of morality is no longer an issue; their generosity with the country's riches amassed through the unrequited slave-labor of the people, is hailed to high heavens as an act of patriotism. Rich robbers have thus become heroes, and honest people are reviled for being ordinary, poor, boring, and unimaginative. When the master dictator and his allies are cornered by critics, and made to panic by true patriots protesting against the regime, they democratically increase prices of essential goods, or make them scarce, as punishment, or a way of giving everyone something to occupy their time and thoughts. Everyone scurries to take advantage of the situation: From market women to petrol dealers, from bank managers to civil servants, they all find bizarre means of exploiting others, by helping the patriotic regime make ordinary air an "essential commodity." The dictator smiles, and sighs in relief. He knows his people perfectly well. And, is it not true that the people deserve their leaders?

I was in Nigeria during the 1993 democratic dance of death. As the government was rolling out its illogical plan to sabotage the process, the minority of committed critics organized marches, and other acts of civil disobedience. In retaliation, the beleaguered regime created fuel shortage, among other items of "protection of people and property." Given the facts that average Nigerians need no adequate public transportation, nor functional telephone service, nor regular electricity, nor steady water supply, nor anything that would make life easy (that was the opinion of one very honorable minister), most people did not complain about the long queues at petrol stations.

I was caught in the quest for petrol one early morning, as I was

217

trying to make a 10 a.m. appointment some eighty miles away from Lagos. In order to be sure of buying petrol, I had arrived at the filling station at 5 o'clock. Not early enough: There were already scores of vehicles in several long lines, waiting for the black gold. I placed my almost 20-year-old Japanese junk of a car behind a shining Mercedes-Benz, bought a couple of weekly magazines sold nearby at double the posted price, and sat calmly in my car, awaiting my turn. The wait lasted merely eight hours. During that short period, I witnessed all sorts of dramas, and was myself an actor in one.

I kept pace with the vehicles crawling ever so doggedly towards the fuel pumps surrounded by vulture-like figures struggling to have their way. I stayed in line. Many of us did. From time to time, I stepped out to stretch my cramped, arthritic legs. I exchanged notions of frustration with other fuel-seekers, among whom was a former sojourner in the United States. Upon learning that I was visiting from there, he let the two fellows behind him get ahead, so that we could follow each other, and have a better chance to talk. He gladly filled me in on the current political situation, how "the political class" was at loggerheads with "the military class:" how "the impasse" could lead to "national calamity," and how "patriots" like himself were most intent on "maintaining our integrity." He declared at the top of his smoke-coated lungs: "This nation's unity cannot, and must not, be debated or mortgaged." A few co-adventurers hissed with disgust as he blew his cigarette smoke into the polluted air, and that fueled his patriotic and analytic zeal. He boasted of what he and others were doing to "save this country." The care with which he glided along his Lexus limousine -"the latest model," he informed me, "not yet available even in America"- must have been symptomatic of the care that he and his co-patriots applied to building "our great nation." I was gradually developing an aversion to the gentleman. Subconsciously, I was leaving a growing space between his car and mine.

Suddenly, I saw a green Mercedes sports car emerge ahead of me. The whole body had not pulled through; only the bulging front end, right there like the bulbous nose of a pimple-haunted bully. The driver, young, nattily attired, and ugly, came out grinning from ear to ear.

I was too shocked to speak. I just stared at him. I tried to keep calm, to ask him politely to go join the queue some fifty vehicles behind. He attacked me as the committed leaders attack their nation's coffers, with a vengeance: I was too old to be driving; my poverty was symbolized by my old match-box of a car; my bald head would make a good road for his beautiful Benz, but I'd probably collapse under its weight, so I should go home and hide, or die. And, it was old men like me that were preventing the great nation from progressing, by setting bad example of poverty for young men such as his good self. At first, some comrades in the struggle for petrol tried to silence the man for being rude: He should have begged me to give him room ahead of me, instead of cutting in. When I objected to such unfair and unreasonable judgment, they turned on me with the anger of people being punished by a patriotic government. My Lexus-riding friend joined them, and said that I must have been away for too long. I had no choice but to let the Mercedes man stay on the line.

Once assured of that stolen position, he took out two big jerry-cans from the booth of his car, and sped to the fuel pumps. Within minutes, he had successfully filled them with petrol. He sold one can for triple the price paid, poured the content of the other in his tank, and drove off with a few choice words of insult thrown at me. Hours after his departure, mouths were still wagging about his extraordinary resourcefulness and victory.

The news in the magazines I was reading, complemented the victor's action and the crowd's reaction. The law of the strongest and swiftest and smartest, must prevail in a land of oppressors and opportunists. While some were talking of justice and dignity, others, more true and tuned to the nation's realities, were echoing the government's call for understanding. You must understand that, as your brother's keeper, you cannot condemn him for his shortcomings, because it may be your turn tomorrow. You must understand that everybody has a family to feed; therefore, if you are in a position of power, you have to take care of your own. You must understand that everybody who, given a chance, does not cheat, or steal, has to be a bastard. Tomorrow is already here today. You must understand.

So, the politicians understand the dictator very well, and cooperate with him to steal the country blind. Likewise, the kings and chiefs, wise traditional fathers, are kind enough to cooperate with him, and the politicians, in claiming a community of crumb-eaters. Everyone loves the nation with a passion. That has to be the only explanation for the resounding, and astounding, success of a blatantly inhuman regime in a country full of excellent minds. It must also account for the ease with which politicians and paternalistic, power-seeking-and-sharing occupants of gilded palaces, declare support, within a period of three months, for three different regimes. That must be the definition of African democracy.

Needless to say, on that adventurous day at the petrol station, I missed my appointment with the publisher. I phoned to apologize, and he was very understanding. I later submitted the manuscript to be discussed and, naturally, I understand why he has not contacted me about it for over six months.

I traveled out of Nigeria while the political and economic crisis continued to grow in confusion. The family and friends that saw me off at the airport, had envy etched on their faces. I expressed the hope for a more irenic time at home in the following year. They collectively exclaimed that I should stay put abroad until further notice.

OF EXILE, ALIENATION, AND COMMITMENT

The events of 1993 are still impacting the lives of Nigerians in 1994. They will continue to do so for years to come. The exodus of men, women, and children from places that need help to those that hardly need it, will not cease until Africa manages to find her way out of the ongoing degradation and devastation. When you are lucky enough to complete an inter-continental phone call, those back home pointedly discourage you from returning there. They want you to feel fortunate for having escaped from that hell to the American heaven. And you, when nobody is watching, or listening, you sigh and thank your stars, too. Yet you cannot forget home. You are caught between there and here. There, the hell of misery for the majority; the den of dictators bashing the innocent into submission and silence; the graveyard of the intellectual stripped of incentive and integrity, as he wallows in poverty. Here, the heaven of credit cards, where you may spend a lifetime of comfort, and die paying debts; the center of civilization, where life has no meaning before the barrel of a gun; the center of a world, where Africa does not count, and is forever painted black like plague, depicted as backward and beastly and dreaded like death. They claim that Africa's glorious past is nothing but a myth. And you, what exactly have you done, what are you doing, to rehabilitate the truth? In 1993, AT & T, America's giant phone company, had to deal with a small scandal: One of its sponsored magazines carried a promotional cartoon using a monkey to depict Africa's participation in the international phone linkage network. African American political leaders spoke out against the insult and, quite magnanimously, the phone company severed relations with the advertising agency. Question: Does that solve the problem? Does that eradicate the West's belief that Africa is populated by monkeys masquerading as human beings? After that phone incident, a member of the American Congress implied that African leaders behaved like savages liable to devour one another. And, no African voice has been heard to complain, or to defend, or to disagree. Meanwhile, shameful stories of African, particularly Nigerian, cocaine-dealers and credit-card frauds are filling the newspapers. For instance, *The Washington Post* published two articles on February 27, 1994. On the first page of the "Style" section, appears "Charlie's Hustle," describing the pitiable experience of an American business man who had received in the mail a proposal from an unknown man in Nigeria. The Nigerian government, it claimed, had mistakenly appropriated $35 million as payment to France for some oil transaction, and the money, yet unnoticed by higher officials, could be made to disappear into the pockets of that eagle-eyed Nigerian and the honest American. All the latter had to do, was to forward his bank account number and tele-transfer instructions, as well as a service charge of a meager $15 thousand. The honest American, very trustworthy and willing to become a multi-millionaire as decreed by the capitalist god, ended up losing his thousands. The article heaped words of scorn on the Nigerian, while pitying the poor American victim. The writer implied that all Nigerians were naturally crooked; on the contrary, the American enjoyed the benefit of the doubt, considered innocent until proven guilty.

The second article, in the "Show" section, was a review of the movie, "Sugar Hill," starring the African American actor, Wesley Snipes. The subject is, drug dealing. Commenting on a scene in a bar where some Nigerians refuse to do business with African Americans whom they sneeringly call, "cotton pickers," the critic writes: "The slave trade of today is the drug business, and the kinds of Nigerians who now sell heroin are the same kinds who sold other Africans centuries ago." (G6) Here again, the racist generalization needs no comment.

Under the present circumstances, it may be time for both Africans and African Americans to come together, and one is not talking of high officials from both sides of the Atlantic, because they have always been together in making deals beneficial to them as individuals, or classes.[7] On several occasions, you find yourself telling a lie about your identity. And you wonder why nobody in the West ever proclaims in public fora the contributions of African scholars and experts to the socio-economic progress of Western countries.

The issue has to do with place, space, and time. The South African writer and scholar, Es'kia Mphahlele, after twenty years in exile (1957-1977), decided to return home. Some people accused him of having sold out to the apartheid regime. Collaboration, or commitment? Mphahlele does see an inevitable compromise in his return: "My return is a compromise between the outsider who did not *have* to be bullied by place in other lands (and yet wanted a place, badly) and the insider who has an irrepressible attachment to ancestral place. Like the rest, I must submit to the pull of place, I must deal with the tyranny of time." (*Afrika My Music*, Johannesburg: Ravan Press, 1984 :11) While abroad, he saw some positive effects of exile: "Lying to the white man who employed me or who processed my life was a natural thing to do before I left South Africa. I learned to be relatively at ease with whites abroad, and I did not have to lie in order to survive. *I could sell my labour on the best market.*" (Ibid: 6-7, emphasis mine) The South African's circumstances and condition are of particular interest to me because, unlike those of us who were so fortunate to have freedom on the palm of our hands only to be so stupid as to transform it into a new form of enslavement, those down there have long suffered from an inhumanism never known by us. In our part of Africa, white man was master, but he never reached the point of making us feel inferior for being black. Maybe that is why we went ahead and created our own white man through ethnophobia and, interestingly enough, this new creation, or creature, has been facilitated with the help of the white man himself.

If Mphahlele can talk of exile in those terms, if he can appreciate the loss of place, it is because he was already being treated back home as an outsider, and he was committed to regaining what had been stolen from him. In exile, he was determined to go back and continue the struggle to the end. On the other hand, those of us searching for greener pastures in the West, are merely spoilt foster-children disgruntled with lost privileges and prepared to borrow a place anywhere. Classic vagrants, wanderers of the world, we are less concerned with questions of commitment to our community than with reclaiming our comfortable life-styles. Quite adaptable, we create our own spurious space which, in actuality, is borrowed, or stolen. With credit-cards in hand, we find whatever we want, materially. In a way, we are also fortunate for being able to go home again with nobody there to hold a gun to our heads, provided, of course, that we do not meddle in matters that are no business of *dignified* -read, spineless- intellectuals. Such is our existence, as we sit on the fence and criticize the crooks in power, and the helpless masses at their mercy, but are hardly ready to lift a finger against them. And I can hear many cowards, like myself, saying that it is not worth the trouble.

At home and abroad, we fit Fanon's description of that bourgeoisie "upholding and justifying the action of politicians" (*The Wretched...*: 217), "utilizing techniques and language which are borrowed from the West" (223), bankrupt caricature of European bourgeoisie. Taking the example of African literature, one finds that African critics have gradually been gravitating (you know, upward mobility, as a matter of superioration) towards Eurocentric theories. Gone are the days when activists were calling for pan-African aesthetics. To ensure validity in the right circles, and to put bread on the table, you must espouse the latest theories as preached from the pulpit of the progressive school of thought, by paternalistic experts that are the natural successors of post-independence imported engineers who, in their countries, were mere technicians. You do realize that your compromising stand is despicable, but you feel better than those caught in the belly of the neo-colonial beast back home. Now, are you really better off? In moments of soberness, when we all descend from the pedestal; when we quit being civilized puppets, and become ordinary, sad souls playing games with the present, and fearful of facing the future; when we speak in our mother-tongue, because the languages that we affect, and perfect, sometimes to hide our heritage, cannot express our deepest desires and the hopes hidden but no less haunting; in those rare moments of perspicacity and honesty, we actually reveal a certain envy for those left behind. We wish to join them, sit with them, and map out strategy for a struggle that would use all of our capabilities for the good of the community, including ourselves. Yet, there remains a basic bad faith in our actions; for, when we think of such concerted efforts, we do so out of our frustrations and failures within the so-called civilized setting of exile: We are recognized as *aliens* (legal, or illegal) as soon as we show our faces and speak, because we are black, and non-European. We are treated as second-class, even though we are doubly qualified to do the work we are employed to do. We are simply a sick, sad, and selfish lot.

CONCLUSION: MORE QUESTIONS THAN ANSWERS

The thought of community has become lost upon many of us; yet, any thinking African knows that it is one factor that has made for our survival as peoples for centuries of suffering and subordination. When my father referred to community, he always took his time to emphasize the collective stand of the colonized against the colonizer; the togetherness of families raising children who were never known to be orphans; the responsibility of the successful ones pulling up others who were less fortunate; the understanding by the rich, that they had nothing if others were poor; the commitment to building the nation, together.

Writers could easily keep alive the attachment to their community. For them, imagination facilitates the linkage. Professionals would find it more difficult, however. In every case, there ought to be ways of maintaining the connection, except one sees one's Africanity as an accident of history best forgotten as part of a nightmare. University professors could be adjunct teachers in institutions at home; thus, they would not only maintain contact, but continue to contribute to the construction of a now sagging education system. I once suggested such an affiliation in regard to the Nigerian university where I was employed before running away. I thought it was a useful idea, to stem the tide of the brain-drain that continues to exacerbate the debilitation of institutional structures. My suggestion was considered an affront by certain officials who must have been angered at their own inability to get away.

It takes courage to face conditions of misery and death. The runaway intellectual is no doubt a coward, but he does not have to be courageous to make the re-connection with home. He has probably not been in danger of losing limb, or life. The millions that do, do not know the road to the airport, or they are already dead. We may consider ourselves to deserve better than to be forced to flee after years of preparation with the hope of becoming participants in planning and implementing constructive programs. Could it be that we were foolish dreamers not realistic enough to note that the very history of our countries had reserved for us life on the verge? If that is true, we must blame ourselves for doing nothing to make rectification, and move from the margin to the center.

Living in exile is, for some of us, a burden, an act of resignation to damnation, and a betrayal. All the same, home is too hot to handle. But, have we the right to keep complaining and criticizing from here, sitting cosily in our financed town homes, and driving our bought-on-credit luxury cars? The African writer remains a pitiful protester, and his words, those words that once served as weapon against the enemy from afar, have been stifled by circumstances dictating compromise. They have become hollow, like the sting of a snake stripped clean of its poison, and reduced to performing in circuses. The poet-politicians (generation of patriots that obtained independence), were focused in their fight against a known adversary. Our generation has never been that lucky: The identity of the enemy is blurred, and we do not have the privilege to combine the private and the public personae; or, rather, when we do, it is out of a compulsion to survive. We cannot escape the issues of compromise and individualism. Do you want, can you afford, to lose the opportunity to help yourself, and your loved ones? If you die now, who will care for them? And how about the community? What do you do, when everyone is telling you to stay abroad, so that you may send them the almighty dollar which, unknown to them, poor fools, you do not have, except on credit, or as remuneration for a job that is killing you slowly, physically, or psychologically?

When my father was still a believer in the community, he did not take cognizance of the ideology of self-preservation, and self-promotion, in a system where you compete with everything that you own, or steal. When we contemplate the community now, we actually look down on *those people* for whom we have no more than pity. With apologies to Fanon, how can we respect those who look up to us as saviors sent from Civilization? How can we learn from them, when they now behave as if we, alienated intellectuals, exiles, bastardized bourgeois, are the epitome of dignity, success, and everything that they want to be? How can the people lead, when they are dying to be led by those raping and robbing them?

What, in the long run, would be the role of the writer in neocolonial Africa? Granted that he does not run away from the battlefield at home, one can only hope that, by means of his work depicting the plight of the people -even though they cannot read what he writes!-, he would remain their voice, their comrade-in-arms, a humble contributor to their cause. But, then, pessimists would remind us, as well they should: "Perhaps the function of writers, apart from mirroring their societies, is to be bad-tempered, to grumble, and to protest, but there is not very much they can do about the real direction of society." (Lewis Nkosi, in Per Wastberg, ed., *The Writer in Modern Africa*, New York: Africana Publishing Corporation, 1968: 47) Nkosi's thirty-year-old statement has lost none of its distressing forthrightness and relevance. Maybe he is right, that no amount of protest can stop politicians from prostituting and pouncing upon the people. Maybe one should simply be silent and thank God for being alive. Silence, however, is death for those who must speak, and one cannot afford to die just like that, even in one's cocoon of credit cards, and corn-flakes, and chitlings, and salad, and saloon-cars, everything made possible by almighty capitalism.

So, we wait, and watch, and continue to call for changes in the hope of going home again. But there remains that increasing fear of death in exile. We all know of an African who, de-programmed of his home's hideous problems, became a citizen in a Western nation. He had never returned home in over three decades. One day, he died, alone in his sitting-room, while watching CNN. Generous, conscience-stricken compatriots (afraid that they might be next?!), put money together, put his body on a plane that took him back home to be buried.

Notes

1. Written in 1994.
2. Es'kia Mphahlele, *Afrika My Music*, Johannesburg: Ravan Press, 1984.
3. Ngugi wa Thiong'o, *Writers in Politics*, London: Heinemann, 1981: 78.
4. Chinua Achebe, "The Novelist as Teacher," in G.D. Killam, ed., *African Writers on African Writing,* London: Heinemann, 1973: 3.
5. Frantz Fanon, *The Wretched of the Earth,* tr. C. Farrington, New York: Grove Press, 1963: 197.
6. Nigeria has established a reputation for trying to buy other countries' friendship, support, and respect, in the same manner as its government "settles" individuals. The "settlement" syndrome notwithstanding, clashes, personal, political, and military, remain the order of the day. For example, the Cameroons, former appendage to Nigeria, has been fighting it out with its bigger brother, over the oil-rich Bakassi peninsula. France, the cunning ex-colonizer, is taking sides with the small country in this late-century "scramble for Africa."
7. See, Femi Ojo-Ade, ed., *Of Dreams Deferred, Dead, or Alive*, Westport: Greenwood Press, 1996, for critical studies by Africans, on the relationship between African Americans and Africa. A necessary corollary to that text will be, a study on the relationship between Africans and America.

CHAPTER 24

BRAZIL'S BAHIA AND THE YORUBA CONTINUUM

I am a Yoruba, I cry in Cuban Yoruba.
Since I am a Yoruba from Cuba,
I want my Yoruba tears to spread
I want the happy tears
Emanating from me to spread, to rise.[1]

These [Oshogbo, Oyo, Ile-Ife] are African-
Brazilian people's spiritual centers, our
places of pilgrimage. We need no Meccas
or Jerusalems. Our home in Africa is ready
to receive us with our own pilgrimage points.[2]

History shows that Brazil is demographically and culturally an African country.[3]

E ni se ire se e fun ara re
E ni sika se e fun ara re
Ire ko ni sai gbe ni, ika ko ni
sai ka onika, bi inu ba mo esinsin
onika kole kun ni.[4]

INTRODUCTION: YORUBA ROOTS
OF THE AFRICAN DIASPORA

With the infamous crime called slavery begun some years after the
so-called discovery of America by Christopher Columbus, Euro-

peans embarked upon their systematic dehumanization of Africans with the collusion of some contemptible African chiefs and kings and various surrogates of oppression, all pimps aiding and abetting their people's prostitution which, sad to say, has continued into the dusk of the twentieth century. Among the victims of the Trade were the Yoruba of West Africa. While figures will remain debatable regarding representation of the ethnic groups constituting the human cargo forcibly uprooted and carted across the Atlantic, one fact has proven incontrovertible: of all the nations resettled in the African diaspora, the Yoruba nation has had the most significant and most lasting influences, at all essential levels of existence, social, political and cultural. That Yoruba has so deeply impacted the lives of Africans in the diaspora is due, not just to accident or chance, but to the late arrival of Yorubas in the diaspora, and the very nature of the culture and civilization, its virility, its adaptability, and generally engaging qualities.

One only has to travel to the Americas and the Caribbean, to those areas where Blacks (Africans) have become permanent settlers (Cuba, Haiti, Jamaica, Trinidad and Tobago, the United States, Brazil), or where they once constituted an important group deliberately diffused or destroyed by European immigrants and Eurocentrist rulers and other overriding factors (Argentina, Colombia, Peru, Venezuela), to witness the Yoruba presence. In the United States, each and every aspect of African culture assumed by the African American has a Yoruba input -names, clothing, habits, music, the totality of community- which, we must admit, has been mixed, and rightly so, with other elements to form a particular and peculiar African-Americanity. The revolutionary sixties would be a truly eye-opening period for studying the impact of Yoruba culture on the United States. Due to the influences of the mainstream (the American Dream), the African American's relationship to Africa has become more socio-political than cultural, which would explain the manifestations of ideas that are supposed to be cultural. For example, the notion of *Kwanzaa* is attached more to East Africa (the Swahili language is the source of it all) than to the West from where the ancestors came. On the other hand, one cannot forget the existence of such a place as Oyotunji village in South Carolina, where Yoruba culture is being reproduced, nor can one overlook the importance of *esusu* groups across the United States: the Yoruba word means, to contribute money as savings with one participant using the bulk sum on each occasion, in a kind of community banking system. *Esusu* also means, coming together as support group, to address the needs of members; such a family exists in Philadelphia, Pennsylvania.

In Cuba and Haiti, among others, Yorubanity is, indeed, more pronounced than in the United States. Haiti's religion, *Voudou*, is without doubt a diasporan form of Yoruba *Ifa*. So also is Cuba's *Santeria*. In both countries, the Yoruba deities, the *Orisha*, are the very ones worshiped in Ile-Ife, Oyo, Ilesha, Oshogbo, Ekiti, Egba, Egbado, Ketu, and other centers. The legends on human creation and community, as related in *Ifa* are similar to those recounted in Haiti and Cuba. The *Nanigo* (cf. *Anago* = *Yoruba)* of Cuba, members of the sect called *Naniguismo*, believe in *Olorun*. Among the best known *Orisha* are: *Ochun, Chango, Oyaa, Ogun, Yemaja.* Bamboche (cf. Bamgboshe in Yoruba) describes thus the origin of the world: "In the beginning, there were only Olorun and Olokun. They were the first. Olokun and Olorun are of the same age. Olokun was the origin of Yemaja. Of Yemaja and Agaya were born the other Orichas, the intermediaries between the Creator and his creations. For a long time, Olorun and Olokun fought for the domination of the earth. There were many battles between the Saints. Each time that Olorun sent something to the earth, Olokun appropriated it..."[5] And the fascinating story goes on and on, reminding all true Yoruba children of the wisdom of *Odu Ifa.*

In short, Yoruba religion, the essence of culture, has never seized to survive and to guide the lives of diasporan Africans. Contrary to what has unfortunately occurred in the ancestral home, the primacy of religion has been maintained according to the original tradition whereby every facet of human existence is imbued with religiosity. In Africa, modernity is in fashion, particularly among the visible and vocal Western-educated, self-proclaimed civilized groups. Modernity has meant psychological abandonment of one's roots for the supposedly superior civilizations symbolized by Christianity and Islam. It is an open secret that the same singers of psalms in the church seek out the shrine of the *babalawos* (Yoruba traditional priests, and doctors) when the going gets really tough, when no one is watching. The irony is not lost on any intelligent observer; for, one would have thought that the diasporan Africans, enslaved and constrained to adhere to Catholicism or other forms of Christianity, would be the ones who, after all these centuries, would hold no respect for African religion.[6]

YORUBA IN BRAZILIAN CULTURE

Meanwhile, the consolation is, that in the countries of the diaspora, Yoruba culture has continued to thrive. We have chosen to address the specific example of Brazil because Brazil has the second largest population of Blacks in the world, after Nigeria. That may come to many as a surprise. The country perhaps best known for football and the samba rhythms choreographed by the fleet feet of players like the king himself, Pele, is, indeed, demographically an African country! Among the population, Yoruba is definitely the most influential culture. As scholars, activists and others have remarked, it is impossible to determine the exact number of Africans transported to Brazil, thanks in part to the Brazilian Finance Minister Ruy Barbosa's instruction of 1891, to burn all existing documents on slavery.[7] It is also problematic to know how many Blacks are in today's Brazil, thanks to the government's policy of deracialization-miscegenation-*branqueamento* (whitening or ethnic cleansing): it all depends on whose opinion or analysis and how the reality is being configured. The result of that policy -vaunted by some and vilified by others- is that most Brazilians, even the truly black, have been alluding to themselves as mulatto (*pardo*), or white (*branco*), or simply as Brazilians (*brasileiro*, which would be the ideal of a non-racial, human society), while running away from black (*negro*) like a plague.[8] To quote John Henrik Clarke, the remarkable African-American scholar-thinker, "the uniqueness of the Brazilian case is that Brazil is an African state with a smiling white minority forever announcing nonracialism and practicing none of it." (Preface to Abdias do Nascimento, p. ix) These brief remarks on race and color in Brazil are necessary in order to fully appreciate the miracle of survival of African culture.

From the beginning of slavery in about 1515 until its abolition in Brazil (1888), the culture grew relentlessly and, today, it has become part of the very air that people breathe. Let us allude to a few lived examples. This critic, on his first visit to Salvador-Bahia in 1981, was welcomed by men and women uncannily resembling the family and friends that he had left back home in Lagos. He was taken to several *Candomblé terreiros* (compounds housing shrines and communities practicing Yoruba religion) where he was welcomed with *obi* (kola nut) and *omi* (water). The *iyalorixa* (Ifa priestess and head of the household), decked out in her flowing white attire and beautiful beads, sat regally on the throne-like chair, reminding the visitor of the kings and queens, and the priests and priestesses back home. And the old woman spoke to him and led songs in Yoruba. An *ogam* (a non-initiated high official in the house) conducted an orchestra of adept drummers. A bevy of beauties danced and the priestess then led them in performing rituals to welcome their brother and son and father; for, in their opinion, the African, the Yoruba, was a representative of their ancestors. He was mesmerized. He felt as if he were back in the days of his youth, when his grandfather used to let him into his hut or take him to traditional ceremonies, which his father, product of the colonial school and a civil servant, had forbidden. That first visit has been followed by several others to Salvador-Bahia, the slaves' point of entry from Africa, and still the center of Yoruba culture.

On another occasion, in that same city, another Yoruba professor, a staunch Catholic, upon informing his hosts that he was the son of a king, was astonished to witness a spontaneous ceremony befitting royalty, with the song, *ki le nfoba pe, oba o, oba alase* (how dare you disrespect the king, the king with power and authority?), ringing in his ears, with libations poured, with prayers solemnly voiced to Ogun, the deity to whom his family was traditionally attached. And, on his way out of the shrine, he caught sight of a beautiful, black woman sitting on the street-corner frying *acarajé*. He walked across and was offered a taste; it was no different from the *akara* balls that he used to eat for breakfast in his Nigerian ivory-tower.

That is Salvador-Bahia, a Yoruba city, as cosmopolitan as Lagos, as traditional as Ile-Ife and Oyo, as immersed in shrines as Oshogbo. The Yoruba religion has been given a Brazilian name, *Candomblé*. The word has a combination of African sources: Kimbundu, *ka* = custom; Kikongo, *ndombe* = black person; Yoruba, *ile* = house.

So, it connotes the house of worship, the shrine, the religion of Black people. The Bantu and Yoruba sources of the word would not surprise anyone who knows that these two nations are the most outstanding of those that went to Brazil. As already stated, however, Yoruba is the one nation that has attained preeminence.[9] There exists in Brazil an official federation of traditional religious groups. On the whole, there are over two thousand (2,000) groups in Bahia. Yoruba-based ones number over a thousand (1,000). Names do not lie. *Ile Axé Opo Afonja, Ile Maroialaji (Alaketu), Ile Iya Nasso Oka, Ile Axé Omi Ya Masse (Gantois), Ile Axé l'Oya, Ile Axé Omi Da,* these are the names of a few of the Houses (*ile*). Each of them has a known history, some dating back many years, thus underscoring their perennialness and permanence on the Brazilian landscape.

Ile Axé Iya Nasso Oka, or *Candomblé do Engenho Velho* (Cult of the Ancient Genius) is generally considered as the oldest in Bahia. It belongs to the Ketu nation (Dahomey-Benin Republic), although it actually encompasses all the various groups of the Yoruba nation because, according to observers, the Ketu House, "in one form or the other, gave birth to all the others and was the first to function regularly in Bahia."[10] It was founded about 1830 by three women from West Africa, Adeta (or *Iya Deta*), *Iya Kala* and *Iya Nasso.* Marcelina followed them as head. Then came the cleavage: Two sisters, Maria Julia Conceiçao and Maria Julia Figueiredo, vied for the position. The latter, by tradition rightly next in line (as *Iya Kekere*), won out. The loser left in anger to establish another House, the present-day *Candomblé do Gantois.*

Meanwhile, Figueiredo was followed by Mãe Sussu, or Ursulina, at whose death another scission occurred between the daughters. Sinha Antonia, the rightful head, was beaten to the post by Aninha. Sinha Antonia and her supporters founded a new House, *Axé Opo Afonja.* From this panoramic view, one learns that *Casa Branca* is, indeed, the oldest cult in Bahia, the mother of all cults. One also notes -and this is of significance- an astonishing similarity between the contest for religious leadership and the rivalry for the throne among different arms of the royal family in Yorubaland. Thirdly, one is struck by the presence of women at the helm of power in the religious community in Brazil. Here again, one is reminded of the female roles in traditional Yoruba society: Only ignorant foreign "experts" would continue to claim that African women are on the periphery while, for centuries, they have been at the epicenter of society.

An explanation is given in the write-up by Antonio Agnelo, for the nomenclature, *Iya Nasso*: "Nasso is not a proper Yoruba name; before, it was a private, honorific title of the coast for the Alafin of Oyo, king of all Yoruba. In 19th century Bahia, among all those of Yoruba origin, those from Oyo inclusive, nobody would use the title of Iya Nasso without authority. It can therefore be affirmed that, if in the Bahia of the beginning of the last century someone was so named, that person was certainly a priestess of Sango in the ancient city of Oyo, and not from Ketu." What is essential in the above statement is the fact that both Ketu and Oyo belong to the Yoruba nation. Through the oldest *Candomblé* community, both have kept alive their affinity and linkage. The inclusive evolution in Bahia is not surprising. Today, one of the most respected *Iyalorixa* is Olga Alaketu (the queen of Ketu).[11]

The inclusiveness of Yoruba culture is due to its strength in galvanizing what may at one time have been differing or opposing forces, to form a harmonious whole. It is also a mark of solidarity among the slaves who succeeded in becoming one in spite of the enslavers' desperate efforts to keep them apart. The uniting power of Yoruba is noticeable in the specificities of African religions established in Brazil, and the identities of the deities. Yoruba religion has become the generally accepted one, the symbol, the standard, the centripetal force. We must not forget that *Candomblé* is a generic term for the practices of all Africans from all nations, Yoruba, Bantu, Ewe, Fon, Angola, and others, each with its own particularities. Yet, Yoruba has come to symbolize the concept, giving as it does its deities to all the nations. Yemanja, Xango, Ogum, Oxum, Ibeji, Obaluae, Obatala, Omolu, Exu, Oxala, Oxossi, Oxunmare, Egum, Iansa and, of course, Orixa, these are the deities known and revered by Brazilians. What has happened in Brazil and elsewhere (cf. Cuba and Haiti) is the incorporation of the beliefs and practices of other nations into the personalities of Yoruba deities. Certain gods are no longer always the ones worshiped on the ancestral continent, even though the names may be the same.

Furthermore, certain gods, unknown to, or forgotten by the continental Yoruba, have been added to the list. To take but two examples, Iansa is not common in Yorubaland. She is Sango's wife and bears resemblance to Oya, another wife of Sango's. Exu, while retaining the characteristics of trickster and messenger between human beings and the Supreme Being, has become in Brazil the spirit of the crossroads and, in the Bantu-based cult of *Umbanda*, he is identified with the devil of Christianity complete with horns, trident and red cape. These changes are only natural in the process of planting one's roots anew in a strange, foreign land.

Candomblé ritual and ceremonies, music, songs, dance, and the life of the community, are replete with Yoruba cultural antecedents. The maxim quoted at the head of this essay belongs to the oldest House in Bahia. At every ceremony, in every compound, one hears Yoruba songs.[12] The instruments are Yoruba: *bata, agogo, ilu, xequere.* Sacrifice is regarded as a necessary ritual, to seek one's deity's support and sanction, to clear the way for a better future. Besides *carnaval*, that annual event in which the poor and destitute feel free to mingle with the rich and the mighty, in which the poor are made to feel fulfilled and to take leave from their everyday hell in order to enjoy a taste of heaven,[13] perhaps the biggest ceremony is the annual sacrifice to Yemanja, on February 2. The beach becomes a sea of white (the deity's color), with beautiful, black women leading the way to the water in honor of the queen of the sea and the most prestigious of the deities.

YORUBA RELIGION AND CULTURE: THE SACRED AND THE SECULAR

Ceremonies, such as the Yemanja festival and carnival, regularly provide proof of the overall Africanity and, precisely, the Yorubanity of Black Brazil; for, as is well known, existence is a combination of the secular and the sacred, with the latter remaining at the roots, giving depth to lived experience and underscoring the absolute power of the Supreme Being. More than the Yoruba remaining on the ancestral continent, African Brazilians have maintained that essential religiosity of our people and, unlike the former, they have been able to retain real commitment to the culture. Carnival samba schools called *blocos* constitute an excellent example.

These *blocos afros* (e.g. *Oju Oba, Ile Aiye, Male Debale, Alaketu, Olodum)* not only participate in the very competitive carnival celebrations, but also are well organized at the socio-economic levels, thus understanding the need to use culture as springboard for popular progress. The best known of these Bahian groups is *Bloco Olodum* (the word is probably derived from *Olodumare*, God, but could also have taken its meaning from the Yoruba word meaning, one engaged in festivities, in celebration, which is a constant in Yoruba culture), founded in 1979. From a small group hardly distinguishable from the many others vying for popularity, *Olodum* has grown immensely in the past several years. It is now a household name, an internationally acclaimed entity which, to all intents and purposes, is a vast commercial conglomerate. *Olodum* is also a very popular musical group; a record company; a dance school; a clothing company; a publishing house; a school for children and professional apprentices. In a word, it is big business faced with the dilemma of where to draw the line between cultural conscientization and commercial exploitation. *Olodum's* musical-cultural troupe has toured many countries but has yet to visit Africa, although, as at this writing, plans seem to have been completed for a tour of South Africa. In one of its publications (there is *Boletim Olodum* among others), it is stated that "today, *Olodum's* main struggle is against poverty that is taking its toll on our country; and [*Olodum*] wants all currents of socio-economic action against poverty turned into a firm and decisive action to bring an end to misery."[14]

That is a lofty and most honorable objective. Unfortunately, it is easier said than done. It is becoming more and more apparent that conquering the Blacks' misery in Bahia and the rest of Brazil is beyond the capabilities of a cultural group evolving into a money-making machine. Apart from the handful of youths snatched from the jaws of poverty and fatalism, the majority cannot escape from the stagnant, stultifying ghetto called Pelourinho. The throbbing rhythm of *Olodum's* drums and the magnificently syncopated sounds may be no more than a passing respite, or an opium helping the victims to forget heart-rending realities. *Olodum's* blossoming commercialism within the largely capitalistic setting, has become a big part of Brazilian tourism.

Tourism helps to disseminate culture, but its spirit of materialism also encourages cultural bastardization. In Bahia, Yoruba culture is a victim of sensationalist sell-out. *Candomblé* leaders often complain of the problem, which is not surprising because the religion requires secrecy in order to safeguard its ideals of mystery, faith, and fate. It is not uncommon to see foreign tourists armed with their cameras and camcorders shooting sacred ceremonies and thereby reducing them to folkloric festivities. Curiosity is increasingly becoming the main quality of so-called converts. Faith is running the risk of being evinced by fantasy. *Candomblé* is featured on popular television. Religion is losing its roots in the hands of fake *pais de santo* (priests) who, after a short sojourn in Nigeria (Ile-Ife, Oyo, Oshogbo), return to Bahia as certified experts in *Ifa* ready to construct their own shrines, to heal the sick, to serve as shepherds for the children of *Orixas*. Mãe Stella de Oxossi, leader of *Ile Axé Opo Afonja*, in protest against the folklorization of the religion and the naked ambitions of some priests and priestesses, once resigned from the National Institute of Afro-Brazilian Tradition. She stated: "Candomblé is a religion and not a folklore. These days it's the fashion to display beads and claim to belong to the cult, and all the scientists want to research and write on Candomblé, so that any book on the subject is like a cookery book. I don't want to be a radical, but it's the reality: nowadays, many different persons are infiltrating the faith which, in the past, used to be a thing for the common people, born and bred in the faith and it is clear that the indiscriminate entry of politicians, artists, intellectuals, in short, persons of another social and cultural level, depreciates the religion, which is being transformed into the ornamental and folkloric object."[15] Mãe Stella's concerns have hardly been addressed. The lack of attention is but symptomatic of a widespread attitude towards matters African and Black at the higher rungs of the societal ladder.

The growing number of charlatans claiming to be priests is both positive and negative: on one hand, it shows the importance of Yoruba culture and religion; on the other, it shows how low the religion has fallen in esteem. This negative side is made all the more disturbing by the action of certain *babalawos* in Yorubaland exploiting the genuine interest and hunger for knowledge on the part of Brazilians for their own selfish, financial ends.[16] This critic has also met Yoruba priests in Brazil as they scramble to make a dollar by divinating and preying upon the gullibility of believers convinced that every Yoruba son or daughter visiting their community is "the real thing."

So as to authenticate and promote Yoruba culture and to build and reinforce bridges, the International Congress of Orisha Tradition was founded in the late seventies under the leadership of Wande Abimbola, a renowned priest and scholar and former Vice-Chancellor of Obafemi Awolowo University, Ile-Ife. The Congress, particularly in the 1980s, served as focal point for constructing a genuine cultural structure bringing together Africans from the continent and the diaspora, to celebrate and deliberate, and to seek solidarity in the struggle to survive in the world as children of Olodumare. Bi-annual meetings were held in Ile-Ife, Salvador, São Paulo and Buenos Aires (where two groups of worshipers were founded, to the surprise of many who had never known of the existence of African culture in Argentina), with other conferences holding in New York, Havana and elsewhere. However, the Congress has fallen on hard times. It is now in a state of near stagnation due to several events and circumstances all of which underscore the great difficulty of making real progress in a world where African culture is considered inferior. In the glorious 80s, the Congress was a masterpiece of solidarity. One still recalls the zealous exchanges, the magnificent plans, the determination etched on every face, the joy of being... together.

Salvador remains the symbol of one's memories of those times past, as well as the hope for times to come, because the realities of Yoruba are there, perpetually and absolutely. *Oxumare House, Edificio Ogum Onire, Ogunja, Edificio Logun Ede, Teatro Yemanja, Orixas Center*, these are some of the names of buildings, places, streets, and city-sectors in Salvador. Individuals are proud to tell you their Yoruba names, such as *Nike, Oke, Tomiua* (the name of the present leader of *Casa Branca*). In addition to the ever popular *acarajè*, Bahian cuisine is full of many other Yoruba delicacies. And one notes that in religious sacrifices and rituals, the essential ingredients are still called *epo, omi, obi, atare, oti, efum, orobo...*

The following is a brief comparative list of Brazilian (Portuguese) and Yoruba words. Quite a bit of the information here is found in John T. Schneider, *Dictionary of African Borrowings in Brazilian Portuguese* (1991).

Portuguese	Yoruba	Meaning
aba (ababa)	agba (agbagba)	elder(s), in religion and generally
ababa	agbada	vase, wide-necked container
ababaloalo	babala(w)o	Ifa priest
abara	abara	small, spicy cake of grated beans wrapped in banana leaves
abo	agbo	Ram
acaraje	akara	bean cake fried in palm oil with spicy sauce (Yoruba *je* = eat)
agogo	agogo	bell, percussion instrument
axe	ashe	power, spiritual foundation, faith in realization of hope; in Brazil, each of the sacred objects on the Candomblé altar; also, name of group; the word has become very (maybe, too) common, now used in everything.
arioko	ara oko	"bush" (ignorant) person; stranger attending Candomblé ceremony out of curiosity
camba	kamba	control, contain; amulet placed behind door to ward off evil spirits
canafo	kan naa fo	someone who speaks; in cult, an old priest of Ifa, god of divination
chugudu	shigidi	malevolent spirit; black magic rites, with black hen as fetish
cufar	ku	to die
ebo	ebo	sacrifice; offering to a deity
ebo	egbo	pounded corn, corn meal and palm oil, with beans
efo	efo	vegetables; typical Bahian

		cuisine of vegetables, shrimps, palm oil and fish
eleba	elegbara	possessor, title of Eshu; Eshu agbara, force, power
eparrei	eepaa (eparipa)	exclamation of terror, announcement of Ogboni fraternity members in procession; greeting by devotees of Candomblé god, Iansa
iale	iyale	elder wife; in Brazil, favorite wife
iao	iyawo	wife; title of girl initiated in Candomblé immediately after her ritual bath, wife of the orixas
irukere	irukere	oxtail fan; emblem of Oxossi, god of hunters and forest
ixe	ishi/ishin	tree with edible fruits; central post of Candomblé house
jagunco	ajagun	soldier, warrior; *jagun*, title of descendants of warriors; pejoratively, bad man, tough, body-guard of mill or of plantation owner
laguidiba	lagidigba	black beads worn by women around waist; used in ritual for the deities
mocoto	bokoto	dish made of cow's knuckles
Nago	Nago, Anago	Yoruba; used pejoratively in secular connotation as a lousy person; note also, gege (from Yoruba, ajeji), foreigner, to Yoruba; now used for Ewe, Fon nations; pejoratively, strange, abnormal; in Jamaica, nango; Trinidad, Haiti, Sierra Leone, nago; Cuba, anago.

Oba	Oba	a. River in Yorubaland; goddess, one of Sango's wives; b. King; the twelve priests of Xango in Axé Opo Afonja, representing the ancient priests of Oyo
ogo	ogo, ego	a lot of money; in Brazil, a kind of fool's gold; scepter, magical object of Exu
opele	opele	Ifa divination artifact
oquico	akuko	cock; in Brazil, chicken
oriki	oriki	praise song, family history through list of qualities; greeting for particular deities
orobo	orogbo	fruit used in religious ceremonies
orunco	oruko	name; naming ceremony of revelation of Orixa to initiate
peji	pejo	assemble; main altar of sanctuary decked out in ornaments
umulucu	muluke	dish of black beans cooked with oil and shrimps
xaxara	shasha	smallpox marks; sheaf of straw pieces decorated with sea shells, for Omolu, god of smallpox
xequere	shekere	calabash covered with cowries used as musical instrument

As for the names of deities, one finds many, including the following: Egum, Exu, Ibeji, Iemanja (Yemanja), Iansa, Ifa, Obaluae, Obatala, Oxala, Ogum, Omolu, Oxossi, Oxum, Oxunmare, Xango, among others.

YORUBA CULTURE AS BASIS FOR REVOLUTION
One does not have to be an etymologist to capture the deep-rooted relationship between Yoruba and Brazilian Portuguese. Now, language is a function of culture. Proof of that is the brief analysis that we have done on religion. Another indisputable proof is a close

look at the socio-political development of Black Brazil. In their continuous struggle for freedom, African Brazilians look up to several role-models in and out of their country. The greatest and the most respected of them all is Zumbi, head of state of Palmares located in Serra da Barriga in what is now known as the States of Pernambuco and Alagoas. Palmares was a self-declared independent state of maroon (revolutionary) slaves who resisted the Portuguese and Dutch colonialists for a century (1595-1696). Scholars have provided data showing the very strong Yoruba components of the revolutionary state known as *quilombo*. The word means, maroon society, similar to others in Cuba, Haiti and elsewhere, all examples of the slaves' heroism and constant efforts to regain and retain their independence and humanity. "Quilombo" brings to my own mind the Yoruba, *ki lo nbo*, that is, "what's happening/going to happen/what's approaching?" It would thus be a password, a call to everyone to be alert, indicating the slaves' solidarity and readiness to keep away the enemy, and to stand up to any adversaries. The word has become part of the lexicon of Brazilian society, specifically the Black community fighting to assert their freedom. *Quilombismo*, a derivation, is the philosophy, the ideology, the ideal of Black revolution. In the late 40s, Abdias do Nascimento founded a newspaper, *Quilombo*, and in 1980 he published a book, *O Quilombismo*, in which he analyzes the history of African-Brazilian revolution and urges Blacks to develop their own ideology, using the African system as practiced in Palmares as a springboard for their organization. Now, Palmares, as rightly stated by critics, was not a one-culture state: "However 'African' in character, no maroon social, political, religious or aesthetic system can be reliably traced to a specific tribal provenience; they reveal, rather, their syncretic composition. The political system of Palmares, for example, did not derive from a particular central African model, but from several."[17]

One cannot disagree with Price's notion of syncretic formation, even though I would prefer to talk of a synthesis, so as to underline the harmony and oneness sought and attained. The fact of oral tradition does not help any effort at particularizing cultural contributions. Which does not remove the fact that Yoruba was a cohesive force in Palmares. In organizing the society, the Yoruba system of *obaship* was used and, interestingly enough, the *oba* was elected bearing in mind his prowess and leadership qualities. Zumbi, the last king of independent Palmares, was, indeed, a *Balogun*. Wole Soyinka, Nigeria's Nobel laureate in literature, has mentioned the significance of Ogun in maroon societies: "Ogun for his part becomes not merely the god of war but the god of revolution in the most contemporary context (...) As the Roman Catholic props of the Batista regime in Cuba discovered when it was too late, they should have worried less about Karl Marx than about Ogun, the rediscovered deity of revolution."[18] Zumbi's exploits recall those of Ogun and the organization of Palmares makes one think of the great Yoruba kingdoms. If Ogun was of vital importance, it did not preclude the essential roles of other deities; for, the state was not geared towards wars (circumstantial) but was constructed to forge a community enjoying perpetual peace, prosperity and stability (essential).

A basic aspect of that essence is religion. Here again, it was largely predicated upon the teachings of Ifa. In his book, *Zumbi dos Palmares, a Historia que não foi contada* (Rio de Janeiro: Sociedade Iorubana da Cultura Afro-Brasileira, 1988), Eduardo Fonseca Junior traces the history of Palmares and Zumbi. He describes in-depth the religious system, including the ritual performed at every meeting of the elders in the oval-shaped chamber "with walls made of palm-leaves and a long central pole called *opanla*." (p.143) Among the priests present were: Bumbushe and Bambushe called "Baba Alapala, egungun" (p.145). The latter, during the deliberations, would speak Yoruba: "Vodum Oluwo, ti orile ede Mahii, loci be niti Ijoba Balogun Zumbi" (Oluwo, great traditional leader of the Mahii nation, is leaving for the kingdom of the Great Warrior, Zumbi). The other elder asks: "Ki leui l'oruko Ijoba Zumbi?" (What is the name of Zumbi's kingdom?) The response: "Palmares m'okurim." (Palmares, my son.)

Fonseca Junior lists the names of inhabitants of Palmares, such as Akinbiyi, Dotsun, Dumdum, Shegum. He informs us that the name, Zumbi, is of Ewe/Fon (Togo/Dahomey) origin, meaning, immortal, fantastic, divine. The linguist, John Schneider (*Dictionary...*, p. 295), claims that the name probably owes its origin to Kikongo (Congo), meaning, god. Meanwhile, Fonseca Junior notes that Zumbi himself has been identified as coming from the Yoruba nation. From that perspective, his original name, we are told, was

Ogundele. All these discrepancies notwithstanding, Zumbi's extraordinary actions and the civilized system established in Palmares have led to his and his state's recognition among today's Blacks and in Brazil as a whole, so that November 26 is a national day.

In areas of agriculture (plurality of crops), socio-political organization (democratic monarchy), and the total culture (importance of African deities and the committee of elders), Yoruba has helped to promote and project a revolution that has continued into the end of the 20th century. Yoruba pride and progressiveness, its adaptability and concept of harmony, contributed to the creation of the greatness of Palmares, while its spirit of self-respect and self-affirmation is helping the contemporary Black community to move forward in what is called *negritud* (Negritude).

It is not accidental that one of the great architects of Brazil's Pan-Africanism, Abdias do Nascimento, has proudly declared the impact of his sojourn in Nigeria on his struggle. The text of his acerbic dismantling of Brazilian racism, *O Genocidio do Negro Brasileiro* (1978) was first presented as a lecture at Ile-Ife, cradle of Yoruba culture. With regard to Zumbi, in the current Black struggle in Brazil, he has been categorically declared to be Yoruba. A controversial position, to be sure; but, one must admit that it does have definite, positive objectives: it is in the best interests of African Brazilians mired in the depths of racism and economic dispossession to seek strength from a respected culture that would therefore serve as symbol and springboard for revolution. The Brazilian action is similar to that of the great regretted Cuban poet, Nicolás Guillén. When the poet declares, "I am Yoruba," he does not mean a biological, categorical filiation, but a resounding expression of pride in a culture that, through its excellence and strength, represents the ethos of all those carried across the Atlantic.

CONCLUSION: OF CONTRIBUTIONS AND CONTRADICTIONS

In considering the impact of Yoruba life and culture in Brazil, one should never forget that inclusiveness, not exclusivism, is of foremost importance. That is exactly what Pan-Africanism connotes. The condition of African Brazilians demands such a conceptualization of culture. Abdias do Nascimento reminds us:

"The color of our skin, in all its varied and sundry shades, functions only as a badge of our African origin, the root of our identity. *Mulato, cafuso, negro, escurinho, moreno*: all the famous euphemisms converge toward this identity, which the ruling elites in Brazil have always tried to disclaim. Therefore, when we are denied a job or shown the service entrance, it is not only our skin color that provokes the discrimination, but above all the African identity announced by the color of our skin." (71-72) If Yoruba culture rightly represents that proud African identity, it is sometimes unfortunate that the positive image is not encouraged from within the ancestral continent. In spite of the aforementioned activities of the Congress of Orisha Tradition, Ifa as a religion has long been relegated to the role of secondary support whose quality is mired in shadiness and the cover of darkness. The presence and progress of our traditional religion in Brazil and other diasporan societies is therefore largely due to the resilience and faith of the diasporan Africans themselves. One is nonetheless consoled by little hints of success or re-awakening on the African continent: for example, in January 1996, the government of the Republic of Benin enacted a law recognizing voudou as an official religion. Hopefully, other countries, particularly Nigeria, will come to realize that our own religion has as much validity as any other, and maybe more, for our own reality.

The solidarity within the Brazilian Candomblé noticed by several researchers[19] is somewhat deceptive when one thinks of the competition for prominence among the innumerable *Ile Axé*. The religion is being exploited by self-serving material-minded adepts, a good number of whom have not been properly trained and initiated. For the good of the religion, there ought to be more cooperation among members of the cult, as well as between them and their brothers and sisters in Africa. The Orisha Congress could help in this regard. Without order and regulations, there is always the danger that Candomblé will continue to drift, that it will remain on the periphery in a society with majority Black population but with no representation in the political establishment.[20] Once again, it cannot be over-emphasized that African culture must be brought to the center. As Abdias remarks, "the African cultural matrix is still seen as exotic and classed as folklore, while European norms and values prevail in Bahian society." (p.146)

During this critic's several visits to Brazil, there invariably comes a moment of sorrow and shame, when African Brazilians fail to assert themselves, when they do not recognize the realities of racism described in this essay, when they do not seize the instant to use their powerful religion and culture as force of revolution. Unlike in Africa, their chances for doing this are enormous because Candomblé, the racist underpinnings of Brazil notwithstanding, has a great deal of socio-political, and economic, potential. The priests and priestesses are already the psychologists and doctors of the poor; more importantly, they have to become leaders working hand in hand with secular comrades to lift the people out of their socio-political and economic hell.

One wonders whether the kind of lack of organization noticed among the end-of-twentieth-century continental Yoruba might not be a negative characteristic carried over by the African Brazilian. That laid-back, merry-making, carnivalesque attitude, that fatalism couched in a certain resignation to fate and to the wishes of the Orisha, that propensity for laughter when one ought to cry out loud and say an emphatic no to the forces of dehumanization, could they be the shared heritage of the Yoruba on the West African coast and the descendants of slaves in the Brazilian diaspora? Lived experiences, because they are so tragic, can easily lead one to pessimism.

Yet, one cannot afford to despair. The African Brazilian offers reasons to hope, what with the ever-present notion of axé,[21] the spiritual foundation of the religion and culture, the power to realize dreams and desires, to foresee future bliss, the will to transform hell into heaven on earth and, finally, the faith in one's abilities and the deities' willingness to accede to one's prayers. *Ashe*!

Notes

1. Nicolás Guillén, *Obra poética*, tomo 1 (La Habana: Instituto Cubano de Libro, 1972), p. 114. (Translation from Spanish mine.)
2. Abdias do Nascimento, *Africans in Brazil, a Pan-African Perspective* (Trenton, NJ: Africa World Press, 1992), p.63.
3. Ibid., p.88.

4. The official maxim of *Casa Branca*, one of Bahia's oldest and most important African religion (*Candomblé*) houses. The language used is Yoruba. Translated, it means: Whoever does good does it for him or herself; same for whoever does bad. Good and bad have their respective repercussions. If your soul is clean, the fly of evil will stay far away from you.

5. Lydia Cabrera, quoted in Femi Ojo-Ade, *On Black Culture* (Ile-Ife: Obafemi Awolowo University Press, 1989), p.167.

6. For further discussions on the issue, and on Yoruba influences in the Caribbean, see *On Black Culture*, pp. 85-102; 164-174.

7. Abdias do Nascimento, p. 89.

8. In my book, *Being Black, Being Human* (Ile-Ife: Obafemi Awolowo University Press, 1996), I have studied this phenomenon in-depth. In his book quoted earlier, Abdias do Nascimento has also made very insightful remarks on the question.

9. See Martin Casanova, "The Negro in Latin America," *Présence Africaine*, 24-25 (Feb. 1959), pp. 328-333.

10. Quoted from Antonio Agnelo Percival, "Notícia sumaria sobre a Casa Branca," published by the House and handed out to visitors. Antonio is president.

11. According to a copy of the unpublished biographical data put together and given to this critic by Ieda Machado Ribeiro dos Santos, professional librarian and Cabinet Director at the Bahian historical center, Fundação Gregório dos Mattos, Mãe Olga is a descendant of the Ketu princess, Ojaro, founder of *Ilé Maroialaji* (better known as *Alaketu*). Olga became the head of the House in 1948 and has collaborated with individuals and groups, including the University's Afro-Oriental Center, in promoting African culture and religion. Olga visited Nigeria in 1974 and 1977. Note that Nasso, indeed, exists in Yoruba; for example Akinaso.

12. Researchers of African-Brazilian religion often refer to the strangeness of the songs heard at Candomble ceremonies (cf. John Schneider, *Dictionary of African Borrowings in Brazilian Portuguese,* Hamburg: Helmut Buske Verlag, 1991, p.xii). While it is true that the singers themselves do not understand many of the songs, it is important to emphasize that the language is easily recognized as Yoruba, *ijinle Yoruba*, the authentic, ancient language dating back to the beginning of slavery in the sixteenth century. An analogy would be the experience of the Quebecois in Canada. In their case, they have been fortunate to maintain their language and culture, while the African slaves in Brazil were forced to (almost) forget.

13. The Brazilian carnival takes place in February or March of each year, depending on the date of Easter. It enjoys a worldwide reputation as an event marked by pomp and promiscuity on a grand scale, where total freedom and joy exist. A showcase for the ideal of a nonracial and non-class society, perhaps; the celebration, however, shows the superficiality and surface-only happiness hiding the realities of racism and social oppression and deprivation at the roots of that society. With regard to Yoruba culture in that setting, it is true to say that *carnaval* often has Yoruba themes, honoring the deities and depicting historical and cultural events.

    For example, Antonio Rosario, *Carnaval ijexá, notas sobre afoxés e blocos do novo carnaval afrobaiano* (Salvador, BA: Corrúpio, 1981), has done an excellent study of the Yoruba (Ijesha) groups involved in Bahia's carnival.

14. Quoted from *Olodum, grupo cultural,* tom/91. It is noteworthy that, unlike other groups, *Olodum* has remained in the same place where it was founded, in Pelourinho, the slave quarters of Salvador; thus, it has retained its popular roots. (Translation from Portuguese, mine.)

15. "Folclorização do culto afro preocupa ialorixa," *Tribuna da Bahia,* Oct.16, 1987. Translation is mine. An African-Brazilian intellectual who once taught Portuguese at Obafemi Awolowo University, Ile-Ife, Antonio Vieira da Silva, makes a cogent point in support of the positive intellectual and artistic presence in Candomblé, in his unpublished presentation at the 2nd Conference of the International Congress of Orisha Tradition, held in Salvador-Bahia in July 1983: "Relevância social dos Orixas nos Cultos Afro-Brasileiros." Among those he lists as being deeply influenced are: Abdias do Nascimento, the dramatist-activist-politician to whose work we have referred in this essay, Gilberto Gil and Clara Nuñes (singers), and Carybé (artist). Music is one area where Yoruba cultural impact is most visible. Bahia's radio is constantly resonating with names of Orishas and Yoruba words come up again and again. For example, there is a record/compact disc, *Afro Brasil,* Verve, 1990, with the following song-titles: *Uma historia de Ifa (Ejigbo); Malé Debalé; Um canto de Afoxé para o bloco de Ilé; Ilé Aiyé; Ifa um canto para subir; Two naira fifty kobo; Ijexá, filhos de Gandhi, etc.* Note the references to the religion (Ifa); to Ijesha and to Ejigbo, two areas deep in Yorubaland; to Afoshe, the power to predict, to make desires and dreams come true; to Ile Aiye, the earth, the world; and to Nigeria's currency, the naira and kobo.

16. From time to time, individual leaders complain aloud. Announcements are made about investigating and dealing with cases of fraudu-

lent priests. For example, see Ogam Gilberto A. Ferreira, "Asiwaju" (editorial), in *Umbanda e Candomblé*, ano 1 no. 6, 1987 p.2.
Everyone involved in Candomblé would appear to agree that some form of regulation is necessary for establishing shrines. For the case of the *Egungun* cult, see Julio Braga, *Ancestralidade Afro-Brasileira, o culto de baba egum* (Salvador, BA: Edufba/Ianamá/CEAO, 1992):, pp.100-101.

17. Richard Price, *Maroon Societies: Rebel Slave Communities in the Americas* (Baltimore: Johns Hopkins University Press, 1976), p.29.

18. Soyinka, *Myth, Literature and the African World* (London: Cambridge University Press, 1976), p.54.

19. For example, Antonio Vieira da Silva, "Relevância social dos Orixas nos cultos afro-brasileiros."

20. The lack of organization at the religious level permeates the other facets of life. With a bit of purposeful, united action, the African Bahians can easily have elected not only a Black mayor for the city of Salvador, but a state governor.

21. Cf. Abdias do Nascimento, *Axés do sangue e da esperança* (Rio de Janeiro: Achiame, 1983).

CHAPTER 25

AFRICA IN THE YEAR 2000: PROSPECTS AND CHALLENGES*

-Did we fight for freedom to eliminate one another?[1]

- We are no longer your monkeys! (...) No Congolese worthy of the name will ever be able to forget that this independence has been won through a struggle (...) We have known the atrocious sufferings (...) of those exiled in their own country. Their fate was truly worse than death itself.[2]

-*Eni ti a fe sunje ko gbodo f'epo para ko joko tina.*[3]

-The West shouts, but soon enough holds its tongue.[4]

- The isolation of exile is a gutted warehouse at the back of pleasure streets.[5]

AFRICA, "THE LAST UNTAMED CONTINENT"

While expressing my sincere gratitude to Wisconsin's African Students Association for inviting me as keynote speaker, I recall my last visit to this campus some twenty years ago, as a young man attending the annual conference of the African Literature Association. The evolution of myself, Africa, the United States of America (generally referred to as America) and, indeed, the world during that period, provides adequate data for the discussion in which I would like to engage you today. We are here to diagnose the state and situation, the conditions and circumstances, the disease and the dilemma afflicting a patient named Africa, Mother Africa, to find out what she is today and what she would be tomorrow (and I insist on *tomorrow* because, contrary to our dream of longevity, the year 2000 is but a short breath away). And we may be fearful of tomorrow, like the debtor praying for the pay-up day to never come. As the Yoruba say, *o pe, o ya, ogun odun si nbo a kola.* (Twenty years will soon become tomorrow, just one day away.) So, our interest is, to know what our yesterday was; what today is, and what tomorrow will/would/could be: It all depends on the doctor's identity, his/her state of mind, training, affinity, hopes and dreams, or even a hidden agenda! Let me warn you that I, far from being a doctor in this exercise, am actually a patient...

When I came to this university in 1977, I presented a paper on the late South African writer, Bessie Head. I received a standing ovation while at the same time starting a controversy over the issue of African Woman's condition, including the matter of circumcision. *The Milwaukee Journal* (April 3, 1977, p.6) interviewed me and, to say the least, the report was quite interesting. In this address, we shall review, among other themes, what has transpired between then and now, in regard to the African Woman. As a preview, we would note that the voice of the Western feminist, once a whisper in the 70s, has evolved into a scowling, scolding shout and, as in several other cases, the Africans, male and female, have followed the mistress and the master, and some have disappeared beneath the sands of the Sahara.

Before we begin our prognosis in detail, that is, by appreciating our past (glorious, real, not some dead fossil excavated by civilized anthropologists to prove its primitivity and disprove its superiority), and by tracing its debasement and near destruction into a shadow of our self, and the metamorphosis of the shadow into a present prepared by colonizers quite successful in bludgeoning and bastardizing our brains through the *mission civilisatrice* birthing Franco-, Anglo-, Luso- and other pseudo-Africans unaware of their alienation; before we unravel the mysteries of our present predicament and tragedy, to project a future out of the seemingly endless tunnel, let us look at Africa with the jaundiced eye of the *civilized.*

Before coming here, I decided to watch again the award-winning docu-drama, "Roots." You probably remember one of the scenes on the boat, when the young Alex Haley was a sailor. He informs his superior in the kitchen of his dream of faraway Africa, home of his ancestors. The latter, shocked, comments: "Africa! All I know about Africa comes from watching Tarzan in the movies." The connotation is quite clear: Africa symbolizes savagery. In 1996, America is still fixated on that same symbol, maybe more so than ever before. Perhaps the ultimate insult to an African American is, to tell him or her to go back to Africa! Look around you. *The Washington Post* of February 11, 1996 reported a meeting between the French extreme-rightist and racist, Jean-Marie Le Pen, and his Russian brother, the ultra nationalist Vladimir Zhirinovsky. Both great men, great patriots, discussed their plan to bring closer Europe's far right. They foresaw the possibility of war between their two countries over NATO expansion into Eastern Europe. Zhirinovsky, full of "jokes [and] bonhomie," said: "We will send in the Chechens. France will send her African Negroes. Jean-Marie will be in Paris drinking French wine, and I will be in Moscow drinking vodka. From time to time, we'll phone each other to tot up how many Chechens and Negroes have been killed." (A27)

In the United States, what matters is the image and its impact on the gullible public: "You gotta sell, baby!" As you sit before the small or big screen, or read your dailies, you witness the unmasking -never intentional, hardly conscious- of a monster that you had been made to believe was put to death by the lethal injection of legislation. Look around you. You will find the renaissance of racism, the re-birth of bigotry and, as it was in the beginning, so it is now, Black, that is, Africa, is the bearer of the burden. Prestigious *Time* magazine had emblazoned in red on its cover of September 7, 1992, *The Agony of Africa*. The cover-story was titled, "Africa: The Scramble for Existence" (did the journalist think of the notorious scramble for our unfortunate continent?), with an accompanying 19th century picture of Burkinabe miners sifting for gold, and the statement, "Rich in resources, Africa has been kept poor by bad government." (40-41) On other pages were the usual vomit-inducing, prize-winning pictures: naked, big-bellied skeletons paraded as children; gun-wielding, wild-eyed "rebels;" giant vultures voraciously eyeing a woman cutting up some gaunt-looking meat (of a human being, some imaginative readers might conclude!); corpses piled on a wheelbarrow waiting for mass burial; a horde of starving human beings held in check behind iron-bars "wait patiently for food to be distributed by the International Red Cross..." Finally, in another article, "In African-American Eyes" (53), the brilliant journalist warns those harboring any pride or hope for the ancestral motherland: "Now is time to face some unpleasant truths under the veil of romanticism." The message is, that Africa is sunk in perpetual savage disorder and drift, and African Americans should thank their stars for being saved by almighty Civilization (the audience, hopefully, recognizes the irony in the use of this word). Interestingly, almost two years after *Time*'s special issue, another prestigious publication, *The Washington Post* (Sept. 4, 1994, p. A1), carried a front-page story, "Africa in Agony," mentioning a basic fact often ignored or downplayed by those suffering from bad memory, hypocrisy, or blatant wickedness: "Africa largely disappeared from the agenda of the major powers *after the conflicts that interested them came to an end*"(emphasis mine). We must add a point of clarification, that interest in Africa has always been out of the desire to exploit and to control (capitalism or communism) and, to achieve these civilized objectives, any means was, and is, deemed necessary, including the most base and the most beastly.

We have a most recent proof of America's sole interest in economics, as far as Africa is concerned. *The Journal of Commerce* (Feb. 15, 1996) reports on President Clinton's new plan for Africa, "a place where most people earn well under $1,000 a year, where one of every two citizens is illiterate and one in 10 has access to electricity, where the foreign debt often exceeds the nation's output." In other words, sub-Saharan Africa is underdeveloped and has to be developed. Clinton has set up an interagency Africa Trade and Development Coordinating Group. Commerce Secretary Ronald Brown has traveled to Africa on a "historic mission." European businessmen have been put on notice that Europe's 40% share of the sub-Saharan import market is no longer acceptable. United States' share of the booty, presently less than 8%, must be boosted and Brown, an African American, has lobbied on behalf of American companies bidding on a combined $9.2 billion in contracts. As an after-thought, mention is made of a "change [that] has begun to sweep the continent," in regards to "democracy."

If we have spent time to emphasize the *image* of Africa presented to the foreign (precisely American) public, it is to make you aware that the myth of our savagery, our backwardness, our beastliness, is very far from dead. As Walter Rodney (*How Europe Underdeveloped Africa:* 251) notes, colonialism (and slavery) made Africans *objects of history:* "Colonialism had only one hand -it was a one-armed bandit." The mission to civilize us has succeeded immensely. The myth of Africa has been so well promoted that many of us have not only internalized but manifested it in our psyche and conduct. Listen, for example, to the statement by one charismatic Father of the Ivorian nation, Houphouet-Boigny: "Colonialism was a good thing for Africa. Thanks to it, we have one united Ivorian nation, rather than 60 tribes who know nothing about each other." (Ayittey, *Africa Betrayed*, St. Martin's Press, 1992: 192) We would like to de-mystify any other thankful son of colonialism; to debunk the lie about Africans as having no prior knowledge of democracy before the coming of the European; to analyze our present problems of poor leadership as basic irresponsibility aided and abetted by their foreign mentors' obdurate economic imperialism; to proffer actions and attitudes capable of helping us become what we once were, that is, makers of history.

Before discussing what has happened to the history made by us, let me bring to your attention another image of overwhelming impact: that of a Nissan television advertisement, captioned, "Africa, The Last Untamed Continent," with the gorgeous car emerging among a bevy of beasts in the legendary African jungle, maybe as proof that our animals, too, can drive cars... At least, the thing invites you to go on safari!

THE PAST: A LOST CIVILIZATION?

Before you purchase your ticket for that summer flight to Exotica, let us explore together the real civilization of Africa which our civilizers would rather relegate to the footnotes of history or, preferably, disregard because it gives evidence of humanity, if not of superiority. This evidence is found in books that Westerners refuse to read: several by Cheikh Anta Diop,[6] the text to which I refer in this lecture being *The Cultural Unity of Africa, The Domains of Matriarchy and Patriarchy in Classical Antiquity* (London: Karnak House, 1989); Ivan T. Sertima, *They Came Before Columbus* (Random House, 1976), and the already quoted Walter Rodney. Two recent books have captured the content of our past and suggest a way forward from our present predicament: George Ayittey's *Africa Betrayed* (1992) and Herbert Ekwe-Ekwe's *Africa 2001* (Reading: International Institute for Black Research, 1993).

These African (not Africanist) researchers show categorically that Egypt, "humanity's first documented civilization" (Ekwe-Ekwe: 60), was Black.[7] They affirm and confirm Africa's original qualities, and control of her heritage. They show that our civilization was a colossus: "Instead of presenting itself to history as an insolvent debtor, the Black world of the Egyptian is the initiator of the 'western' civilization flaunted before our eyes today. Pythagoran mathematics, the theory of the four elements of Thales of Miletus, Epicurian materialism, Platonic idealism, Judaism, Islam, and modern science, are rooted in Egyptian cosmology and science. To his great surprise and satisfaction, [the Black African reader] will discover that most of the ideas used today to domesticate, atrophy, dissolve, or steal his 'soul', were conceived by his own ancestors." (Ekwe-Ekwe: 61)

African civilization was a humanism, with emphasis being placed on the welfare and survival of the human. Diop (108) meticulously analyzes the much debated condition of the African woman. Matriarchy was the system in many societies. "Matriarchy is not an absolute and cynical triumph of woman over man; it is a harmonious dualism, an association accepted by both sexes, the better to build a sedentary society where each and everyone could fully develop by following the activity best suited to his physiological nature. A matriarchal regime, far from being imposed on man by circumstances independent of his will, is accepted and defended by him." Patriarchy came as a result of outside influences, specifically Islam and Christianity, as well as Europe's secular presence. We again quote Diop: "The African who has been converted to Islam is automatically ruled, at least as far as his inheritance is concerned, by the patriarchal regime. It is the same with the Christian, whether Protestant or Catholic. But in addition, colonial legislation tends everywhere to give an official status to these private choices, as is attested by a verdict delivered at Diourbel in 1936 by the Commissioner Champion, regarding the inheritance of the lands of the village of Thiatou, near Gaouane." (113)

As for polygamy, we must declare that it is not only in Africa that it has been practiced; it was common among the upper classes in German aristocracy, in Greece, in Asia, and in Egyptian royalty. At the level of the mass of the people, in Africa, monogamy was the norm; indeed, Diop points out that it was as an attempt to deceive themselves about their social rank that some in the lower class became polygamists. (see Diop: 114)

With regard to the alleged ill-treatment of African women, Diop uses the matriarchal conception to show up the lie. Matriarchy implies a kind of rigidity in the daily lives of man and woman. By the division of labor, man did tasks involving "risks, power, force and endurance; if, as a result of a changed situation due to the intervention of some outside factor -cessation of a state of war, etc... the tasks of a man came to be whittled down, so much the worse for the woman: she would nonetheless continue to carry out the household duties and others reserved to her by society. The diminution of the tasks of the man comes from the suppression of national sovereignties which causes the disappearance of a large fraction of the tasks of responsibility (...) The European travelers who crossed Africa like meteors often brought back piteous, striking descriptions of the fate of these poor women, who were made to work by their husbands, while the latter rested in the shade. In contrast, the Europeans who have visited Africa and stayed there for a greater or lesser period of time, are not sorry for the African women: they find them very happy." (115)

African woman was not relegated to secondary or second-class roles. Witness the life of Queen Hatshepsout of Egypt, "the first queen in the history of humanity" (Diop: 103). Her reign, marked by an all-inclusive ideology, is to be contrasted with that of the Amazons whose legend has been used to show women's superiority over men. Diop informs us that the Amazons living in Libya belonged not to a sedentary, Black nation but to a nomadic, European group. Their society had nothing matriarchal; "it reflects rather, although it is only a legend, the unpitying and systematic vengeance of one sex on another." (Diop: 108)

In matriarchal Africa, married women retained their names. The adoption of the father's name for the children stemmed from Arabic influence (the Islamization of West Africa began with the

Almoravidia movement in the 10th century). The importance of Mother in all of Africa is an indisputable fact: "The accent is always on the mother proper, 'the mother who bore me.'" (62) The Ashanti say, "To show disrespect to a mother is equivalent to committing a sacrilege."

The system of government in precolonial Africa was, democratic. It is true that kingdoms proliferated, with kings, queens, and chiefs. However, the head was not a dictator. To be king, one had to possess "the greatest vital force in the kingdom" (Ayittey: 52). For example, in selection of a Yoruba king, "the main objective was to select the best candidate, and the qualities that were most important were good character, unselfishness, and the willingness to listen to advice." (Ayittey: 58) Sanctions were brought against a dictatorial or despotic king and he could be destooled, sent into exile, or even killed. "Enstoolment and destoolment were the right of the people." (Ayittey: 61) The chief was no autocrat. He played a consultative role. He ruled in conjunction with an inner council, a council of elders, and the village assembly. All in all, traditional society had a pattern of checks and balances against tyranny.

The bond between the individual and the community, referred to as communalism -not to be confused with communism-, permeated the society. Nonetheless, contrary to the misconception that the emphasis on the group meant the individual's loss of importance, the truth is, that rights and responsibilities went hand in hand. "The individual at every stage of life had a series of duties and obligations to others in the society as well as a set of rights: namely, things that he or she could expect or demand from other individuals." (Rodney: 45) Freedom of expression, the right to criticize authorities, these were normal aspects of a human being's existence (see Chancellor Williams, *The Destruction of Black Civilization*, 1987: 174). For policies and decisions, consensus was the norm, not majority, winner-takes-all, Eurocentric democracy. "The process of consensus-building ensured that minority positions were not only heard but also taken into account in negotiations." (Ayittey: 72)

As far as religion was concerned, we know how much fun our detractors have had with references to animism, stone-worship, paganism, and other habits fit for the sub-human savages that our society was supposed to breed. Which does not remove the fact that African traditional religion (cf. *Ifa* of the Yoruba) is more human and humanist than many others. *Odu Ifa*, the corpus of Yoruba religion, contains much more wisdom and ideal of a happy life than you will ever find in the Bible or the Koran. According to Diop and others, the teachings of Egyptian religion have been imitated in the two latter texts.

Now, the rich African civilization briefly described above became the object of various "civilizing missions," begun by Arabs and continued by Europeans. The results have no doubt been devastating. From slavery through colonialism to neocolonialism, freedom has become fettered; our culture, shackled; our civilization, shattered, shocked into subservience to Europe. Call it the final frontier of the process of development. And some would jump for joy at the mission accomplished.

Europe, become the superior adventurer and conqueror (note: any declared universalism is but a euphemism for Eurocentrism), will not relent in her racist, self-gratifying actions and attitudes. As some of us are becoming aware, "there will always be racism in the West and elsewhere." (Ayittey: 6) Hence, we would do well to desist from explaining away all of Africa's problems in terms of the racist paradigm, or the constant cankerworm of imperialism. A valid advice, but one that also underscores the gravity of our sad condition.

DECOLONIZATION AND NEOCOLONIALISM: OF LEADERS AND LYNCHERS

The question I would like to ask is this: With our civilization having been stripped of its glory, leaving us with a carcass of which we are supposed to be ashamed, what must we do? First, let us review what our leaders have done, and are doing. The struggle for independence apparently led to freedom and nationhood. Freedom-fighters, patriots, nationalists, they were all heroes ushering us into new heavens on earth. Some had the gift of the gab, brilliant brains molded into perfection at the colonial school. They sat at the round table with the colonizers with whom they held "constructive negotiations." Others, fiery fighters, guerrilla warriors, shamed the invaders into submission. Whether through armed or armchair struggle, Africa finally attained Independence. Disappointingly, it led to an era of neo-colonialism, of neo-dependence, of what Ayittey calls a betrayal of Africa by our leaders. "For many countries independence meant only a change in the color of administrators from white to black." (Ayittey: 100) Ayittey blames "the nationalists and elites" who led us to independence for not "building a national consensus." (209) I beg to disagree: There was no nation to begin with, and many so-called nationalists were stooges of Europe, or pseudo-patriots; hence, the impossibility of building a consensus.

In order to understand the depth of today's economic devastation and socio-political dilemma, let us bear in mind that:

1. the "nations" were/are mostly artificial creations, mere geographical entities consequential to the whims and caprices of the scramblers for Africa, who were not in the least interested in the cultures and survival of the "savage tribes jumping from tree to tree in the African jungle."

2. Africa's natural resources were, and are, abundant: "It has 40 percent of the world's potential hydroelectric power supply, the bulk of the world's diamonds and chromium, 30 percent of the uranium in the noncommunist world, 50 percent of the world's gold, 90 percent of its phosphates, 40 percent of its platinum, 7.5 percent of its coal, 8 percent of its known petroleum reserves, 12 percent of its natural gas, 3 percent of its iron ore, and millions upon millions of acres of untilled agricultural land. Without [Africa's] essential minerals [manganese, copper, bauxite, nickel, lead, cobalt which is critical in the manufacture of jet engines, rhodium, palladium, vanadium, titanium], many industrial plants in the West would grind to a standstill." (Ayittey: 2-3) No other continent is blessed with such natural wealth and diversity.

Our leaders, from independence in the late 50s and early 60s until now, in 1996, have been at the vanguard of economic wastage, looting of treasuries, daylight robbery in all its forms, material dipsomania, megalomania, and an insatiable craze for power. To retain power, they have used and used up people, through sinecures and contracts with astronomical "mobilization fees" (which means, the contract does not have to be fulfilled once the up-front percentage cash has been paid, often in foreign currency), political patronage rewarding sycophants and all sorts of "patriotic" praise-singers and, for the minority rejecting manipulation, death, or the threat of it, by means of a prelude of torture, psychological or physical.

African leaders are a bunch of peremptory, paternalistic, reactionary reprobates. They are pompous and paranoid and prepared to live forever as fathers of their still-born nations. The list of profligacy is endless. Houphouet-Boigny's almost $400 million basilica at his village, Yamassou-krou (Ivory Coast). Emperor Bokassa's $20 million crowning ceremony in the Central African Republic. Arap Moi's $200 million KANU political party headquarters with a four-storey statue of himself, in Kenya. Abacha, in Nigeria, where morality goes by the name of Corruption. And there are many magnificent projects, such as chains of hotels meant to attract foreign tourists in countries where millions are dying of hunger and disease. And there are myriad white (or is it black?) elephant projects, supposedly meant to begin technological development, but which are never completed, never functional, never, indeed, considered essential beyond the billions in foreign exchange to be made and stashed in Swiss banks. We call the madness, *transferred technology*.

These leaders, lynchers *par excellence*, approve of no criticism. Whether "comparatively civilianized and domesticated" (Soyinka in *Index of Censorship*, 1988: 8) or outrageously brutish, a dictatorship remains just that: a clique of ambitious animals never giving people a chance to breathe, ready to rule over a wasteland as long as they remain in power. And our people's freedom has been locked away as an aberration of an unpatriotic period. The South African Desmond Tutu declares: "It is true that God's children suffer because there is less freedom in their countries than during the colonial times." (In Ayittey: 97)

There is oppression galore. It is necessary to erase from our minds the myth of ideology as playing a role in Africa's tragedy. The irrelevance of ideology is adequately documented by Ayittey (116): In 1990, there were 25 military dictatorships; 19 civilian dictatorships; 2 monarchies; 2 white-only rule (in South Africa and Namibia, which, of course, is no longer true); 4 indigenous African consensual democracies (Senegal, Botswana, Mauritius, and The Gambia). Of this last number, we may actually question the cases of Senegal and The Gambia, even with regard to 1990.

I stated earlier that democracy did exist in traditional Africa. Today, we are being told otherwise, that we have to be taught like savage children trying to catch up to the *civilized* adults from the West, sprinting ahead at jet-speed. Our leaders compare rather well to their masters and mentors; one might even say that they are worse, that is, more vicious in their attempts at manipulation, and misrepresentation. Mobutu of Zaire once declared: "Democracy is not for Africa. There was only one African chief and here in Zaire we must make unity." (*Wall Street Journal*, Oct. 14, 1985: 1) When his Western masters insisted on democracy, the "Father of African Authenticity" shifted gear: "Zaire's one-party state system is the most elaborate form of democracy." (Ayittey: 210) An oxymoron? I call it arrant nonsense! Other leaders, claiming to be socialists, or Marxists, confuse communism (with its emphasis on ideology) with communalism (humanity, human beings, and the community). In some countries, there have been claims of "grass roots democracy;" only it has been imposed from above, often by a military regime. We all know that these leaders, servants of foreign masters, are eager to listen to them, and to *prove* to them, by any means necessary, besides truthfulness, that the wind of democracy *a la West* is sweeping through the continent and that they, committed messiahs, patriots and nationalists, are leading the way.

It is in the name of democracy and the commitment to the national, popular cause, that our presidents-for-life sit tight in their marble mansions, and that the military plot and execute coups and counter-coups. Meanwhile, scorched-earth files of battered economies blot the landscape. Civil wars break out in a few spots and, when they end, the country returns to the status quo. If they do not end, maiming and murder continue, and the combatants, all calling themselves revolutionaries, proclaim the usual refrain, *a luta continua*. And there is a so-called revolution everywhere. Ghana, for example, is undergoing "Rawlings' revolution." And we note that the revolutionary has put on enormous weight, naturally, consequential to hard work and accumulating wisdom, or could it be the weight of gold and diamonds? He certainly wears it all very well. And we think of Liberia's Sergeant-turned-General Samuel Doe whose decade-long destruction of his country's economy led to his death, naked and missing an ear and other body parts, his bloated body under the feet of drunk renegades, including women, posing as revolutionaries. Ethiopia's Mengitsu, who in 1974 overthrew the dictatorial pseudo-deity, Emperor Selassie, installed Marxism and nationalized everything "for the benefit of the mass of the people," only to fall into an absolutism outstripping his predecessor's. He was forced to flee to Zimbabwe in 1991. And there was Sekou Toure, Guinea's once respected nationalist who defied General de Gaulle's order to stay with France, declaring, "we prefer to live in poverty in liberty to riches in slavery." (Ayittey: 100) Toure gradually entrenched a dictatorship with death-squads, detention, and economic destitution. When he died in 1984, 25 percent of his compatriots were in exile. Those caught in the concentration camp called home were living "in poverty in slavery!" To this endless list may be added Togo's strong man, Eyadema, who seized power about a quarter of a century ago through the barrel of a gun, and has enjoyed strong support from his foster-parents, the French, in eliminating any real, or imagined, opposition.

In these unfolding dramas of murder and mayhem, one may easily be tempted to forget the role of foreigners, either by their commission or omission. African leaders' irresponsibility is amply condoned by imperialists. A few examples would suffice. The United States bases its policy on economic interest combined with anti-communist phobia.[8] The result: collaboration with, and cover for, pro-West regimes, no matter how inhuman they may be. With the end of the cold war, any form of coherence in American policy in Africa has almost disappeared. Except for the hot market in South Africa, interest has been on the wane. Burundi, Somalia, and Rwanda, may burn; they will never arouse as much concern as Bosnia. Communism is no longer a threat. Besides, in the best days of communism, the Soviet Union hardly did anything concrete; its actions were "ill-conceived and ill-executed, half-hearted and meanly meager, or plainly conditioned by non-African considerations." (Peter Calvocoressi, *Independent Africa and the World*, New York: Longman, 1985: 88) Soyinka comments on the "double standard in the arrangement of conscience which seems to operate sincerely in the rich European world but only on a token level in Africa." (in *The Toronto Star*, Aug. 25, 1992: A17)

Africa's problems have remained distant, remote, and unimportant, to America and Europe. It is an open secret that Switzerland serves as bank for many an African chief robber's secret accounts. Britain also holds billions of stolen pounds sterling. Ayittey (263-4) quotes a 1991 official change to a 57-year-old Swiss secrecy law, repealing "Form-B" accounts to reveal names of clients. We are told that, in 1992, a Russian official who had stolen from public coffers was extradited from Switzerland to Russia. Does anyone wonder why African countries have not benefitted from that new law? If, and since, these leaders are daylight robbers, why do their civilized account-keepers not exercise the democratic right to act responsibly on behalf of the long suffering people? Our so-called African leaders, as expected, have refused to pull all stops to bring the culprits -including themselves, one daresay- to justice. I recall the 1994 offer of the Swiss ambassador to Nigeria: He said that his government would provide a list of Nigerians with bank accounts in Switzerland, *if only* the Nigerian authorities made the demand. He is still awaiting a response! While in office, the famous "iron lady" of British politics, Margaret Thatcher, claimed that five individuals were rich enough to pay off Nigeria's multibillion dollar debts, at a time when everyone was seeking relief from the "First World" lenders. Again, one may wonder why the British prime minister did not use her power to reveal the names of those money-bags. The late Kwame Nkrumah's comment is appropriate here: "African capitalists are still the junior partners of imperialism. They receive the crumbs of investment profits, commercial agencies, commissions, and directorships of foreign-owned firms. In these, and in many other ways, they are drawn into the web of neo-colonialism." (*Class Struggle in Africa*, New York: International Publishers, 1970: 33)

Ekwe-Ekwe (90) mentions the same imperialistic collusion and silence, the "creeping [and] accelerated genocide" committed against Africa. The World Bank, the International Monetary Fund (IMF), multifarious multinationals, are all agents of Africa's underdevelopment. For example, the ballyhooed Structural Adjustment Program (SAP), always forced upon African countries by IMF, has never succeeded in solving our economic problem. On the contrary, SAP is constantly sapping the society's strength and ability to survive. It has never stopped the siphoning of national riches to Europe and America. Nigeria is an excellent case in point.

Potentially Africa's richest country, Nigeria is a conglomeration of nations with only the colonial legacy to show as a sign of solidarity. It is a unique example of the impossibility of defining institutions, or analyzing events logically or rationally; for, the set-up is as convoluted as the various combinations of cultures that hardly have anything in common. In Nigeria, you cannot confidently distinguish between the military and the civilian orders (both have now designed the very democratic system of "classes") because both are blatantly political and politicized. Once a military ruler himself (1966-1975), Yakubu Gowon declared with apparent, praiseworthy perspicacity: "The military should not get itself involved in politics. The sooner they leave the stage the better, or else the people may rise up against them." (Ayittey: 137) The same Gowon had to be forced out of office by his underlings who were fed up with his dithering posture couched in patriotic blabbering about some concern for stability and gradual, lasting democracy.

Nigeria's uniformed buzzards would not have lasted this long without the cooperation of civilian vultures ready to prey upon anyone, including their own family, so desperate are they to feed on crumbs scattered in the corridors of power. Nigeria invents new vocabulary and offers new definitions by the day. We now have a military *class* working with the political *class* to patriotically free the moribund country of its petro-dollars. For the peace, unity, and stability of our dear nation, we must annul free and fair elections so as to cause chaos, which would give us a chance to begin again, and work slowly but surely towards our goal of self-destruction. We have *new-breed* politicians replacing the old who are their fathers and friends without whom they cannot even breathe. The judiciary, the vaunted last hope of the common people, is caught in the game of graft and greed common to the powerful sworn to an oath of justifiably sucking innocent people's blood.

No wonder a *Washington Post* reporter titled her article, "In Nigeria's Confusion, Military Coup Looks Like Democracy" (Dec. 4, 1993: A24). The confusion is visible at both the upper and lower levels of the society. The Yoruba say, *Esin iwaju ni ti ehin nwo sare* (the horses behind synchronize their speed to that of the lead horse). Nigerians obviously imitate their leaders' wise ways. It was Zaire's Mobutu, definitely a very wise leader, that once advised members of his party: "If you steal, do not steal too much at a time. You may be arrested. Steal cleverly, little by little." (Ayittey: 233) Those at the bottom of the ladder envy the robbers at the top, and pray everyday to the Christian or Moslem Almighty to give them the opportunity to emulate them, or, at least, to benefit from their patriotic largess. The economy keeps going down the drain, while Europe and America, beneficiaries of cheap oil and raw materials, as well as free market for their democratic technology, watch with a satisfied smile, the dissipation of a potential threat to their program of underdevelopment of our continent. A whole nation, the Ogoni, is being physically eliminated from the face of the earth, because they dare complain of being exploited and enslaved on their own land: Their punishment is perhaps meant to serve as warning to other unpatriotic dissidents, that is, those demanding their rights to basic, human life, freedom and justice.

All the threats of sanctions against Nigeria must be a sad joke, because only a brain-dead optimist would expect his enemy to help him escape from the shackles of enslavement serving the singular purpose of promoting the latter's supremacy. So, Nigeria's transition to democracy and national reconciliation may last until the end of the 21st century. Soyinka, accused by some of being an alarmist, has warned of possible disintegration. One would hope that it would not come to that. Nonetheless, the Nobel laureate's prediction may not be far-fetched, considering the alarming speed at which the country is descending towards the precipice. Everyone has some sorry tale to tell about the "flying elephant": There are, the battered economy,[9] rigged or aborted elections, feudal oppression and repression; harassment of known and suspected opposition; massacre of minorities, all perpetrated by a self-proclaimed leadership hugging absolute power and guilty of irresponsibility and unaccountability. The Ogoni case is the most resonant example of the mess created in Nigeria by the British. Is Soyinka right that "we may be witnessing, alas, the end of Nigerian history"? ("Nigeria's Long Steep, Bloody Slide" (*The New York Times*, Aug. 22, 1994: OP-ED) If one were to be cynical and doubt the commitment of those who can make a change, one would say that Soyinka is not being an alarmist, but a dreamer. For, how would change come when gun-toting tyrants and bazooka-wielding bandits are zealously supported by sweet-tongued puppets and sycophants and self-prostituting politicians also serving as pimps of an unwary people? In that culture of silence and collusion, of suffering and smiling, and of self-survival, where terror reigns, it might take a miracle to bring about change. Perhaps that is why many people, born again into the belly of the beast, spend hours on end praying assiduously to God. Do you blame them? Those that resist, die; cowards live, even if in shame. And I can never forget that night in a hotel room in Illinois after a long day at some literature conference. That was the first and last time I ever met Ken Saro-Wiwa. We got into one of those discussions about writing, politics, commitment, and the rest. His pipe emitting smoke and dangling from the tip of his thick lips, he scolded me, and those like me, with his subtle but serious humor. He said we all ought to return home to lead the many struggles begging to be begun, instead of sitting pretty harvesting dollars, and the despair of exile. I argued that some of us needed to be on this side, but both he and I knew one side of me was a stinking coward, lying through my teeth. And I warned him, ominously: "Those people will just kill you for nothing!"[10]

THE INTELLECTUAL GRAVEYARD

Does it then mean that the activists, the committed critics of our criminally minded leadership and our decadent society, are doomed to die for nothing? Current realities would appear too daunting, except for the truly courageous. Matters are not helped by the presence of an African intelligentsia ever willing to be bought over by brigands in government. We, African intellectuals, indeed, the bourgeois, are a shameless lot made of what I call a combination of the *wasted generation* (Soyinka's description of his generation), the *washed up generation* (mine, the one after his), the *wishful generation* (directly after mine), and the *wanting generation* (two removed from mine). The last, the youngest, is perhaps the most unfortunate, because the young ones are supposed to represent the future. As it is, our young intellectuals, bright but blighted by the iniquities of their elders, are wanting in will. Their only desire is, to abscond from the cauldron of scorching misery at home, that is, if they are not already considered lucky to have been born abroad.

Walter Rodney (36) identifies the bourgeois collaborators of African underdevelopment, thus: "The presence of a group of African sell-outs is part of the definition of underdevelopment. Any diagnosis of underdevelopment in Africa will reveal not just low per capita income and protein deficiencies, but also the gentlemen who dance in Abidjan, Accra and Kinshasa when music is played in Paris, London and New York." Strictly speaking, not all of them can be considered intellectuals (some are stark illiterates with wads of money-bills adding to the weight of their bulging bellies), but quite a number are. Think of professors rushing to the presidential palace after every coup, with their padded curriculum vitae, begging the latest savior of the nation for a ministerial appointment, or whatever position is available, because they simply wish to be of service! Think of paperweight academics pretending to be constructive critics, only to become overnight converts to the policies of economic robbery and social rape, once they have got the regime's attention. Think of press men and women and public servants serving each new messiah, ready to line their pockets with pound sterling and dollars in return for cover-up and connivance in crimes committed against the people.

If you read Fanon's indictment of the bourgeoisie (*The Wretched of the Earth*, 1963: 163), you would be nonplussed by how close we still are to the situation of the early 60s, on this the eve of the 21st century. A bourgeoisie without imagination, without a program other than the propensity for robbery, serving as model for a people too trusting, too timid to complain, too corruptible to be lucid. The most tragic characteristic of the African bourgeoisie - and we are thinking particularly of the intellectuals— is our painstaking effort to ape the Euro-American model. The intellectuals symbolize Africa's underdevelopment as we try our best to *prove* ourselves, to prove something to the superior Other. America is heaven; Africa is hell. True or false?

In an article just brought to my attention, and written by a fellow Nigerian, Emmanuel Obiechina ("The Dilemma of the African Intellectual in the Modern World," *Liberal Education*, March/April 1992: 18-21), I found several disturbing assertions. Obiechina is right on the money when he lists, among aspects of our dilemma, one, the Euro-establishment's refusal to admit other voices or accept other cultures' validity, and "the tenacious Eurocentricism that has dominated the world of ideas since the Enlightenment;" and, two, the African intellectual's self-alienation and "tendency to be both 'self' and 'other' simultaneously." However, when he mentions the intellectual's "race with time... as a relative newcomer to the world intellectual stage, just emerging from both the colonial experience and a tradition of thought and experience different from that of the West," and "the question of commitment [when the intellectual is] dogged by the bogey of society's expectations," the scholar-critic himself reveals a certain colonial, and *civilized* mentality that has made him fall prey to the very Eurocentricism that he appears to be condemning. For example, why must we always be trying to catch up? If that is our goal, we had better forget it! Rather than restrict our view to the tree, we ought to contemplate the forest: African culture and civilization constitute a body of knowledge and a way of life which must be studied *sui generis* by Africans themselves, and it is on this basis that we can acquire the ability to adapt whatever we borrow to our own, always conscious of its originality and viability. This entails hard work, reviving and reinforcing our humanism, for example, creating our own literary tradition and critical theories, writing our history afresh, and not merely repeating or refuting Western historical assertions about us.

Reporting on an academic conference in Nigeria, Emeka Anunkor (*The Guardian*, Lagos, March 30, 1984) makes the following cogent comments applicable to many an African intellectual: "The Nigerian scholar unthinkingly believes that it is eminently scholarly to copiously quote white scholars even when he writes on Nigerian politics or social affairs (...) More and more our identity and psyche are distorted; our perception and interpretation of our own internal and external realities become more and more defined and conditioned by these white folks. The spirit of exploration, the drive for creativity and originality becomes cruelly blunted and numbed." (See also, Ayittey: 289)

Are African intellectuals lazy? Are we cowardly? Or are we committed to our professions, which cannot preclude -which, indeed, should include- a commitment to our people? I know that the *civilized* answer would be, that there is a universal canon to which we must gravitate... I would, in all humility, submit that charity, as we say, begins at home. Whether we like it or not, if we wish to remain Africans, we must establish or, in some cases, *re-discover an African tradition* before aspiring to become "all-world." We are often too dishonest, too selfish, too shallow, and too alienated -yes, even ashamed!- to lay any claim to our Africanity.

Take, for instance, the language debate. Just as we have apparently accepted the inferiority of our religions (if you are not a Christian or a Moslem, then you are a pagan!), so also have we tacitly agreed that our languages are but dialects of no relevance to the "modern" world. I remain convinced that we can, and should, encourage some African languages to develop naturally, to cope with the exigencies of contemporary society. After all, minority languages proliferate in Europe, and Japanese is good enough for technology, so why not Kiswahili or any other former languaged? Future generations would benefit from it as galvanizing force.

In my opening remarks, I alluded to African women's writing. It is but one area where we have allowed foreigners to lead the way and, yet, we complain of people usurping our roles within our culture, or of relegating us to the position of interpreters and messengers for foreign "experts." Why do African critics hardly read African women's literature? Would it be true that we consider women inferior, or irrelevant? Facts of our history show that, in African civilization, women have always been considered as human beings, not as sex objects, or beasts of burden. Nonetheless, since we have in a large measure refused to assume and interpret our culture, the myth of our dehumanizing of African women has taken hold in the so-called modern society. Note that I am not restricting my comments to men, because women are also engaged in the modernist (or is it post-modernist?) misinterpretation.

Those at home in Africa complain of lack of research material and funding. They also complain of the growing misery. You either join the ranks of robbers, or run away, if you do not want to rebel and be killed for nothing! The number of Africa's drained brains in Euro-America must be in the millions. I shall not waste time on the group that Ayittey (288) calls the "lost tribe," that is, the *civilized* ones perfectly settled here, who have given up the ghost of ever returning home. I am concerned with those of us who, in our different, often weird, ways, are still attached to home, and would not wish to die abroad like a child unworthy of his father and mother. We worry because of the isolation of exile, the despair, the desperation, life on the verge, the irrelevance, the perpetual questions about lost community, indeed, the hope for the millions caught on the other side and, irony of ironies, the fact of their humanity as against our own *materiality*... A horse is never too tired to run the final race home. And, can you imagine, you, blessed with the strength of youth, seeking firm footing in this civilized sand, and us, the ageing, reeling from our lost battles, fighting against senility and irrelevance, can you imagine us all being given our marching orders from this our plastic haven? Can we, shall we, go home again? We must appreciate the anger of someone such as Soyinka because, at his age, he ought to be back there, for the makers of our future to drink from his well of wisdom. Somehow or another, we must understand this: We can only live, not just exist, at home; hence, the task is ours to do whatever we can, and whatever has to be done, to make home livable.

CONCLUSION: OF SOLUTIONS AND RESOLUTIONS
You are probably tired of my negativity, and wondering whether I would have anything heartening to tell you today. You will forgive me for telling the truth and, hopefully, you will appreciate my desire to consider you as my brothers and sisters, and, indeed, my children; and, we all know that when members of a family put heads and hearts together to discuss and to seek solutions to their problems, they come away looking gloomy and thoughtful, because they have told one another the bitter truth. This is a Yoruba adage. So, what do we want for our dear Mother Africa? Where do we want her to be in the year 2000? Where do we ourselves want to be? I insist that it is a matter of urgency. Tomorrow never comes for cowards and debtors; however, for the courageous determined to seize their destiny from the forces of destruction, tomorrow comes too soon. The 21st century is tomorrow, and we have no time to waste.

First and foremost, we must find the courage to assume our destiny. We have no right to ask questions about Africa's future without a commitment to going back home. As a friend of mine said the other day, you have to put your money where your heart is. If it is not possible to return now, we should begin to do something concrete, cooperatively, to support and encourage the process of change. Talk will not tame tyrants. Words will not win a war. Rhetoric cannot eliminate misery. I am in agreement with A.M. Babu in his postscript to Walter Rodney's masterpiece, *How Europe Underdeveloped Africa* (316), that Africa's problems will not, cannot, be solved by foreigners, and that we must have the resolve to do it ourselves. "Our action must be related to our concrete experience and we must not give way to metaphysical hopes and wishes-hoping and wishing that the monster who has been after us throughout our history will some day change into a lamb; he won't."

Ayittey (35) proposes building on certain elements of our civilization, some of which I have alluded to in this presentation. He affirms: "[Africa's] salvation lies in returning to these roots and building upon its indigenous tradition of participatory democracy and free village markets." He also believes that we should "give Africa back to its traditional rulers." (228) However, I totally disagree with this last suggestion, because we know how tarnished are today's traditional rulers, modern messengers and handmaids of tyrants. The first idea, regarding collective democracy, would be more acceptable, with one condition, perhaps the most complex and, some would say, impossible: that Africa's national map be redrawn. In certain countries, the colonial legacy of sham nationalism stands to continue to impede peace and progress and, if sincere discussions are not held, even the year 3000 would still see such countries embroiled either in civil war, or in the usual hypocritical posture of patching together incongruities, and this scenario might even not occur, if the invading forces of imperialism succeed in emptying the continent of its riches and turning it into a vast desert. National realignment ought not to be such an inconceivable measure; is it not being done in Europe? After all, African brotherhood and sisterhood is a widespread attitudinal reality. I recognize the difficulty of the attendant economic restructuring, particularly when it involves the possible loss of natural resources to some nations. I am also aware of the possible loss of existing infrastructures. Nonetheless, some form of discussion, and modification, would serve a very useful purpose. Short of restoring original nations, new systems of governance, such as authentic federalism, confederacy, and regionalism, should be adopted. If the right to choose is given to the people, as it should be, I am convinced that the present configurations will be altered. Of course, we are well aware that our dear dictators will do everything to avoid such debate. With concerted resolve, the people will succeed in railroading their agenda for everlasting rule. Will the West cooperate in this design for real freedom? Will Africans be able, finally, to choose our real leaders? Will intellectuals, public servants, the press, and the mass of the people, all committed citizens of their nations, show integrity? Will there be independent labor unions? And government accountability?

To embark on the arduous journey from our present hell towards our own heaven on earth, we must begin by a process of decolonization. It is most common to say that Africa's problem is leadership. An incontrovertible fact: I have given examples of profligacy, irresponsibility, and inhumanity, on the part of leaders-lynchers feeding on the flesh of the people they are supposed to serve and protect. Yet, that fact cannot be deemed absolute, because dictators' fancies are always fed by collaborators, as well as the people who, by suffering in silence, help the murderous messiahs to remain in power. You might say that Africa is already independent, and wonder why I am talking of decolonization. Note, however, that Africa is far from being free. The most insidious aspect of colonialism is the pulverization of our psyche by almighty *civilization*. Physical wounds, visible, fixed, real, are easy to heal; physical, geographical borders are also relatively easy to liberate. On the contrary, the psychological, invisible, unfathomable, always prove intractable, and Africa's biggest problem is psychological. The minority mentality being exhibited at all levels must make many a Westerner smile with satisfaction. Sometimes, we seem to accept, by our actions and attitudes, the possibility that God deliberately created us to be second-class citizens of the world!

Decolonization entails a painful process of deprogramming our soul to make us believe in our culture and civilization, and in our ability to make history. One big mistake that we have made is, to think that freedom for Africa was achieved, once and for all, the day each country (and I refuse to call most of them nations) hoisted a flag, and sang a song of praise about a dream that died before it was born. We quickly forgot that another form of (internal) colonialism, the enslavement of our people, had achieved alienation and confusion from which the slaves never freed themselves. If we had learnt any lesson, we would have realized that freedom from slavery and colonialism (a mental disease) must be a continuous process, so that the sick may not slide back to the hallucinatory sphere where the master is in control. Let me take the example of religion and that, yes, religion has a great deal, if not everything, to do with life here on earth. Religion was an essential weapon of colonization, and it remains so in these days of imperialism. As the devastation continues, we are waiting for the International Red Cross, or Crescent, to feed our refugees, to save them from being massacred. Who would have thought that the scramble for Africa's soul would be happening at the end of the 20th century? I am told that Christianity is one of the fastest growing religions in the world, and that its greatest progress is being made in Africa. What happened to African religions? They are very much alive in the diaspora, if only Africans would wean themselves from their civilized slumber, and show respect for beliefs that their brothers and sisters hold very dear.

With the process of decolonization will come a reevaluation of our development policies. Up till now, the West has been fooling us into believing that it is the expert on democracy, and that we should learn, as good students do. But, as I have tried to show, the West is not in a position to teach us. Once we have removed the civilized blinkers from our eyes, we shall be ready to choose. "It would be best if Africans themselves make their own case for reform. (...) It is up to the African people to decide which political and economic systems are the most workable for them." (Ayittey: 352) I support Ekwe-Ekwe's rejection of Europe's "developmentalism," which has contributed to our present state of neocolonialism. Agricultural revolution and "re-development" ought to be our goal. "We do not want to catch up with anyone," as Fanon proudly declared. (314) We must look inwards, produce food for ourselves, use our own resources instead of exporting them to our exploiters. Self-sufficiency can be achieved. China and Japan managed to build and develop out of their own volition. Africa need not continue to transfer technology. African leaders have been begging the West to reschedule debts, and to grant new ones. Rather, we should not pay any debts which, to a large extent, are non-existent, or are part of our stolen legacy. Rather, we should seek reparations.

In conclusion, Africa must strive to achieve solidarity with the African diaspora. The call has been made before. Listen to Es'kia Mphahlele (*The African Image*, New York: Praeger, 1974: 121-2): "Africa knows very little about its diaspora. Poets who talk about slavery at all stop on the West African coastline, at the seaside slave dungeons. The educational programs of Africa do not allow for systematic study of the African diaspora, e.g., its literature, history and sociology. More Afro/Americans and Caribbeans must visit Africa; Africa must open her doors to them. They should get to know Africa as she is, not as a mere grand idea. We must create a climate that will help us understand what it is we expect of each other. We have long exhausted the reserves built up by the early Pan-African congresses. And the need for frequent circuses has passed."

Past efforts at pan-Africanism failed, because we did not recognize the essential continuity of the reintegration. In addition, the diasporans felt a certain superiority vis-a-vis the continentals who, for their part, were too proud to believe that those from abroad could claim to be in a position to help. Today, we are talking of *mutual help*, interdependence between two sides of a family racked by racism and exploitation and condemned to live various ramifications of a macrocosmic colonial condition. Our captors and mesmerizers have never wanted us to come together, because they know our potential. Of course, they would tell us that the idea of Mphahlele is effete, just as they always tell us that the disease of racism has been resolved. For those Africans lured by the green pastures of the West, we must seize the opportunity to concretize the relationship with our brothers and sisters as a prelude for the liberation, and re-construction of Africa. I have talked of mutual help in this process because, in the final analysis, African-Americans, African-Brazilians, African-Caribbeans, will all benefit from a free, progressive Africa. The African-American jazz trumpeter, Wynton Marsalis, in his current teaching about the history and importance of jazz, remarks that there can be no jazz without America. I say he is wrong, that he should rather say that there can be no jazz without Africa. Just as there can be no diaspora without Africa; and no Africa without the diaspora.

*Keynote address delivered on March 2, 1996, at the symposium of the African Students Association, University of Wisconsin, Madison, USA

Notes

1. Waruru Kanja, Kenya's minister of information and broadcasting, in Parliament after the mysterious murder of the very popular foreign minister, Robert Ouko; in George Ayittey, *Africa Betrayed,* New York: St. Martin's Press, 1992, p. xv.
2. The late Patrice Lumumba, Zaire's (then and now again the Congo) first president, in June 1960, at the independence ceremony, in response to King Baudouin of Belgium; in Ayittey, 98.
3. Yoruba saying: A person that his/her enemies wish to burn (destroy) should not soak himself/herself in gasoline and go sit by the fire.
4. Wole Soyinka, Nigeria's Nobel laureate in literature, in *O Estado de São Paulo,* Nov. 16, 1995, p. A10.
5. Arthur Nortje, in Cosmo Pieterse, *Seven South African Poets,* Heinemann, 1971.
6. Cheikh Anta Diop, *Pre-colonial Black Africa,* Westport, CT: Lawrence Hill, 1987; —*The African Origin of Civilization: Myth or Reality,* 1974; —*Civilization or Barbarism,* New York: Lawrence Hill, 1991.
7. Western assault on any attempt to valuate African civilization has not abated. For instance, a new book by the reactionary scholar, Mary Lefkowitz, *Not Out of Africa: How Afrocentrism Became an Excuse to Teach Myth as History* (Basic Books), is making the rounds of academe. The racist title, a take-off on another racist text made into a movie, "Out of Africa," is to be noted. When the author waves off the oft quoted respect of the Greek Herodotus for Egyptian philosophy and science as "his own respect for the Egyptians, and his own desire, as an anthropologist, not to feel superior in every way," Leftkowitz reveals her own disrespect and superiority complex. The belief here is that civilized scholars will devour the text and quote copiously from it. For the reactionary, myth can, of course, replace history.
8. The list of "Third World" dictators and murderers pretending to be patriots that have been propped up by the United States, is truly astounding: Somoza (Nicaragua); Marcos (Phillippines); Shah (Iran); Mobutu (Zaire); Tubman-Tolbert-Doe (Liberia), to name a few.
9. An example of Nigeria's ridiculously low esteem is the battle with the Cameroons for the oil-rich Bakassi Peninsula. Surprisingly, the small Cameroons, once annexed to Nigeria, poses such a great threat.

Naturally, France, the ex-colonial master, is siding with the Cameroons. In a scenario fit for farce, the Nigerian government announced that, after a recent round of talks, the armed forces of the two sides of the skirmish "staged a joint military exercise... with the aim of promoting good neighborliness." (Reuter). The mediator in the dispute is none other than the embattled president of Togo, Eyadema. [1998: The Bakassi case is yet to be resolved by the International Court at The Hague.]

10. I have done an in-depth study of the life and work of Saro-Wiwa: Femi Ojo-Ade, *Ken Saro-Wiwa, a bio-critical study*, New York: Africana Heritage Press. [Note that, in 1998, the Ogoni example is being followed by several other groups in the oil-producing areas. Protests are being organized by youths who seize oil depots, and prevent the foreign companies from exploiting the "black gold." Reports of official killings of individuals are emerging, bringing to mind the Saro-Wiwa tragedy.]

NIGERIA'S FIRE BRIGADE APPROACH

Time alone, time will tell
You think you're in heaven
When you're living in hell
(Bob Marley, late Jamaican reggae artist)

I am writing this in a hotel room in Salvador-Bahia, Brazil, upon arrival for another of those academic gatherings where intellectuals are made to feel relevant but where some, like me, always remember what they would like to, but cannot, forget: home. News about Nigeria or, indeed, Africa as a whole, is hard to come by in Brazil, a nation intent upon denying its Africanity (with the majority of its population being *tainted*, by the African blood, and the verb is used deliberately), declaring its attachment to the *First World* symbolized by almighty *Estados Unidos*. Just as over there, stateside, the zeal to report on Africa is always displayed for tragedy, such as, starvation in the Sudan, conflict and death in Somalia, ethnic cleansing in Burundi, self-destruction in Liberia and Sierra Leone, and conflagration and confusion in the Congo. Even South Africa, darling of the West, cannot escape: The television is inundated with news of violence in th townships. The journalistic style is simple and straightforward: Lay emphasis on the negative, in order to show that Africans are naturally savage, and are in need of pity, and help.

It was therefore not at all surprising that my Brazilian friends and colleagues welcomed me with words of sympathy about the latest scoop on Africa, the fuel-induced conflagration in the Nigerian delta, which has consumed the lives of well over five hundred poor people. Actually, news of the event found me at my outpost in the United States; hence, I've had the opportunity to compare the American and Brazilian reactions and, very importantly, to reflect on the tragedy. The American press went into details of how men, women, and children were turned into walking flames as they were siphoning fuel from a burst, or deliberately broken, pipe after, maybe, some careless soul had lit a naked fire nearby. The surrounding hospitals were immediately flooded with burnt bodies, while hundreds of others transformed into charcoal littered the charred earth. When news broke of an imminent visit to the disaster area by the head of state, many of the maimed fled their hospital beds, or floor, out of fear of being arrested and put away, perhaps forever, by the government that has threatened to deal with the *saboteurs* who, however, remain accused, anonymous, and at large.

The head of state did arrive -a rarity in a country where rumor often refuses to become reality- to commiserate with the people, and to assess the situation. He promised a thorough investigation, and payment of hospital bills, but no compensation for any of the victims, or their families. To Mr. Head of State's words, the American journalists have added those of some surviving victims, lamenting total loss of livelihood, denying active participation in the fuel-looting, or, simply crying out for help, perhaps best expected from heaven. Although the Brazilian publication has not been as comprehensive as the American, it has kept tag on the increasing number of the dead. Of course, one knows that, within a week (that would make it two weeks after the tragedy), the matter will disappear from the press, to be replaced by either silence, or another tragedy, or atrocity, from a continent considered incapable of managing its affairs.

This latest Nigerian tragedy makes me think of the *fire brigade*. A group of employees brought together, not through professional apprenticeship and interest in saving endangered lives, but as a result of self-interest in keeping their own bodies and souls intact in a society where, too often, employment is a privilege. A brigade of beggars. A corps of carpenters, and plumbers, and experts in other areas, except fire-extinguishing. A brigade with neither discipline, nor desire, least of all the equipment to combat the ever-increasing number of conflagration, in a society where, in order to ensure the everlasting secrecy of high public crimes, the safest action is to torch the accounts department. Thus, Nigeria's twenty-five storey Independence skyscraper suddenly lit up on one beautiful night; as did the NITEL (telegraphic communications) building, and others that cost billions to build, and the repair of which has been a continuing catastrophe. Imagine a twelve-foot ladder propped up against the wall of a burning giant of a building. Imagine fire-hoses without water. Imagine fire-trucks with stuttering engines, or without fuel to make them function. Imagine firefighters battling against all odds, praying to just stay alive in their fire-prone apparel. Such was the sight at the most recent pipeline disaster where hundreds of the victims probably had reached heaven, or hell, before the fire brigade was informed of the tragedy: Imagine a dead telephone line, and the messenger asked to take the request for help by hand, jogging along the road, and in the opposite direction, due to the hallucinatory consequence of a whole day without a meal.

Nigeria has made an art of the fire brigade approach in resolving its myriad problems. In essence, problems are allowed to pile up and then, suddenly, a one-time solution is applied. Unfortunately, like the fire at Jesse that destroyed hundreds of precious lives and land, the solution always arrives too little, too late. Moreover, it often happens that the purveyors of the solution are not only incompetent; they are also uninterested in bringing an end to the problem. At best, they would like to be seen to be trying their best when, in truth, they are doing their worst. At worst, they do not care whether the fire is put out or not; they may actually prefer the latter situation, so that others may die, and they continue to survive, and stay in power, with the right to decide who would live, and die.

Let us consider the situation that led to the Jesse catastrophe. Everyone now knows that Nigeria is the world's sixth producer of oil. The way this fact has become common knowledge is, in itself, a source of shame. From the instant explorers struck *black gold* in commercial quantities, the country's elated, pretentious rulers seemed to have decreed that every citizen stop working hard, and begin to think of spending the wealth. Soon enough, people obeyed the patriotic pronouncement by declaring themselves born-to-be millionaires, chosen by the Almighty as the world's spendthrifts. No wonder, wherever we Nigerians used to go, our identity preceded us. Western business people welcomed us with very open arms. None of them complained, until oil prices began to falter, and then to plummet, and Nigeria's fortunes with them. The very zealous partners of the good old days, have become today's critics of our corruption. To be sure, we have no right to blame them, because they were taking care of their own interest. Since ours was, to spend, and destroy, without thinking of the future, we have a right to suffer the consequences, as we are doing at places such as Jesse. If Nigeria's refineries were functioning properly, gasoline products would be readily available, and there would be no reason for people to rush to a burst pipe to siphon the *essential commodity*. If the oil-producing areas were adequately compensated for the billions of dollars worth of oil taken out of their land, and for the ecological devastation and unfathomable health hazards, there would be no danger of sabotage that might have led to the oil-leak. On the contrary, the past few years have witnessed official delinquency and wastage, and a mixture of misappropriation and mismanagement of funds and facilities. Rather than repair the rickety refineries, the government gave cash to certain individuals who, in their magnanimity, deposited large sums in their personal accounts abroad, and used the rest to import cheap fuel hazardous to the health of both machines and humans. The recently deceased dictator, perhaps a failed magician, used to decree that fuel be present in the pumps within twenty-four hours. Some patriots hailed him as the messiah. Meanwhile, protesters in oil-producing areas, before the Jesse tragedy, were summarily silenced, temporarily, or forever.

Other actions reek of the same fire-brigade tactics. The democratization process remains flawed, in spite of the West's avowed support. By eschewing the idea of a broad-based discussion of the national question, popularly called a sovereign national conference, Nigeria is trying to douse the fire of freedom with the palliative of zoned presidency which, according to general opinion, will be ceded to a Southern candidate. A similar measure has been implemented in the workers' conditions of service: In September 1998, federal employees' salaries were greatly increased (in certain cases, by as much as 600%), and everyone ran off to the bank with big bundles of naira. Although it is too early to tell the effects of the cash boom on the people and the system, one already notices the confusion caused by the government in failing to plan before executing the new salary structure. After employees at the state level had cried foul, because they were excluded from the windfall, especially in those states that provide most of the money being distributed, the federal government decided to set up a committee to review the policy. Even if arrangements are made to include all public employees in this sharing of *the national cake,* it would not eradicate the proletariat's chronic poverty, abominable conditions of service, and overall low standard of living.

Regarding higher education, the government decided to decree viability of universities by reducing costs. The reasoning is very interesting: If there is no adequate funding, some of the institutions would simply rot, and die; and candidates for enrollment, whose numbers continue to far outstrip available space, are expected to become less ambitious, and to learn to be modest, as third-world citizens ought to be! That realistic policy, of encouraging Nigerians to cut their educational coat according to the country's underdeveloped size, is in line with what a federal minister stated a few years back, that average Nigerians, that is, the vast majority, do not need electricity, water, and transportation. Now, only a stranger to the country's pragmatism, would fail to applaud the eminent official's declaration. The idea, the ultimate in *fire-brigadism,* is that, in order to prevent problems from arising, the people must be protected against the hazards caused by what other countries consider useful and essential. You know, electricity can lead to death by electrocution; water can be a source of flood; cars and buses can easily cause accidents. Hence, a government that saves its people's precious lives by that most natural means, must be congratulated!

Another piece of disturbing news has just been flashed on the internet: Students at Obafemi Awolowo University, where I was once employed, decided to take matters into their own hands, when a colleague of theirs died as a result of cholera which, in their opinion, could, and should, have been avoided if the authorities had paid attention to simple hygiene on campus. The angry students went on ramrage, and took as hostages the deputy vice-chancellor and fifteen other professors in various positions. These future leaders of Nigeria have probably learnt their lessons well from their professors. They have realized that their university, once reputed to be among the best in Africa, is not being run by a bunch of brigands, that is, members of a fire brigade interested in short cuts and quick millions: Instead of repairing toilets and roads, instead of maintaining delapidated infrastructures, they prefer to embark on constructing capital projects costing billions of dollars, as showpieces of excellence and prosperity. For those who can hardly see, or who prefer to see the shadow and to overlook the substance, such brilliant constructions would easily hide the rot and the stench being lamented by those who used to know the real, excellent institution. Imagine a skyscraper constructed on quicksand, by a carpenter; and designed, not by an architect, but by a draughtsman, a pseudo-professional claiming to be an expert. As the structure begins to crumble, the owners, proud of their beautiful edifice, a replica of some ultra-modern building in temperate climes, call in a cook to modify the component parts, you know, the way one adds spice to the delicacies at the presidential mansion. So, at Ife, the students may be thinking of eliminating the unfortunate administrators and professors, and replace them with brand-new ones, in the hope that the latter would use some Nigerian magic to clean up the mess at the university. (For a very thought-provoking symbolism of the ill-founded, and ill-fated, Nigerian House, see Wole Soyinka's recent lecture upon his brief return to Nigeria, "Soyinka Redesigns Nigeria," Oct. 16, 1998).

Just imagine: If there were no vehicles and other gadgets using fuel products, Nigeria would be much better off. Every pint of oil would be exported abroad. The country would be much richer. The powers that be would thus be in a position to buy everything needed, particularly, brains. And, significantly, there would be no tragedy, such as the one that occurred at Jesse.

INDEX